Nörr · Stiefenhofer

Takeover Law in Germany

Takeover Law in Germany

A Handbook and Practitioners' Guide

Editors:
Dr. Rudolf Nörr
Dr. Alfred Stiefenhofer

Coordinating Editor:
Dr. Markus Stadler, LL.M./M.B.A

Authors:

Prof. Dr. Holger Altmeppen
University of Passau, School of Law

Dr. Tobias Bürgers
Attorney at Law

Iliana Duderstadt
Solicitor

Austin Dunne
(Translation of the Takeover Act)
Solicitor

Dr. Gerald Reger
Attorney at Law

Dr. Dieter Schenk
Attorney at Law
and Tax Advisor

Dr. Markus Stadler, LL.M./M.B.A
Attorney at Law

Verlag C.H.Beck München 2003

Verlag C. H. Beck im Internet:
beck. de

ISBN 3 406 49507 9

© 2003 Verlag C. H. Beck oHG
Wilhelmstraße 9, 80801 München
Druck: Nomos Verlagsgesellschaft
In den Lissen 12, 76547 Sinzheim

Satz: Druckerei C. H. Beck Nördlingen

Umschlag: Siegfried Bütefisch, Schlaitdorf

Gedruckt auf säurefreiem, alterungsbeständigem Papier
(hergestellt aus chlorfrei gebleichtem Zellstoff)

Vorwort

Mit dem zum 1. Januar 2002 in Kraft getretenen „Übernahmegesetz" hat der deutsche Kapitalmarkt erstmals einen umfassenden und bindenden rechtlichen Rahmen für öffentliche Angebote zum Erwerb von Wertpapieren erhalten. Diese in Deutschland neue Rechtsmaterie für den Praktiker übersichtlich darzustellen, haben wir uns mit diesem Buch zur Aufgabe gemacht. Es ist vornehmlich an Berater außerhalb Deutschlands im Bereich Mergers & Acquisitions und Capital Markets gerichtet, also Investmentbanker, Rechtsanwälte und Unternehmensberater. Trotz des Charakters als Handbuch soll das Werk zugleich einen wissenschaftlichen Beitrag zur Entwicklung des Übernahmerechts in Deutschland leisten; auch für deutsche Rechtsanwälte und Juristen in Rechtsabteilungen von Banken und Unternehmen wird sich in der täglichen Praxis ein Griff zu dem Werk lohnen. Die Autoren nehmen zu einer Reihe von ungeklärten Rechtsfragen Stellung, wobei wir uns bewußt auf besonders praxisrelevante Fragestellungen beschränkt haben. Für Anregungen sind die Autoren stets dankbar, wir bitten diese zu richten an: markus. stadler@noerr.de.

Die Autoren danken Herrn Rechtsanwalt **Wolf Stumpf** und Herrn Rechtsanwalt **Stephan Philbert** für ihre wertvolle Mithilfe.

Foreword

The Takeover Act, which came into force in Germany on 1 January 2002, provided the German markets for the first time with a comprehensive and binding legal framework applicable to public offers for the acquisition of securities, so-called „Tender Offers." In this book, we have undertaken the task of providing the professional with a clear overview of this new legal material. Our aim is mainly to assist advisors such as investment bankers, lawyers and business consultants outside Germany who act in the areas of mergers and acquisitions and the capital markets. We believe that the book will contribute to academic discussion about the development of the takeover law in Germany, and that consultation by German lawyers and legal consultants to banks and businesses in their daily practice will prove worthwhile. The authors state their opinions on various unresolved legal issues, thereby deliberately confining themselves to questions of particular practical importance. The authors are always grateful for suggestions, which may be sent to: markus.stadler@noerr.de.

The authors gratefully acknowledge the assistance of **Wolf Stumpf**, Attorney at Law, and **Stephan Philbert**, Attorney at Law.

Table of Contents

Preface XV

Chapter 1
The Corporate Structure of a German Stock Corporation

1. Corporate Governance	1
a) The Two Tier Board System	1
b) The Supervisory Board	2
c) The Management Board	4
d) The Shareholders' Meeting	4
2. Shares and Capital	5
a) Voting Shares and Non-voting Shares	5
b) Issue of New Shares	5
c) Contingent Capital Increase	6
d) Authorized Capital	6

Chapter 2
Development of Takeover Law in Germany

1. Situation until 1995	7
2. Takeover Code 1995	7
3. The Takeover Act 2002 ("Übernahmegesetz")	8

Chapter 3
Need for Efficient Takeover Regulations 11

Chapter 4
Takeovers under the new Takeover Act

1. Objective of the Takeover Act	13
2. Scope of Application	13
a) Matters Regulated by the Takeover Act	13
(1) Public offers	13
(2) Securities of the target	14
(3) Admission to public trading	15
b) Takeover Offers	15
c) Mandatory Offers	17
d) International Application	17
(1) Admission to trading	17
(2) International offers	18

3. Structure of the Takeover Act ... 20
4. General Principles ... 21
  a) The Principle of Equal Treatment ... 21
  b) Transparency and Information ... 22
  c) Acting in the Best Interest of the Target ... 23
  d) Duty to complete the Transaction without Delay ... 23
  e) Preventing Market Manipulation ... 24
5. Procedural Overview ... 24
6. Individual Steps in Making an Offer ... 27
  a) The Decision to Make an Offer ... 27
  b) The Takeover Offer ... 30
    (1) The offer document ... 30
      (a) Conditions in the offer document ... 30
      (b) Prohibition of partial takeover offers ... 33
      (c) Content of the offer document ... 33
    (2) Confirming how the offer is to be financed ... 34
    (3) Procedural steps ... 34
    (4) Liability for the content of the offer document and for the statement confirming how the offer is to be financed ... 36
  c) Acceptance Period; Changes to the Offer and Extension of the Acceptance Period ... 37
    (1) Length of the acceptance period ... 37
    (2) "Water-Level" announcements ... 38
    (3) Amendments to the offer ... 38
    (4) Extension of the acceptance period ... 39
  d) The Completion of the Takeover Process and Further Acceptance Period ... 39
  e) Illegal Offensive Tactics ... 40
    (1) Two-tier offers ... 40
    (2) Proxy fights ... 42
    (3) Greenmailing ... 42
    (4) Leveraged buyout ... 43
    (5) Bootstrap offer ... 44
    (6) Golden handshakes and parachutes ... 45
7. Response of the Target ... 45
  a) Development of Law in the U.S. ... 45
  b) The Principle of Neutrality under German Law ... 47
  c) Exceptions to the Principle of Neutrality ... 48
    (1) Shareholders' resolutions ... 48
    (2) Approval by the supervisory board ... 49
    (3) Ongoing business operations ... 49
  d) Statements of the Boards ... 50
8. Defense Strategies ... 51
  a) General ... 51
  b) Structural Defensive Tactics ... 52
    (1) Poison pills ... 52
    (2) Staggered boards ... 56
    (3) ESOPs ... 57

(4) Cross shareholdings of affiliated companies 57
(5) Authorized but unissued share capital – sale by a company of its own shares 59
c) Ad-Hoc Defensive Tactics 59
  (1) Public relations activities 60
    (a) Official statements of the target's boards ("Defense Document") .. 60
    (b) Advertising campaigns 62
  (2) Search for a "White Knight" 65
  (3) Approval by the shareholders' meeting 65
    (a) Shareholders' meeting <u>after</u> publication of an offer 65
    (b) Shareholders' resolutions <u>before</u> publication of an offer 67
  (4) Approval of the supervisory board 68
  (5) Remedies of the shareholders 69
    (a) Remedies for breach of fiduciary duties 69
    (b) Claims in tort 70
    (c) Amount of damages 71
  (6) Remedies of the bidder 71
  (7) A practical note 71

9. Consideration 73

a) Form of Consideration 73
  (1) Consideration in liquid shares 73
  (2) Cash consideration 74
  (3) Other forms of consideration 75
b) Amount of Consideration 75
  (1) Average-price rule 75
  (2) Income/DCF approach – thinly traded stocks 75
  (3) Problems of average-price rule 76
c) "Variable Consideration" 77
d) "Most favored Status of a Bid" and Improved Bids 78
  (1) Pre-offer acquisition 78
  (2) Acquisitions pending the offer 79
  (3) Post-offer acquisition of shares 79
  (4) Form of the price improvement 80
    (a) Pre-offer acquisitions 80
    (b) Acquisitions pending a public offer 81
    (c) Post-offer acquisitions 81
e) Legal Consequences and Remedies for Non-compliance 81
  (1) Remedies of the Federal Supervisory Office 81
  (2) Private cause of action 82

10. Mandatory Offers 83

a) General Principles 83
b) Triggering Events – Controlling Interest 83
c) Exemptions from the Requirement to make a Mandatory Bid 86
d) Consideration 88
e) Sanctions 88

11. Supervision by the Federal Supervisory Office 89

a) Responsibilities of the Supervisory Office 89
b) Other Sanctions 90
c) Remedies 91

Chapter 5
Merger of Equals

1. Introduction 93

2. Relationship of the Reorganization Act to the Takeover Act 94

3. Forms of Merger under the Reorganization Act 94

4. Merger and Anti-Trust Law 95
   a) German Merger Control 95
   b) European Merger Control 96

5. Steps in a Merger under German Law 97
   a) The Decision on the Exchange Ratio 97
      (1) Intrinsic and extrinsic value 97
      (2) Determination of the intrinsic value of an enterprise 99
      (3) Relative valuation of the merging entities 100
      (4) Synergy effects – stand-alone basis 101
      (5) The valuation date 102
   b) Merger Agreement 103
      (1) Minimum content of the merger agreement 103
      (2) Form of the merger agreement 105
      (3) Presentation of the merger agreement to the works council .. 105
   c) Merger Audit 106
   d) Merger Report 106
      (1) The scope of the report obligation 106
      (2) Confidentiality requirements 108
   e) Merger Resolution 108
   f) Capital Increase at the Receiving Entity 109
   g) Notification of the Merger to the Register 109
   h) Legal Protection of Shareholders 109

6. Cross-Border Corporate Mergers 111
   a) Reorganization Act and Cross-Border Corporate Mergers 112
   b) Principles for Cross-Border Mergers 112
      (1) Share exchange 112
      (2) The participating entities come together in a newly formed stock corporation 113

7. Final Note 113

Chapter 6
Squeeze-Out

1. Introduction 115

2. Previous Legal Situation 115
   a) Integration 116
   b) Squeeze-Out Asset Deal 116

c) Delisting 117
d) Control and Profit Transfer Agreements 117

3. The New Squeeze-Out Provisions 118

a) Reasons for Introducing the Squeeze-Out 118
b) Conditions and Procedure 119
   (1) Shareholding of at least 95% 119
      (a) Attribution of indirectly held shares 119
      (b) Pooling of shares in a partnership 120
   (2) Determination of the cash compensation and audit 121
   (3) Passing a resolution on the squeeze-out at the shareholders' meeting .. 122
   (4) Registration of the squeeze-out resolution in the commercial register; transfer of the shares 123
   (5) Holders of options and convertible bonds 124

4. Calculation of the Cash Compensation 124

5. Legal Protection for Minority Shareholders 126

a) Action to Set Aside 126
b) Compensation Assessment Proceeding 126

6. Comparison with other Countries 127

a) Squeeze-Out Procedure not Restricted to Corporations Quoted on the Stock Exchange 128
b) No Prior Takeover Bid Required; No Right of Withdrawal for Minority Shareholders 128

7. Facilitated Delisting due to a Squeeze-out 128

8. Conclusion 129

Chapter 7
Comparison with UK City Code on Takeovers and Mergers

1. Self-Regulation 131
2. Application of the City Code 133
3. General Principles 134
4. Mandatory Offers 135
   a) Obligation to Make a Mandatory Offer 135
   b) Exemptions 136
5. Conclusion 137

Appendix 1: The Act on the Purchase of Securities and on Takeovers 140
Appendix 2: Public Offer Regulation 204

Glossary 217

Index 227

List of Abbreviations/Abkürzungsverzeichnis

AG	Aktiengesellschaft, Stock Corporation
AG	Die Aktiengesellschaft (legal periodical)
AktG	Aktiengesetz, Stock Corporation Act
BAFin	Bundesanstalt für Finanzdienstleistungsaufsicht (Supervisory Office for Financial Services)
BayObLG	Bayerisches Oberstes Landesgericht (Supreme Appeal Court of Bavaria)
BB	Betriebs-Berater (legal periodical)
BGB	Bürgerliches Gesetzbuch (Civil Code)
BGH	Bundesgerichtshof (Federal Supreme Court)
BGHZ	Entscheidungen des BGH in Zivilsachen (official case reporter of the Federal Supreme Court regarding civil law cases)
BKR	Zeitschrift für Bank- und Kapitalmarktrecht (legal periodical)
BMF	Bundesministerium der Finanzen (Federal Ministry of Finance)
BT-Drucks.	Bundestagsdrucksache (bill submitted to the Federal Parliament)
BVerfG	Bundesverfassungsgericht (Federal Constitutional Court)
BVerfGE	Entscheidungen des Bundesverfassungsgerichts (official case reporter of the Federal Constitutional Court)
CFR	Code of Federal Regulations (U. S.)
DB	Der Betrieb (legal periodical)
DStR	Deutsches Steuerrecht (legal/tax periodical)
ESOP	Employee Stock Option Plan
FSO	Federal Supervisory Office (Bundesanstalt für Finanzdienstleistungsaufsicht)
GAAP	Generally Accepted Accounting Principles
GmbH	Gesellschaft mit beschränkter Haftung (Limited Liability Company)
GmbHG	Gesetz betreffend die Gesellschaften mit beschränkter Haftung (Limited Liability Company Act)
GWB	Gesetz gegen Wettbewerbsbeschränkungen (Antitrust Act)
IdW	Institut der Wirtschaftsprüfer in Deutschland (German Association of Certified Accountants)
KGaA	Kommanditgesellschaft auf Aktien (Partnership Limited by Shares)

Abkürzungsverzeichnis

LBO	Leveraged Buyout
LG	Landgericht (Regional Court)
NJW	Neue Juristische Wochenschrift (legal periodical)
NZG	Neue Zeitschrift für Gesellschaftsrecht (legal periodical)
ÖBA	Österreichisches Bankarchiv (Austrian legal periodical)
OLG	Oberlandesgericht (Appeal Court)
RdW	Recht der Wirtschaft (Austrian legal periodical)
SEC	U. S. Securities and Exchange Commission
U.S.C.	United States Code
WiB	Wirtschaftsrechtliche Beratung (legal periodical)
WM	Zeitschrift für Wirtschafts- und Bankrecht, Wertpapiermitteilungen (legal periodical)
WPg	Die Wirtschaftsprüfung
WpÜG	Wertpapiererwerbs- und Übernahmegesetz (Act on the Purchase of Securities and on Takeover Offers – Takeover Act)
ZBB	Zeitschrift für Bankrecht und Bankwirtschaft (legal periodical)
ZGR	Zeitschrift für Unternehmens- und Gesellschaftsrecht (legal periodical)
ZIP	Zeitschrift für Wirtschaftsrecht (legal periodical)

Preface

Takeover Law in Germany

I. Overview

A new Act on the Purchase of Securities and on Takeovers ("Takeover Act") came into force in Germany on January 1, 2002. This Act creates, for the first time in Germany, a legal framework for public tender offers, in particular for the case that a controlling influence over a stock corporation is acquired by means of a public takeover process. Previously a voluntary takeover code, to which many of the quoted companies in Germany had not subscribed, applied.

The Takeover Act is intended:
- to provide guidelines for a fair and orderly bid process, without either encouraging or preventing takeovers,
- to improve information and transparency for the affected shareholders and employees,
- to strengthen the legal position of minority shareholders in the case of a takeover, and
- to harmonize with usual international standards.

The Act applies to public offers for securities of target companies having their registered offices in Germany and admitted on a European stock exchange. Obligations to provide information in the interests of "comprehensive transparency" have been introduced for the offeror, concerning its intentions, its financing of the bid and its financial situation.

II. The Obligation to Maintain Neutrality

1. The New Situation in Germany

By far the most controversial question was and is the behavior required of the management board of the target company, and whether, in particular, it can resort to "defense mechanisms" against a so-called "hostile takeover bid." In this connection poison pills ("Giftpillen"), which are intended to deter an unwelcome investor by issuing shares at a bargain price with the offeror excluded from the issue, are often referred to. In addition, capital increases (e.g. the issue of shares to a White Knight), the purchase of its own shares (self-tender offers) in order to increase the stock exchange price, the sale of the target's "crown jewels," and, not least, the acquisition of a competitor in order to make the takeover difficult under antitrust law, are defense mechanisms successfully applied in the U.S. In practice it has even happened that the management board of a German company spent over 0.4 billion DM on a defense campaign.

In July 2001, a proposed solution at European level according to which the management board of a target company should take an entirely neutral position, failed. The Takeover Act has opted for a more differentiated scheme allowing a limited scope of defensive steps in certain circumstances, and has thereby gained broad support from industry and management, as well as from trade unions. The limitations to the duty of neutrality in the Takeover Act were criticized in that the legislature gave way, on the one hand, to the trade unions' concern to protect jobs endangered in takeover situations, and, on the other, to influential managers concerned to preserve their own jobs, so that the management board is typically in a situation of conflict of interests if a "hostile takeover bid" arises. However, as we will see, the legal scope of possible defensive actions is quite narrow, and, in practice, defensive measures will predominantly be used in order to increase the consideration offered for the target's shares and will rarely prevent a hostile bid from ultimately being successful. Both the Vodafone/Mannesmann and the INA/FAG Kugelfischer cases are vivid examples in this respect. Overall, the Takeover Act provides for a solid level playing field for public takeover bids.

The Takeover Act allows for defensive steps in three graduated stages. First, the management board may of course continue the daily business of the target and take other actions as it would "in the course of due and diligent management of a company which is not affected by a takeover bid." In particular, it may continue to pursue a certain business strategy even if this might impair the chances of success of a takeover offer.

Secondly, the management board and the supervisory board (without the participation of the shareholders' meeting) may take defensive measures which are exclusively for the purpose of preventing the takeover bid. It is true that this provision defeats the property rights of the shareholders who are willing to sell. However, when making the decision on taking defensive steps, the board remains bound by the principle that it must exercise its business discretion in the interests of the company and of the shareholders. In this respect, the fact that the (non-executive) supervisory board must approve defensive measures is in most instances an adequate safeguard against illegal self-dealing of the management board; the supervisory board members usually have only a marginal part of their wealth connected to the company, and will be reluctant to ruin their professional reputations by approving defensive tactics which are to the detriment of the target company and its shareholders. Moreover, the scope of possible defensive measures is quite limited, as the supervisory and management boards may not interfere with the responsibilities of the shareholders' meeting in general.

Thirdly, the shareholders have the opportunity to provide the management board with discretion as far as defense mechanisms are concerned. Such shareholders' resolutions, which are valid for no more than a period of eighteen months, will not play any significant role, as the shareholders will generally not impair reasonable expectations of receiving a sizable premium in a public takeover, and stock markets would punish such resolutions with a discount on the share prices. An uneasy feeling may arise in the case where a dominant majority shareholder, in agreement with the management and supervisory boards, lays the foundation for defensive tactics by means of shareholders' resolutions and corresponding measures by the boards. However, any such shareholders' resolutions will often be subject to legal challenges. It is beyond question that the general meeting may not damage the company in order to ensure a particular structure of the shareholders or to prevent takeovers. The new takeover provisions do not alter this clear legal position, otherwise they would be unconstitutional under the property rights guarantee of the Federal Constitution. Moreover, such potential collaboration between management and a majority shareholder to the detriment of the minority shareholders is inherent in companies with a low percentage of free-floating shares which usually trade lower than the shares of companies with a broadly diversified body of shareholders.

Overall, therefore, the defense opportunities of the general meeting and the management under the new takeover provisions are not extensive.

2. Comparison with U.S. Law

U.S. law takes a different approach in some respects. U.S. securities regulation (the Williams Act with its Regulations 14 D and 14 E) does not impose an obligation of neutrality; when U.S. courts have nevertheless repeatedly emphasized a (differentiated) duty of neutrality, such decisions were based on general (state) corporate law, and in particular in the sense of a fiduciary duty owed by the management to the company and to the shareholders. Accordingly, a takeover bid which is too low should be contested in the interests of the shareholders. The board of management has, in this regard, broad discretion under corporate law, i.e. the (limited) business judgment rule, in order to deflect an inappropriate takeover offer, without damaging the company or its shareholders. As well as the buy-back of its own shares and the issue of new shares under rights plans, which enable the existing shareholders of the target company to acquire shares below value and exclude the subscription rights of the new majority shareholder, can be introduced. Here one speaks of "poison pills," which the management board of the target company can create, while in Germany not even the general meeting can create such poison pills in the articles of association. Overall, U.S. law has a very clear approach as to defensive tactics which are allowed to deflect inappropriate offers provided these do not damage shareholder value by obstructing favorable bids.

III. Mandatory Offer

1. The Legal Position in Germany

The new provisions relating to mandatory offers represent a significant interference in private autonomy. At the threshold of 30% of the voting rights, the Takeover Act deems that the shareholder has acquired control of the company. It must then launch a public tender offer for the acquisition of the remaining shares at a reasonable price.

This obligation to make a mandatory offer does not apply if the controlling shareholder has acquired control by virtue of a public tender offer (under the Takeover Code such takeover offers were therefore called "voluntary mandatory offers"). However, a tender offer that aims at gaining control of the target must, in any event, be an offer to acquire all the shares in the target; a cap with a pro-rata acquisition is not permissible (prohibition against partial takeover offers).

Controlling shareholders who have gained control before the effective date of the Takeover Act (January 1, 2002) are under no duty to make a mandatory offer. It is understood that a mandatory offer may not retrospectively be imposed on them.

In the case of a mandatory offer, as well as in the case of a takeover bid aimed at gaining control, minimum price rules apply, i.e. the bidder must offer a certain minimum amount of consideration based upon average stock prices over a reference period of three months.

The intended protection of the minority by means of this mandatory offer is somewhat questionable in Germany, because compared to other jurisdictions ample minority protection is already provided by company law, according to which a controlling entity may not damage the controlled company to the disadvantage of the minority shareholders. For example, control and profit transfer agreements, which ultimately constitute "temporary mergers," are only possible if minority shareholders are adequately compensated. Moreover, there is within groups a relatively efficient control on the observance of the prohibition to cause damage to controlled entities, as the controlling entity, its management board, its supervisory board and auditors may become criminally and civilly liable if they breach the protection system existing for the benefit of controlled companies and their minority shareholders. However, there might still be controlling influence on a controlled entity that does not reach the threshold of "damage," but which does not nevertheless further the interests of the company and of the minority shareholders; as for this "grey area," one may very well deem the provisions on mandatory offers a reasonable supplement to other minority protection features. On the other hand, an "over protection" may be reached at some point.

Squeeze-out provisions according to which a principal shareholder holding 95% and over of the nominal capital can resolve in a general meeting to transfer the shares of the minority shareholders in consideration of a reasonable cash settlement, were finally introduced in Germany at the same time as the Takeover Act. Though some reservations may exist as to the sense and justification of this squeeze-out procedure – as it represents a significant interference with the private autonomy of minority shareholders who lose their shares involuntarily – its advantage is that awkward minority shareholders, who may be a source of disturbance in such a majority situation, can be removed. At the same time considerable expense is spared by the removal of mandatory minority protection measures. Overall, the squeeze-out procedure is a meaningful novelty in German corporate law.

2. The Legal Position under U.S. Law

The law in the U.S. is in some respects different from that in Germany. In the tender offer rules, no minimum price regulation is given. In the U.S., more trust is evidently placed in the power of the free market. Only the principle of equality of treatment applies, according to which unfair attacks are excluded and the same consideration must be offered to all target shareholders (best price rule). As there is no mandatory offer (except for certain "cash out" procedures in a few U.S. jurisdictions), partial takeover offers are generally admissible. However, there is the obligation in the U.S. to provide considerably more comprehensive information in the offer document (so-called Schedule 14 D-1). The confidence in the capital markets in respect of appropriate pricing is based therefore on the most comprehensive information possible being available to participants on the capital market. Supply and demand should then regulate matters, because all participants are adequately informed and therefore in a position to make free decisions.

IV. The Position in Europe

At the European level at the present time a new directive is being attempted following the failure of that intended in Summer 2001. It is to be expected that the content of such a directive would include most of the provisions of the previous draft of 2001, according to which a strict neutrality obligation was to be imposed on the board as a mandatory obligation, to a significantly greater extent than in Germany under the current Takeover Act. Germany may, therefore, be required to adjust the Takeover Act. However, as in practice the actual extent of defensive measures should remain quite limited, the changes to be expected should not have very significant consequences.

Chapter 1. The Corporate Structure of a German Stock Corporation

The following chapter is a short description of the corporate structure of a German stock corporation focussed on the questions which arise if the stock corporation is the target of a takeover bid. Aspects such as the formation of a stock corporation or the problems related to affiliated enterprises of a stock corporation are not, therefore, part of this chapter.[1]

1. Corporate Governance

a) The Two Tier Board System

German corporate law has established a two-tier board system consisting of the management board and the supervisory board. No person may be a member of both boards of the same company at the same time; equally, no member of the supervisory board may be a registered authorized officer („*Prokurist*") or a general manager („*Handlungsbevollmächtigter*") of the company.[2] As a very limited exception, a member of the supervisory board may be seconded or delegated to the management board; during the secondment, the secondee may not act as a member of the supervisory board.[3]

The reason for this incompatibility of membership on the two boards is the strict separation between the functions and the duties of the two boards: the **management board** represents the company "in and out of court."[4] The **supervisory board** supervises the management of the company and is entitled to inspect and examine the books and records of the company. The law states explicitly that "management duties may not be conferred on the supervisory board."[5] The articles of association may provide, or the supervisory board by majority decision may determine, that certain types of transactions may only be entered into by the company (management board) if the supervisory board has granted its consent. Usually, the articles of association carry a certain list of transactions which require the supervisory board's approval and the supervisory board establishes a further, often more detailed, list of such transactions. Such transaction lists often include the for-

---

[1] Other introductory works to German stock corporations in the English language are Schneider/Heidenhain, The German Stock Corporation Act, 2nd ed. 2000; Matthew/Bender, Business Transactions in Germany Volume 3, New York/San Francisco 2000.
[2] § 105 Stock Corporation Act.
[3] § 105 para. 2 Stock Corporation Act.
[4] § 78 para. 1 Stock Corporation Act.
[5] § 111 para. 4 Stock Corporation Act.

mation, acquisition, sale or liquidation of companies, the acquisition and encumbrance of real estate, major lending and borrowing transactions, and the like. Often, transactions of minor economic importance are excluded from the requirement of the consent of the supervisory board. Should the supervisory board refuse to consent to a transaction proposed by the management board, the management board is entitled to put the decision to the shareholders' meeting which, by a majority of not less than three quarters of the votes cast, may grant the consent and thus overrule the refusal of the supervisory board.

b) The Supervisory Board

The supervisory board consists of three members or a higher number which is a multiple of three, up to a maximum of 21. Apart from special rules for the coal and steel industry, two different scenarios exist under the German codetermination laws:

- If the corporation has more than 500 but less than 2000 employees, one third of the members of the supervisory board must be elected by the employees.
- If the corporation has more than 2000 employees, one half of the members of the supervisory board must be elected by the employees.[6]

Even in the latter case, the members elected by the shareholders are entitled to the chair and the chairman has the casting vote on all resolutions.

The shareholders' meeting may also elect substitute members of the supervisory board in the event that any member of the supervisory board does not complete his term of office.

The members of the supervisory board, except for those elected by the employees, are elected by the shareholders' meeting by simple majority. The shareholders' meeting also determines the term of the supervisory board up to a maximum of approximately five years[7] (usually this maximum term is chosen). During such term the shareholders' meeting may remove without cause any member elected by the shareholders' meeting but only with a majority of three-quarters. The articles of association may provide for a different (higher or lower) majority and for additional requirements, although this is not common. A further way to remove members of the supervisory board is by petition to court by the supervisory board itself. Such a motion requires a simple majority of the members of the supervisory board, but must be based on "cause relating to the person of such member." Such a

---

[6] The special question of holding companies – where the stock corporation itself has less than the 2000 employees but together with the number of employees of its subsidiaries has more than this number – is not dealt with in this chapter.

[7] Four full business years plus the time from the ordinary shareholders' meeting before the first business year until the beginning of the first business year, plus the time from the end of the fourth business year to the following ordinary shareholders' meeting, which altogether makes, depending on the dates of the shareholders' meetings, about five years.

petition may also be brought against members elected by the employees. Finally, members of the supervisory board may resign their office at their discretion; the articles of association usually require that notice of one month be given before such a resignation becomes effective. If the supervisory board does not have the number of members required by law and the articles (for example, following death, dismissal, removal) the competent court can replace the missing members until the shareholders' meeting or the employees (if the missing member is to be elected by the employees) have had a chance to elect a successor. In the case of replacement of one of the members to be elected by the shareholders' meeting, the courts would often follow the (informal) proposals of the major shareholders, in particular if they also indicate an intention to vote for the proposed candidate at the next shareholders' meeting when the term of office of the member appointed by the court expires.

Usually, the court appoints replacement members of the supervisory board only after an interim period of three months, except "in urgent cases." Supervisory boards which are subject to "full" codetermination (50% of members elected by the employees) are always deemed to be urgent cases in this sense since the balance of the same number of board members of both "benches" is an essential element of codetermination.

All members of the supervisory board – including the members elected by the shareholders' meeting – exercise their office independently of the shareholders' meeting. The shareholders' meeting is not entitled to interfere with actions and resolutions of the supervisory board. In addition, the election of the chairman and the vice-chairman of the supervisory board is the sole responsibility of the supervisory board itself.

The quorum for any decision by the supervisory board, if not otherwise set by specific law or the articles, is a minimum of one half of its statutory members (even in the case of an incomplete supervisory board), in any event not less than three members (which means that the quorum of a board consisting of three members requires that all these members always take part in the decision-making).

Usually personal attendance at meetings is required and a supervisory board member may not simply send a proxy. In certain circumstances, however, votes in writing may be accepted from absent members. Resolutions of the supervisory board which are passed in writing or by telephone are only valid if no member of the board objects.[8]

Supervisory boards of publicly listed stock corporations must convene at least twice per half year and whenever the needs of the business require. Members of the management board usually attend, though, purely as guests. The auditor of the company must attend the meeting at which the supervisory board discusses and approves the annual accounts.

---

[8] According to a recent change of § 110 para. 3 Stock Corporation Act, supervisory board meetings held by video or telephone conference count towards the required minimum number of supervisory board meetings, i.e. two meetings bi-annually for public companies and one meeting for private companies.

c) The Management Board

Apart from its duties to supervise the management board and to consent to specific types of transactions, it is the supervisory board which appoints the members of the management board.

The maximum term of the members of the management board is five years. Re-appointments and extensions of the period of office – in each case limited to a further five years – are possible.

The supervisory board may revoke the appointment of a member of the management board only for good cause, such as gross breach of duty or failure to manage the company properly. Business decisions by the member which turn out to be wrong, or a weak performance of the company (or the branch for which the member of the management board is responsible) do not, as such, necessarily justify a revocation. Should the member of the management board question the grounds for his removal, the supervisory board can either call a shareholders' meeting to vote on a resolution of "no confidence" in the member, or implement the removal which is, in any event, valid until rendered invalid by a final and unappealable court decision, which will rarely happen before the term of office of the board member has expired, should all three court instances be exhausted. For all practical purposes, the supervisory board is therefore in a position to revoke the appointment of a member of the management board subject to the company being willing to pay the entire remuneration of the member of the management board as provided in his service contract for the remainder of its term.

The supervisory board usually not only appoints the members of the management board but also defines their responsibilities (CEO, CFO, etc.).

The members of the management board must report to the supervisory board regularly about the business and intended transactions.

d) The Shareholders' Meeting

The function of the shareholders' meeting is to elect the members of the supervisory board (except the members to be elected by the employees under codetermination laws), to ratify the acts of the members of the supervisory board and of the management board, and to appoint the external auditor. In the annual general meeting – which must take place within eight months following the end of the financial year – the shareholders' meeting also must resolve upon the allocation and distribution of distributable profits.

Amendments to the articles, resolutions on increases or (less frequently) reductions of the share capital and the issue of authorized capital and contingent capital increases[9] as well as consents to profit transfer agreements and control agreements with subsidiaries, are the most common additional resolutions passed in an ordinary shareholders' meeting.

---

[9] *See* Chapter 1 no. 2. c. and d. below.

The resolutions of shareholders' meetings are subject to actions to set aside on the grounds of a violation of law or the articles. Such an action does not require any minimum number of shares to be held by the plaintiff. Since certain resolutions require registration in the commercial register to be valid (amendment of the articles, increase of the share capital/issue of new shares, resolutions on authorized capital and so forth) and the resolutions are usually not registered as long as law suits against them are pending, actions have substantial influence regardless of how well-founded they are. Only a few resolutions relating to special forms of mergers may be the subject of special injunction proceedings to determine the chances of any such action.

2. Shares and Capital

a) Voting Shares and Non-voting Shares

Shares are either voting shares or non-voting shares. Voting shares grant one vote per share. "Golden shares" which grant special voting rights are not admissible. Non-voting shares must carry preferential dividend and/or liquidation rights. The number of non-voting (preferential) shares may not exceed the number of voting shares. If the preferential dividend granted for a non-voting share in the articles of association is not fully paid in a financial year (because a sufficient amount of distributable profits has not been generated) and if these dividends are not paid in the first following year, the shares are vested with the same voting rights as "normal" voting shares until the preferential dividends have been fully paid for all outstanding years.

Non-voting shares do not grant voting rights except for:

- resolutions restricting the preferential dividends;
- issue of new non-voting shares which have preferential or equal rights with respect to the existing non-voting shares, except if a rights issue is involved and the holders of the existing non-voting shares are not excluded from the subscription for the new shares.

b) Issue of New Shares

It is not, generally, within the competence of the management board to issue new shares.

The issue of new shares requires a majority of three-quarters of the votes cast in the shareholders' meeting. The articles of association may specify a higher or lower majority and/or other requirements (e.g. approval of the supervisory board) for the issue of non-voting (preferential) shares. The articles of association cannot provide for a lower majority than three-quarters of the votes cast for such a resolution.

The issue of new shares must be by rights issue in order not to dilute the holdings of existing shareholders and the holders of existing shares have pre-emptive rights to subscribe for new shares in proportion to their existing shares except in cases of:

- contributions in kind;
- contributions in cash if the new shares do not exceed 10% of the existing shares and the offer price of the new shares is close to the stock market price of the shares (not more than 3 to 5% below the stock market price).

c) Contingent Capital Increase

The shareholders' meeting can resolve upon a contingent capital increase which lays the ground for the issue of new shares only if the relevant conditions are fulfilled. Contingent capital increases are permitted only:

- to prepare a merger,
- to grant conversion rights to holders of convertible bonds,
- to grant stock warrants to holders of warrant bonds, or
- for stock incentive programs.

d) Authorized Capital

The original articles of association or, more frequently, the shareholders' meeting can authorize the management board to issue new shares. The number of shares which may be authorized may not exceed half of the existing shares as of the date of such authorization. The above-mentioned rules on pre-emptive rights apply *mutatis mutandis* to the issue of new shares based on such authorizations.

Chapter 2. Development of Takeover Law in Germany

1. Situation until 1995

Until 1995, German securities regulations did not contain specific provisions for public tender offers.

Tender offers were merely subject to general corporate law principles which, however, apply to all business acquisitions and takeovers, whether by means of public offers or privately negotiated transactions. Therefore, only a limited legal framework for public tender offers was derived from generally applicable corporate law and securities regulation, such as:

- A limited duty of neutrality towards hostile tender offers is supported by general fiduciary duties of the board towards the company and its shareholders.[1]
- Disclosure to the shareholders and the capital markets was rudimentarily regulated by general corporate disclosure rules.[2]
- A ban on market manipulations within the context of takeover offers.[3]

However, no comprehensive substantive or procedural basis for public tender offers was available. For this reason, the Stock Exchange Expert Commission (*„Börsensachverständigenkommission"*) promulgated guidelines on takeover bids in 1979.[4] However, those guidelines were not binding on the offeror or the target company.

2. Takeover Code 1995

It was not until 1995 that more comprehensive takeover regulations were promulgated, the so-called Takeover Code (*„Übernahmekodex"*) of the Stock Exchange Expert Commission (*„Börsensachverständigenkommission"*). This Takeover Code did not have the binding force of law; it was designed as a recommended procedure for public bids. In the course of its history, the Takeover Code was, however, widely accepted by public companies in Germany. While as of April 2000, only 540 of 933 publicly traded companies had voluntarily accepted the Takeover Code, this proportion sub-

---

[1] §§ 53a, 93 Stock Corporation Act; Schanz, NZG 2000 p. 337, 340; Krause, AG 2000 p. 217, 218; Hirte/Schander in Rosen/Seifert, Übernahme börsennotierter Unternehmen, p. 341, 348; this is the approach that is still prevalent under U.S. law.

[2] § 131 Stock Corporation Act: information rights of shareholders at the shareholders' meeting; § 15 Securities Trading Act: general publication duties for public companies regarding relevant facts.

[3] § 4 Securities Trading Act.

[4] BMF – Nachrichten 6/1979 p. 1 et seq.

stantially increased by the end of 2001; at that time, 802 of 913 companies publicly listed in Germany had adopted the Takeover Code. This relatively high self obligation ratio is partly due to the fact that the German Stock Exchange had made listings in several important large, mid and small cap indices contingent on an unreserved compliance with the Takeover Code. Likewise, a listing on the "Neuer Markt" rendered participants subject to the provisions of the Takeover Code. Both of the recent hostile takeover battles in Germany, the Vodafone/Mannesmann and INA Holding/FAG Kugelfischer cases, were governed by the Takeover Code.

Though a rather basic set of takeover regulations, the Takeover Code already contained the most important principles of the Takeover Act 2002 now in force, such as:

- a strict and expeditious **procedure** for public tender offers;
- relatively ample **disclosure** requirements for the offeror, in particular in the offer document;[5]
- duty of **equal treatment** of the shareholders of the target company;[6]
- **mandatory offers** for controlling shareholders, and fair price rules;[7]
- **duty of neutrality** imposed on the target´s management.[8]

The Takeover Code, which was amended as of January 1998, remained in force until the beginning of 2002 when the new Takeover Act 2002 came into force.[9]

3. The Takeover Act 2002 ("Übernahmegesetz")

The Vodafone/Mannesmann takeover battle was the one important event that finally triggered the creation of a comprehensive body of takeover regulations by the legislature. The final version of the Takeover Act effective as of January 1, 2002 was based on several drafts, the first of which was published on June 29, 2000.[10]

Concurrently, the European Union was working on a "Takeover Directive." The effort to create Europe-wide takeover regulations commenced as early as 1974 when the European Commission hired U.K. Prof. Pennington to draw up a "Report on Takeover and other General Bids" along with a first draft of a Takeover Directive.[11] Following several other drafts (of 1989, 1990, 1996 and 1997), the Council of Ministers finally adopted a "Common

---

[5] Art. 2, 7, 8 Takeover Code.
[6] Art. 1 Takeover Code.
[7] Art. 16 Takeover Code.
[8] Art. 19 Takeover Code.
[9] The Stock Exchange Expert Commission officially rescinded the Takeover Code as of March 4, 2002.
[10] "Diskussionsentwurf eines Gesetzes zur Regelung von Unternehmensübernahmen," published in NZG 2000 p. 844 et seq.; two other drafts followed on March 12, 2001 ("Referentenentwurf") and July 11, 2001 ("Regierungsentwurf").
[11] *See* Zinser, WM 2002 p. 15.

Position" regarding the enforcement of a directive in the area of corporate law regarding takeover offers.[12]

While the first drafts of the German Takeover Act were largely in line with the provisions of this common position, the Directive finally failed in the European Parliament in a stalemate of 273:273 votes. This was mainly due to the fact that the last draft of the German Takeover Act of July 2001 *("Regierungsentwurf")* was not in compliance with the strict and unlimited duty of neutrality provided for in the proposed Directive;[13] although the Takeover Act also contains a principle of neutrality, there are several important limitations allowing defensive actions which contradicted the provisions of the draft of the new Directive. As such, the German Takeover Act came into force on January 1, 2002 as national law with its scope being limited to companies with their registered offices in Germany.

While there are still ongoing efforts of the European Union to create Europe-wide takeover regulations, one can today hardly predict whether and when such efforts will finally put Europe on the track of a common tender offer and takeover law.

---

[12] Common Position adopted by the Council on June 19, 2000 on the 13th EU-Directive on Company Law concerning Takeover Bids (Official Journal C 023, 24/01/2001 p. 1–14).

[13] Art. 9.

Chapter 3. Need for Efficient Takeover Regulations

In general, dense and complicated legal regulations are considered an obstacle to economic freedom and dynamic development. Germany frequently suffers from extensive statutes and over-regulation in many economic fields. However, the opposite seems to be true for regulation of the capital markets.

The U.S. has the most extensive capital markets regulation. While the provisions of the Securities Act of 1933 and the Securities Exchange Act of 1934 are rather basic, the regulations promulgated under the Acts by the Securities Exchange Commission are extremely comprehensive and complicated. Yet, capital markets in the U.S. are deemed to be the most efficient in the world.

This phenomenon of co-existence of extensive regulation and efficiency of capital markets is largely due to the fact that capital markets by themselves do not ensure a level playing field. Extensive regulation is required to deal with information asymmetries inherent in capital markets and conflicts between minority shareholders and investors on the one hand and large institutional investors and the issuers of securities on the other. Minority shareholders will generally not invest substantial amounts of time or effort to control the management of the company as they would carry the full burden and cost of these control activities (so-called "information cost") but only benefit to the small extent of their shareholdings. They would rather rely on other shareholders to exercise control over the management (sometimes referred to as the "free rider problem"), with the result that no minority shareholder will exercise sufficient control, thereby devaluing the shares issued to each of them.[1] Therefore, comprehensive capital market rules are designed to provide for extensive disclosure in order that the market can price securities properly without relying on control activities of shareholders and having to mediate conflicts arising from the separation of ownership from control. In countries with little market efficiency and low shareholder protection, companies with one or a few large shareholders dominate the market,[2] as the high information costs in such countries act as a deterrent to investment by minority shareholders.

These principles apply equally to takeover offer rules. The shares of target companies in capital markets with a lack of protection for minority shareholders generally trade at a discount, as minority shareholders are afraid that they will be forced to accept an underpriced offer. This consequence has been vividly demonstrated by several studies on the difference between prices for preference and ordinary shares of the same issuer. Though preference shares should expect a higher amount of cash flow at a

---

[1] This is a typical case of a so-called "Prisoners' Dilemma."
[2] Pellens/Hillebrandt, AG 2001 p. 57, 59.

reduced risk, they in fact generally trade at a substantial discount.[3] Though the reasons for this are not entirely clear, some analyses suggest that actual or potential private benefits to investors are the immediate cause of these discounts; thus, for example, institutional investors may exert a disproportionately high influence over the company by acquiring a relatively small amount of the issued shares of the company (e.g. 25.1% of the total amount of issued ordinary shares of a company which has 50% preference shares will confer more than 50% of the voting rights) and then create private benefits (e.g. by means of transfer pricing arrangements, changes in strategy beneficial for the investors' other business interests) at the cost of the minority of ordinary shareholders and the preference shareholders. Therefore, the voting rights of ordinary shares have a particularly high value for potential strategic investors. This explanation accords with the fact that the discount at which preference shares are traded diminishes when large shareholders acquire ordinary shares.[4] When this occurs neither an existing shareholder holding a large proportion of voting rights nor a potential new investor will be willing to pay a premium for the voting rights.

One interesting fact is that, according to empirical studies[5] in Germany in 1999, the discount at which preference shares were traded was substantially lower for the shares of those companies which had voluntarily accepted the German Takeover Code. As the Takeover Code is designed to ensure a fair takeover procedure with safeguards against unfair treatment of the minority shareholders of the target company, the capital markets clearly perceive the danger of the takeover procedure being exploited for the private benefit of the bidder or corporate raider and future majority shareholder to be reduced when the safeguards of the Takeover Code apply to ensure fair and equal treatment of the target's minority shareholders. This perception is supported by a comparison of the discounts at which preference shares in different countries are traded. The discounts are highest in those countries with a low standard of minority shareholder protection and lowest in countries with extensive securities regulation and ample safeguards for minority shareholders (e.g. an average discount of 11% was observed in the U.S., 26% in Germany, and up to 82% in Italy).[6]

All this demonstrates that efficient capital markets depend on a comprehensive network of securities regulations designed for the protection of all market participants, so that proper pricing of securities is achieved on the basis of expected cash flow, and that frictions based on the danger of private benefits and agency conflicts are minimized. Takeover offer rules are an essential feature of such efficient securities regulation schemes, and the authors unanimously welcome the decision of the German legislature to finally give the takeover offer rules the force of law.

---

[3] An empirical study in 1994 suggests that the voting right has an average value of 24% of the price of common stock (adjusted for the value of the preferred dividend), Binz/Sorg, DStR 1994 p. 993, 995; Jung/Wachtler, AG 2001 p. 513, 516.
[4] Kruse/Berg/Weber, ZBB 1993 p. 23, 28; Jung/Wachtler, AG 2001 p. 513, 516.
[5] *See* Pellens/Hillebrandt, AG 2001 p. 57, 64.
[6] Pellens/Hillebrandt, AG 2001 p. 57, 58.

Chapter 4. Takeovers under the new Takeover Act

1. Objective of the Takeover Act

The objective of the Takeover Act is to create a framework within which public offers for the acquisition of certain securities (in particular, shares) in Germany can take place. Germany will thereby keep pace with globalization and meet the needs of the financial markets in such a way as to strengthen its position as a commercial and financial center in an increasingly competitive international marketplace. The German legislature *("Bundestag")* specified three objectives of the Act, which were to be met in addition to bringing German law in line with international standards:[1]

- creating guidelines for a fair and orderly bid procedure, without encouraging or hindering takeovers,
- improving information and transparency for the shareholders and employees involved, and
- strengthening the legal position of minority shareholders in the context of takeovers.

In order to achieve these objectives, the German legislature has created a standardized formal takeover procedure, which places considerable restrictions on the offerors freedom to structure the offer in terms of content, procedure and timeframe. A further important effect of the formalization of the procedure is the speeding up of the takeover process: a takeover offer should not distract the management of the target from its duties in operating the business for longer than absolutely necessary.[2]

2. Scope of Application

a) Matters Regulated by the Takeover Act

(1) Public offers

The Act regulates (i) all public offers made voluntarily and (ii) all mandatory (pursuant to the Takeover Act, since intended to result in a takeover) public offers. The public offers must relate to the acquisition (by way of exchange or purchase) of securities of listed stock corporations *("Aktiengesellschaft")* and listed partnerships limited by shares *("Kommanditgesellschaft auf Aktien")* the registered offices of which are in Germany.[3] The Takeover Act therefore regulates takeovers by way of public offers with the

---

[1] Explanatory Memorandum of the Federal Government on the Takeover Act, BT-Drucks. 14/7034 of October 5, 2001, p. 28.
[2] § 3 para. 4 Takeover Act.
[3] § 2 para. 1 Takeover Act.

objective of acquiring control of such companies. The Act additionally regulates any and all other public offers in respect of shares of such companies. This includes offers where the offeror[4] wishes to acquire only part of the shares in the target[5] (without acquiring a sufficiently high proportion of the voting rights to create a controlling stake in the target) as well as offers which effectively consolidate pre-existing controlling shareholdings.

(2) Securities of the target

The Takeover Act applies to public offers[6] for the acquisition of ordinary or preference shares, and also to offers for securities and certificates of a comparable nature (interim certificates, depository receipts) and to offers for securities under which shares can be acquired (e.g. convertible debentures, convertible bonds, warrant-linked bonds and options).[7]

According to a statement of the Federal Supervisory Office[8] regarding a buyback of its own shares by Siemens AG, the Takeover Act is applicable to **self-tender offers**, which, under German law, a corporation may make for shares representing a maximum of 10% of its nominal share capital.[9] This view is in compliance with the wording of the Takeover Act;[10] it is, how-

---

[4] The Act describes the person making the offer as an offeror, a description which can include also a group "acting in concert" or parties affiliated with the offeror; § 2 para. 4, 5 Takeover Act.

[5] The company, the securities of which are the subject of the offer, is referred to by the Act as "the target," § 2 para. 3 Takeover Act.

[6] Although the concept of "public" offers is central to the Takeover Act and to its scope of application, what constitutes an offer to the public is not defined in the Takeover Act. The Explanatory Memorandum of the Federal Government states that the legislature intentionally did not provide a statutory definition: this would be an almost impossible task given the infinite variety of circumstances which might constitute a public offer, and given the danger that providing a definition might encourage individuals to find a way in which to circumvent the definition (Explanatory Memorandum of the Federal Government on § 2 para. 11 Takeover Act, BT-Drucks. 14/7034 of October 5, 2001, p. 33). However, the Explanatory Memorandum does go on to state that one criterion of whether or not an offer is made to the public should be whether it is directed at only a limited number of persons or at many holders of shares. A further criterion should be whether or not an offer is personally tailored to individuals (not generally the case with a public offer) and whether or not the offer contains conditions which would allow the offeror to withdraw the offer if a certain level of acceptances among the target's shareholders were not reached. For detailed commentary on the concept of what is a "public offer" see Fleischer, ZIP 2001 p. 1653 et seq.

[7] § 2 para. 2 Takeover Act. The extension of the Takeover Act to securities is limited by the fact that the obligation to make a full bid, which arises in connection with a takeover offer or a mandatory offer, only relates to shares (§ 32 and §§ 39, 32 Takeover Act).

[8] "Bundesanstalt für Finanzdienstleistungsaufsicht."

[9] § 71 para. 1 clause 1 no. 8 Stock Corporation Act.

[10] Fleischer/Körber, BB 2001 p. 2589, 2593; Oechsler, NZG 2001 p. 817, 818. In the U.S., specific provisions apply to self-tender offers, sec. 13 (e) Securities Exchange Act 1934, 15 U.S.C. § 78m.

ever, questionable whether it is in compliance with the underlying principles of the Takeover Act. The Act does not, in any event, apply where a company repurchases its own shares on the stock exchange.

(3) Admission to public trading

The Takeover Act applies only if the securities of the target company are listed on a "regulated market."[11] However, the Takeover Act also applies to stock corporations the shares of which are listed on the "Neuer Markt" and on other special markets and must therefore be *admitted* to the Regulated Market *("Geregelter Markt")*, but are nevertheless *traded* in the unregulated market *("Freiverkehr")*.[12] This conclusion is correct, in the authors' view.[13] According to the Regulations of the Neuer Markt, admission of shares to the Neuer Markt is conditional on the same shares also being *admitted* to (though not quoted on) the Regulated Market of the Frankfurt Stock Exchange.[14]

b) Takeover Offers

As set out above, the Takeover Act applies to all public offers for the acquisition of shares in the target; however, the Takeover Act contains some specific provisions which apply to takeover offers only:

- The determination of the minimum consideration to be offered to the shareholders of the target is governed only by minimum price rules.[15]
- It is prohibited to limit the offer to a certain portion of the tendered shares (not even pro rata).[16]
- As it is expected that the management board may try to obstruct the takeover, the Act regulates the reaction of the boards of the target (including defensive tactics).[17]

A takeover offer is made when the purpose of the offer is to acquire **control** of the target.[18] A takeover offer is not, however, involved if the bidder already owns a controlling interest in the target and aims to acquire additional shares by means of a public offer.

Control of a corporation is achieved when one shareholder holds at least 30% of the voting rights in the target.[19] Those shares in the target which

---

[11] § 2 para. 7 Takeover Act.

[12] Explanatory Memorandum of the Federal Government on § 2 para. 7 Takeover Act, BT-Drucks. 14/7034 of October 5, 2001, p. 35.

[13] *See* also Schüppen, Die Wirtschaftsprüfung 2001 p. 958, 960; different opinion: Mülbert, ZIP 2001 p. 1221, 1227.

[14] *See* 2.3 para. 1 Regulations of the Neuer Markt.

[15] § 31 Takeover Act.

[16] § 32 Takeover Act.

[17] § 33 Takeover Act.

[18] § 29 para. 1 Takeover Act.

[19] § 29 para. 2 Takeover Act.

have restricted voting rights attached must also be taken into account when calculating whether this threshold has been reached.

It is difficult to fix a threshold at which control can be deemed to be attained by statute, as (on the one hand) the 30% threshold does not constitute actual control (in the sense that it does not confer a majority at the general meeting). On the other hand, however, already less than 30% of the voting rights in the target will often secure a stable majority at a shareholders' meeting, since many shareholders will not bother to attend. Nevertheless, fixing the threshold at 30% does provide the market with a clear and unequivocal figure. A lower control threshold would not allow companies to acquire a minority shareholding (as defined by corporate law) whereas a higher threshold – according to the legislature – would not reflect the practical reality of low attendance at general meetings nor conform to equivalent provisions in other jurisdictions.[20]

In calculating the percentage of voting rights held by the offeror, there may be circumstances in which shares held by third parties will also be treated as being held by the offeror. In addition to the shares of the offeror's subsidiaries[21] being treated as belonging to the offeror,[22] shares will be treated as shares of the offeror in the following cases:

- where the shares are owned by a third party, but are held by that party on behalf of the offeror;
- where the offeror has transferred shares to a third party as security. These shares will not be ascribed to the offeror only if the third party holding the shares is entitled to exercise the voting rights attached to the shares and has declared its intention to exercise the voting rights independently of the instructions of the offeror;
- where the offeror has a usufruct in the shares of a third party;
- where the offeror may acquire ownership of certain shares merely by making a declaration to that effect, without the necessity of an intervention by a third party. This applies particularly to option agreements. Note, however, that most options merely grant the right to demand that the shares are transferred to the option holder.[23] Such option is not sufficient; the option must be designed in a way that upon exercise of the option the shares automatically vest in the option holder.[24]
- Where shares are entrusted to the offeror together with authority to exercise the voting right at the offeror's own discretion unless special instruc-

---

[20] Explanatory Memorandum of the Federal Government on § 29 Takeover Act, BT-Drucks. 14/7034 of October 5, 2001, p. 53. The corresponding laws in France, Italy, Austria, Switzerland and the U. K. also provide a threshold of 30% or one third of the voting rights.

[21] As defined in § 2 para. 6 Takeover Act.

[22] According to § 30 Takeover Act.

[23] In most cases of publicly traded options, those are usually settled by a clearing institution without the shares ever being transferred.

[24] Explanatory Memorandum of the Federal Government on § 30 para. 1 no. 5 Takeover Act, BT-Drucks. 14/7034 of October 5, 2001, p. 54; Geibel/Süßmann, WpÜG, § 30 annot. 20–22.

tions are given by the shareholder. No special depository relationship is required between the shareholder and the offeror. Shares may, therefore, be ascribed to an offeror where the offeror may exercise the voting rights attaching to those shares at his own discretion, in spite of the shares in question being held by a third party, and not the offeror.
- Where the offeror or its subsidiary co-ordinates its actions in relation to its shares in the target with a third party on the basis of a formal agreement or in any other manner (for example, a gentlemen's agreement). This cooperation is not limited to the exercise of voting rights in particular circumstances and includes situations where the parties could be deemed to be "acting in concert."

A subsidiary which falls within one of the above headings will be equated with the offeror. Its shares and the shares ascribed to it will be treated as being held by the offeror.

The Federal Supervisory Office may, on application, permit that shares in the target held by an offeror for trading purposes should not be taken into account in calculating the percentage of voting rights which that offeror holds.[25] However, voting rights attaching to shares which are granted this exemption may not be exercised, if taking them into account would require the offeror to make a takeover offer. Capital investment companies and investment companies are not deemed to be subsidiaries within the meaning of the Takeover Act.[26] Accordingly, shares held by them will not be treated as being held by the offeror.

c) Mandatory Offers

The Takeover Act requires a shareholder who has acquired control over a company other than by means of a public takeover offer to make a mandatory public bid to the remaining shareholders of the target company (see in detail Ch. 4 no. 10). Most of the provisions for takeover offers (in particular, minimum price rules) also apply to mandatory offers. The Takeover Act does not, however, require a mandatory offer if the controlling shareholder has acquired the controlling interest before January 1, 2002, i. e. before the effective date of the Takeover Act.[27]

d) International Application

(1) Admission to trading

For the application of the Takeover Act, the shares of the target (the registered office of which must be in Germany) must be admitted for trad-

---

[25] § 20 Takeover Act.
[26] *See* § 2 para. 6 Takeover Act; cf. § 10 para. 1 lit. a Capital Investment Companies Act and § 15 b para. 2 Foreign Investment Act.
[27] Explanatory Memorandum of the Federal Government on § 35 para. 1 Takeover Act, BT-Drucks. 14/7034 of October 5, 2001, p. 59.

ing on a regulated stock exchange in the European Economic Area.[28] German takeover law therefore applies to the takeover of a stock corporation which has its registered office in Germany, even if its shares are listed solely in other countries in the European Economic Area. The Takeover Act does not apply, however, to a stock corporation the registered office of which is outside Germany, even if its shares are listed (perhaps even exclusively) on a German stock exchange. The same applies to stock corporations whose registered offices are in Germany, but whose shares are listed only on stock exchanges outside the European Economic Area (for example, the NASDAQ). Note that according to bilateral treaties, the registered office may mean the place where the corporation is formed or the jurisdiction under the laws of which the company is incorporated.[29] For example, the Takeover Act does not apply to a stock corporation registered in Munich but formed under the laws of the U.S. State of Delaware.[30]

(2) International offers

The Takeover Act's remit may also give rise to conflict of law issues. These are particularly likely to arise if the target's securities (in particular, depository receipts) are admitted to trading in countries other than Germany, or are owned by residents outside Germany.[31] An offer to acquire such securities can create multi-jurisdictional issues and the laws of several countries, including those of countries outside the European Economic Area, may apply. In this case, the offeror must ensure that it complies with the regulations which apply in the foreign jurisdiction as well as with those provisions which apply in Germany.[32] This may be especially problematic if the foreign law to be applied contains provisions which contradict the Takeover Act and which would consequently prevent the offeror from observing its legal obligations under German law.

An example of a conflict of law issue arises in connection with the U.S. Securities Regulation: U.S. securities law, as a rule, protects all U.S. shareholders. The fact that the registered seat of the corporation is abroad, or that the shares are not traded in the U.S., does not undermine this protection.[33] If, therefore, some shareholders of the target reside in the U.S., the offeror must meet all U.S. procedural and disclosure requirements. The publication

---

[28] § 2 para. 7 Takeover Act: the definition of a regulated stock exchange is given there: included are the Official Listing *("Amtlicher Markt")*, the Regulated Market *("Geregelter Markt")* and regulated stock exchanges in the European Economic Area.

[29] Treaty of Friendship, Commerce and Navigation between the Federal Republic of Germany and the United States of America, BGBl. 1956 II p. 487 and 763.

[30] Treaty of Friendship, Commerce and Navigation between the Federal Republic of Germany and the United States of America, BGBl. 1956 II p. 487 and 763.

[31] *See* Explanatory Memorandum of the Federal Government on § 24 Takeover Act, BT-Drucks. 14/7034 of October 5, 2001, p. 51.

[32] Example: the U.S.-American Rule "Cross-Border Tender and Exchange Offers, Business Combinations and Rights Offerings" of the U.S. American Exchanges and Securities Supervisory Authority (SEC) of January 24, 2001.

[33] Holzborn, BKR 2002 p. 67, 72.

2. Scope of Application

of the decision to make an offer under the German Takeover Act[34] triggers an obligation to prepare and publish an offer document in the U.S. Such publication, however, would violate German law[35] if made before the offer document has been checked and approved by the German Federal Supervisory Office.[36]

The German Takeover Act does take conflict of law issues like this into account. As the German legislator has no power to abrogate the application of the U.S. provisions, an exception to the principle of equal treatment of all shareholders has been provided instead: the Federal Supervisory Office may permit the offeror to exclude from the offer shareholders residing in countries outside the European Economic Area.[37] Such "disclaimer" is an exception to the prohibition against limiting public offers to certain shareholders.[38] Within its discretion,[39] the Federal Supervisory Office must decide whether it would be unreasonable to expect the offeror to make an offer to all holders of the target's shares. The practice to be adopted by the Federal Supervisory Office has still to be determined. Nevertheless some predictions can be made: if foreign provisions apply which conflict with the German provisions so that compliance with both is not possible, the Federal Supervisory Office will grant an exemption. On the other hand, if compliance with both is indeed possible, but would incur higher costs, an exemption will not, in principle, be granted.[40] Nevertheless, we should not expect that the Federal Supervisory Office will generally grant exceptions for certain countries with rules conflicting with the German Takeover Act.[41] On the contrary, the Federal Supervisory Office will carefully examine the circumstances of each case. For example, the Federal Supervisory Office has indicated that it will generally not allow the exclusion of U.S. shareholders. If less than 10% of the shareholders of the target reside in the U.S., the offeror migth indeed be released from many procedural and information obligations under applicable U.S. securities regulations.[42] If more than 10%, but less than 40% of the shareholders of the target are U.S. holders, the offeror might still be released from these obligations;[43] the decision is within the discretion of the SEC. In these cases, the Federal Supervisory Office will probably reject an application for exemption for

---

[34] § 10 Takeover Act.
[35] Holzborn, BKR 2002 p. 67, 74.
[36] § 14 para. 2 Takeover Act.
[37] § 24 Takeover Act.
[38] § 32 Takeover Act.
[39] Geibel/Süßmann, WpÜG § 24 annot. 11.
[40] Explanatory Memorandum of the Federal Government on § 24 Takeover Act, BT- Drucks. 14/7034 of October 5, 2001, p. 51.
[41] Dissenting opinion: Geibel/Süßmann, WpÜG § 24 annot. 16.
[42] Regulation 14D-1(c): "Tier I Exemption;" in order to benefit from the Tier I Exemption, the bidder may offer U.S. holders only a cash consideration, even if other shareholders are offered shares. That, on the other hand, might conflict with the principle of equal treatment under the German Takeover Act as German and other European shareholders may claim the cash consideration as well.
[43] SEC, International Series Release No. 1171, II. C., "Tier II Exemption."

U. S. holders.[44] A compelling problem is that the offeror must provide the facts that would justify an exception, e. g. the offeror must show that more than 10% of the shareholders of the target are U. S. holders.[45] This is quite difficult because in the case of bearer shares the offeror has no information about the identity of the shareholders.[46] Even if the target has issued registered shares, the offeror has no right to examine the share register.[47] All that remains are informational enquiries to brokers and dealers; however, such enquiries could tip off the capital markets that an offer will be launched for the shares of the target.

Moreover, the above exemptions apply only to all-cash offers. The offeror must not only comply with the U.S. tender offer rules but also with the registration requirements under the Securities Act if shares are offered as consideration. In this case, a registration statement must be filed with the SEC. The offeror is exempt from this registration requirement only if U.S. shareholders hold no more than 10% of the target's free-floating shares.[48]

3. Structure of the Takeover Act

The central subject matter of the Takeover Act is the takeover procedure[49] followed by implementation provisions and sanctions for violations.[50] After setting out general provisions and definitions, followed by a section setting out the jurisdiction of the Federal Supervisory Office in the first two parts of the Takeover Act, the third part of the Act[51] deals with the general rules which apply to all offers for the acquisition of securities. It deals (for instance) with issues such as the prerequisites to making an offer and the minimum content and form of an offer, together with the individual procedural steps required, including in the case of competing bids. Part four[52] sets out additional specifications which are solely applicable where a public offer is made with a view to gaining control of the target. These specifications include:

- the circumstances in which shares with voting rights will be deemed to be held by the offeror;[53]
- the consideration to be provided to the shareholders;[54]
- the options open to the management board and supervisory board of the target in responding to an offer.[55]

---

[44] Holzborn, BKR 2002 p. 67, 75.
[45] Explanatory Memorandum of the Federal Government on § 24 Takeover Act, BT-Drucks. 14/7034 of October 5, 2001, p. 51.
[46] Geibel/Süßmann, WpÜG § 24 annot. 3.
[47] § 67 para. 6 Stock Corporation Act.
[48] 17 CFR 230.802; "Rule 802 Exemption."
[49] Parts 1 to 4 of the Takeover Act.
[50] Parts 5 to 9 of the Takeover Act.
[51] §§ 10 et seq. Takeover Act.
[52] §§ 29 et seq. Takeover Act.
[53] § 30 Takeover Act; *see* Ch. 4 no. 2. b. above.
[54] § 31 Takeover Act.
[55] § 33 Takeover Act.

Part five of the Takeover Act sets out details of the obligation of the offeror to make a public offer in the event that a controlling shareholding in the target has been acquired. It also sets out the particular rules which apply to such a mandatory offer, in addition to those already contained in parts three and four. This "building block" structure of the Takeover Act means that all offers to purchase which fall within the remit of the Takeover Act are subject to the same fundamental rules, and that additional special provisions apply to takeover offers, and to mandatory offers, where these arise.

4. General Principles

The offer procedure is dominated by five general principles.[56] These principles are to be observed in all offers for the acquisition of securities. They reflect the original aims of the legislature and are to be used as guiding principles in the interpretation of the individual provisions of the Takeover Act:

- holders of all securities shall be **treated equally**;
- all necessary information shall be given to the shareholders of the target and **transparency** shall be maintained throughout the transaction;
- the management board and supervisory board of the target must act in the **target's best interests**;
- the transaction shall be completed **without undue delay**;
- the market shall **not be manipulated**.

The Takeover Act prescribes a clear, formal, step by step procedure to protect the target's shareholders, who – in the context of a takeover – are commonly regarded as the party in greatest need of protection. The Act therefore aims to ensure the observance of the basic principles which are given such prominence at the beginning of the Takeover Act.

a) The Principle of Equal Treatment[57]

The general principle of equal treatment of holders of securities[58] provides that holders of any security of the same class[59] are to be treated equally. It ensures that all shareholders of the target may dispose of their

---

[56] § 3 Takeover Act; similar principles are found (for example) in the general principles of the City Code on Takeovers and Mergers applicable in the U. K. and in § 3 of the Austrian Takeover Act.

[57] Corresponding U. S. provision: U. S. Rule 14D-10, 17 C.F.R. § 240. 14d-10.

[58] § 3 para. 1 Takeover Act. The legal implications of the general principle of the equal treatment of shareholders are found, inter alia, in §§ 19, 31 and 32 Takeover Act.

[59] The general provision on equal treatment of shareholders in § 53 a of the Stock Corporation Act was not adequate, as this only bound the company to treat its own shareholders equally and did not regulate the position of the individual shareholders as between themselves. For this reason, legal commentators have, as far as shareholders were concerned, relied until now on the duty, which exists between shareholders and which is generally recognized in corporate law, to act in good faith.

shares on equal conditions. In particular, the principle of equal treatment prevents the conditions of the offer being varied during the takeover process. An offeror may not induce the target's shareholders to accept the offer, whether by varying the structure of the conditions of the offer or by granting financial inducements. For this reason, "two-tier" and "front-end-loaded" offers[60] are not permitted. Other types of bids which offer different levels of consideration – depending on the timeframe in which the bid is accepted by the shareholders – are also forbidden.

b) Transparency and Information

The legislature has placed particular emphasis on the creation of transparency for the benefit of all participants involved in the offer process. All holders of securities in the target must be given sufficient time to consider the offer and all relevant information on the offeror, to enable them to reach a properly informed decision regarding the disposal of their shareholding. They must have the opportunity to evaluate the (often considerable) documentation relating to the offer and to weigh up the matters which are crucial to their decision. The duty of the offeror to provide detailed information to the target's shareholders is designed to counterbalance the fact that the offeror will already have carried out its research and will have an extensive amount of information at its disposal. The requirement for transparency within the takeover process[61] is reflected in several individual provisions of the Takeover Act.

For example, the offeror must publish its intention to make a public offer without delay.[62] The offeror must set out the offer clearly and in detail in an offer document.[63] In particular, the offeror must set out the financing of the offer and state its plans for the future of the target and the target's business, as well as the plans it has for its own enterprise (see in more detail Ch. 4 no. 6. b. (1) below).[64] Throughout the offer process and after the expiry of the acceptance period, the offeror has a continuing obligation to provide information.

Certain obligations to provide information apply not only to the offeror, but also to the target's management board, which must be provided with information by the offeror. As the opinion of the management board of the target regarding the offer is of considerable importance to the shareholders (in particular, whether the board welcomes or rejects the bid), the man-

---

[60] *See* Ch. 4 no. 6. e. (1) below.
[61] Specified in § 3 para. 2 Takeover Act.
[62] § 10 Takeover Act.
[63] Corresponding U. S. provisions: Rule 14 D – 3 and Schedule 14D-1/14D-9; § 14 (d) (1) Securities Exchange Act 1934, 15. U. S. C. § 78 n.
[64] Explanatory Memorandum of the Federal Government on the Takeover Act, BT-Drucks. 14/7034 of October 5, 2001, p. 29, gives examples of information which might be viewed as pertinent, such as a planned change of registered office or location and other matters which will affect the employees, their employment conditions and their representation.

agement board must issue a reasoned statement setting out its position on the offer.

The legislature also attaches similar importance to keeping the employees informed. The management board of the target must pass information provided to it by the offeror on to the employees or the employees' representatives without delay. If the employees wish to comment on the offer, the board must publish this comment together with its own statement.

c) Acting in the Best Interests of the Target

The management board and the supervisory board of the target must act in the interests of the target throughout the offer process.[65] The general duty of corporate boards to act in the interests of the company (embodied in the German Stock Corporation Act) continues to apply. This principle is particularly important in the context of defense mechanisms which may be deployed to block a takeover offer.[66]

d) Duty to complete the Transaction without Delay

The legislature has placed particular emphasis on ensuring that the offer process can be dealt with speedily. Public offers are, (as the example of Mannesmann/Vodafone clearly illustrated) liable to have considerable adverse effects on the target and can deflect the attention of its management away from the day to day running of the business and, consequently, from pursuing its strategic aims.[67] This is exacerbated by the fact that the management board and the supervisory board are limited in their scope of "normal" action as a result of the duties imposed on them by a takeover offer. In relation to actions which could prevent an offer from being successful, the target's boards are subject to special legal obligations. For this reason, the offer process must be handled as swiftly as possible, so that the target company is not hindered in pursuing its business for an unreasonably long time.[68]

In addition, the offer process necessarily entails a certain amount of uncertainty and insecurity as to the target's future and its prospects. This period of uncertainty should be kept as short as possible in the interests of the offeror, the shareholders, the target and, not least, the capital markets.

The principle of managing a speedy transaction[69] is evident in many other provisions of the Act. For example, time "windows" within which the indi-

---

[65] § 3 para. 3 Takeover Act.
[66] § 33 Takeover Act.
[67] In the Explanatory Memorandum of the Federal Government on § 3 para. 4 Takeover Act, the legislature points out that the takeover procedure may be intentionally initiated to hinder the business of the target and the pursuit of its business goals, in particular due to the limitations which arise under the special obligations imposed on the management board and supervisory board, BT-Drucks. 14/7034 of October 5, 2001, p. 35.
[68] § 3 para. 4 Takeover Act.
[69] § 3 para. 4 Takeover Act.

vidual steps of the offer process (for instance, filing the offer document) must be carried out ensure that the transaction is handled as expeditiously as possible. Any legal proceedings which are brought in connection with the offer are also to be dealt with as rapidly as possible. As a rule, proceedings should be disposed of by means of a hearing in a court of first instance only. Proceedings relating to administrative matters and regulatory breaches are to be brought in one court only, namely the Oberlandesgericht for Frankfurt am Main, which has jurisdiction for the Federal Supervisory Office.

e) Preventing Market Manipulation

The general prohibition on the creation of market distortions[70] is intended, *inter alia*, to prevent shareholders (as recipients of an offer) from being induced to make decisions which are not supported by facts. Individual examples of this concept are the prohibition on insider dealing[71] and on share price manipulation.[72]

5. Procedural Overview

The beginning of the offer process and (more particularly) of the takeover process takes place, according to the Takeover Act, in two stages. The takeover process commences with the publication by the offeror of its decision to make a bid.[73] The second stage is the preparation and publication – after examination by the Federal Supervisory Office – of a so-called offer document, which contains the actual offer.[74] The offer document will state, *inter alia*, the acceptance period within which the shareholders of the target may accept the offer. The takeover process ends when the acceptance period expires. The offeror must then inform the shareholders of the result of the takeover process.

Simplified timetable

Time	Action	Details
	Pre-announcement	Investigation of target by offeror, approach to management of the target (if bid is not hostile from its very inception)

---

[70] § 3 para. 5 Takeover Act.
[71] §§ 14, 38 Securities Trading Act.
[72] § 88 Stock Exchange Act.
[73] § 10 Takeover Act.
[74] §§ 11, 44 Takeover Act.

	Start of the offer process under the Takeover Act		
	On firm intention to make a bid	**Announcement**	• Notification to the Federal Supervisory Office ("FSO") and the relevant stock exchanges; followed by • announcement to make a bid in a national stock exchange gazette or an electronic banking information system; followed by • notification to the target's management board
4 weeks	Within 4 weeks of announcement	**Offer document to FSO**	Dispatch of the offer document to the FSO for review and approval (or prohibition).
2 to 3 weeks	Review period of up to 10 working days, extendable by further 5 working days	**Publication of offer document**	Following approval by the FSO: • Publication of the offer document on the Internet and in a national stock exchange gazette; • copy of the offer document to the target's management board; copy to the target's works council/employees.
4 to 10 weeks	During acceptance period: 4 to 10 weeks	**"Water level announcements"**	Publication of the acceptance rate on a weekly basis; during the last week of the acceptance period on a daily basis.
		Statements of the target's boards	Statements of the target's management and supervisory boards ("Defense Document" in hostile takeover cases);

Time		Action	Details
			without undue delay after publication of the offer document.
		Shareholders' meeting of the target	The target's management board may call a shareholders' meeting for approval of defensive steps with a two-week notice period (in this case, the acceptance period will automatically be extended to the maximum of 10 weeks)
		Defensive steps	By the management board with approval of the supervisory board (and the shareholders' meeting, if applicable).
2 to 12 weeks*	Extension of the acceptance period, if any	**Improvement of the offer**	Until the last working day of the acceptance period, the terms of the offer may be improved; if the improvement is announced within the last two weeks of the acceptance period: automatic extension by two weeks. Shareholders who have already accepted may withdraw and accept the improved offer.
		Competing offer	If a competing bid is made during the acceptance period, the acceptance period of the original offer is extended to expire at the end of the acceptance period of the

Time	Action	Details
		competing bid. Shareholders who have already accepted may withdraw and accept the competing offer.
2 weeks	Further acceptance period of two weeks, if offer was already successful	**Last chance to accept**	Shareholders have a last chance to accept if the offer was already successful (i.e. the required acceptance ratio has been achieved).
	Final publication of acceptance rate	Without undue delay after further acceptance period.
	**Completion of the offer: ~ 10 weeks to 6 months*** (after satisfaction of other conditions, if any, such as antitrust approval)
one year	Within one year of publication of acceptance rate	**Improvement of consideration**	If bidder acquires shares in the target at a higher price than offered in the offer document the difference must be paid to all shareholders who accepted the offer.

* May be longer in the case of several competing offers.

6. Individual Steps in Making an Offer

a) The Decision to Make an Offer

The takeover process is set in motion by the decision of the interested party to make a takeover offer. As soon as an offeror has made this decision, it must be made public without undue delay.[75] The statement need only state that the offeror has made the decision to make an offer; it need not set out the conditions of the offer or details of the offer itself. The requirement to publish the decision to make a bid is intended to provide the public as soon as possible with information which is of interest to the market, and, in doing

---

[75] § 10 para. 1 Takeover Act, which is in turn based on the "ad-hoc publication" requirement in § 15 Securities Trading Act.

so, to prevent insider knowledge and market distortions from being exploited. The shareholders of the target are also given time to adjust to the possibility of the target being taken over and to adopt their own investment strategy accordingly. The announcement of the intention to make an offer is usually followed by a period for preparation of the offer document, checking and ascertaining details of how the offer is to be financed. The offeror is given four weeks in which to prepare the formal offer, at the end of which the offer document must be sent to the Federal Supervisory Office.[76]

In practice, it will be difficult to establish the exact point at which the obligation to publish arises. This will be particularly significant where the decision-making process of the offeror is in several stages and requires the approval of various committees. From the wording of the Act, one must conclude that where the offeror is a company, the intention to put forward an offer originates within the company's administration and not from the shareholders. The offeror may (in effect) be obliged to publish its offer even though the approval of its shareholders' meeting is required but has not yet been obtained. In these cases, the offer should be made subject to the approval of the offeror's shareholders' meeting, which is to be obtained prior to the expiry of the acceptance period.[77] If the offeror had to wait for the decision of the shareholders' meeting and the offeror were a stock corporation, the offeror's intention to make a takeover bid would be common knowledge among the offeror's shareholders in the time taken to call the general meeting and announce the meeting's agenda. This might result in market distortions taking place in advance of the public offer.[78]

In ascertaining at what point in time in the staggered decision-making process an offer must be published, the principles developed in connection with the general disclosure rule[79] should be applied.[80] In deciding whether to make an offer (during which time the offeror will obtain and assimilate a great deal of data regarding the current position of the target and the relevant capital markets, and will analyze the effect of any offer), no obligation to publish will arise. Otherwise, public offers would be rendered practically impossible.[81] In principle, it is more likely that the last step in the offeror's decision-making is crucial to the issue of when to publish: the point at which the offeror becomes obliged to declare that it will make a public offer will therefore, as a rule, depend on the final decision of the offeror's manage-

---

[76] § 14 Takeover Act.

[77] §§ 18, 25 Takeover Act.

[78] In accordance with § 10 para. 1 clause 3 Takeover Act, the Federal Supervisory Office may, on application, permit that the publication of the offer be made only after approval by the shareholders' meeting. A condition for doing so is that (in the interests of avoiding market distortions) the confidentiality of the offeror's intention to make a bid is guaranteed. This exception could be applied to companies with a limited circle of shareholders, where the shareholders' meeting does not need to be called by public announcement.

[79] § 15 Securities Trading Act.

[80] See Explanatory Memorandum of the Federal Government on § 10 para. 1 Takeover Act, BT-Drucks. 14/7034 of October 5, 2001, p. 39.

[81] See Liebscher, ZIP 2001 p. 853, 860.

ment board, or (in the case of a stock corporation) on the approval of the supervisory board, where this is required under corporate law.[82] The obligation to announce an offer is triggered when the offeror's intention to make a takeover offer has been so firmly established that it is no longer financially viable for the offeror to back out of this plan.[83] This prohibits the offeror from abstaining from or delaying in making an offer on grounds of requiring formal ratification of a decision to make an offer by the supervisory board. If in doubt as to the best course of action, the offeror should seek clarification from the Federal Supervisory Office.

The publication need only state that the offeror intends to make an offer and which of the target's securities will be affected. The offeror is not obliged to include details of the offer[84] (for instance, the form and amount of the consideration).[85] However, if the key points of an offer have already been determined, these should be published in the interests of providing early and comprehensive information to the target and to the markets. The offeror can thereby avoid the requirement of publication[86] if such information would have a considerable influence on the stock exchange price irrespective of the offeror's announcement to make an offer.[87]

The decision to make an offer should be published in German in at least one national stock exchange gazette *("Börsenpflichtblatt")* or by means of an electronically operated information distribution system.[88] Immediately prior to the publication, the offeror must inform the Federal Supervisory Office and the management of the German exchanges, on which the securities of the offeror or of the target are listed, of its intention to take over the target. On receiving this notification, the exchanges should be able to suspend trading in the relevant securities, if necessary. Following publication, the offeror must inform the management board of the target without delay of its decision to make a takeover offer. The target's management board must then inform its employees and/or the relevant works council, if any.

The offeror's duty to publish its decision to make a takeover offer makes it difficult (in advance of a takeover offer) for the offeror to gradually build up a shareholding in the target. This applies equally whether shares are acquired via a stock exchange or by any other means. While it is acceptable for an offeror to acquire shares in the target in anticipation of staging a takeover, publication of the intention to make a takeover offer must not be delayed or withheld by the offeror because of this. Breach of the obligation

---

[82] Explanatory Memorandum of the Federal Government on § 10 para. 1 Takeover Act, BT-Drucks. 14/7034 of October 5, 2001, p. 39.
[83] *See* Liebscher, ZIP 2001 p. 853, 860.
[84] § 10 Takeover Act.
[85] § 10 Takeover Act.
[86] § 15 Securities Trading Act.
[87] While § 10 para. 6 Takeover Act clearly states that § 10 Takeover Act is a special provision in relation to § 15 Securities Trading Act, this applies only insofar as a publication under § 10 Takeover Act is made; Explanatory Memorandum of the Federal Government on § 10 para. 1 and 6 Takeover Act, BT-Drucks. 14/7034 of October 5, 2001, p. 39 et seq.
[88] § 10 para. 3 Takeover Act.

to publish[89] constitutes an administrative offense and is punishable by a fine.[90]

The offeror may acquire shares in the target whilst preparing its decision to make an offer. Equally, the offeror may begin, or continue, to acquire shares once it has made public its intention to take over the target. However, it should be borne in mind that such advance acquisitions[91] may have the effect that the offeror is obliged to pay consideration for the takeover in cash only; the offeror may forfeit the option of paying in liquid shares.[92] The attribution provisions[93] should also be borne in mind in this context.[94] Additionally, the price paid in such advance acquisitions could influence the minimum consideration to be paid in the takeover offer itself.[95] A potential offeror must also ensure that it serves a general notification[96] each time a particular shareholding threshold is reached in respect of these advance acquisitions. The first notification threshold of 5% in the target effectively prevents the offeror from secretly acquiring shares in the target.

b) The Takeover Offer

(1) The offer document

The formal binding takeover offer of the offeror is made by publishing the so-called offer document, the content of which is regulated in detail.[97] The offer document must be presented in German and must be published, after approval by the Federal Supervisory Office, on the Internet and in a national stock exchange gazette.[98] The offer document (which should set out the takeover offer and its conditions in full detail) is intended to provide the target's shareholders and employees and the capital markets with the particulars and precise content of the offer, the financing of the takeover and the offeror's reasons for proposing the takeover. The offer document represents the main body of the implementation of the provisions on transparency and of the information obligations[99] which permeate the entire takeover procedure. The offer document should put the target's shareholders in a position where they can make an informed, considered judgment, based on all relevant information, as to whether to dispose of the investment or not.

(a) Conditions in the offer document

As the publication of the offer document represents the actual making of the takeover offer, the offer must (in principle) be binding. The offeror may

---

[89] § 10 Takeover Act.
[90] § 61 Takeover Act.
[91] § 31 para. 3 Takeover Act.
[92] § 31 para. 2 Takeover Act.; *see* Ch. 4 no. 9. a. (2) below.
[93] § 30 Takeover Act.
[94] *See* Ch. 4 no. 2. b. above.
[95] § 4 Public Offer Regulation; *see* Ch. 4 no. 9. d. below.
[96] §§ 21, 22 Security Trading Act.
[97] § 11 Takeover Act.
[98] § 14 para. 3 Takeover Act.
[99] § 3 para. 2 Takeover Act.

not merely demand that the target's shareholders make their own offers to the offeror.[100] Given the potential consequences of the takeover bid for the target, and in the interests of the target being able to continue its day to day business as smoothly as possible, the target should not be subjected to the uncertainty of non-binding takeover offers. For this reason, the offer cannot contain a proviso which allows it to be revoked or withdrawn. Neither can the offer be made subject to conditions which the offeror or a party acting on its instructions, would be able to fulfil themselves.[101] In contrast, conditions concerning events beyond the control of the offeror are generally admissible. As the offeror is also undertaking considerable risk, it must have the opportunity to protect itself to a certain degree. It is a matter of interpretation as to which types of conditions are admissible within the principles of the Takeover Act.

The offeror must take into account that the takeover may be rejected or burdened with qualifications or conditions by the Federal Cartel Office or the European Commission. Often, the takeover offer has already been implemented when the decision of the relevant competition authority is made.[102] This presents problems of reversing the transaction. The offer should, therefore, be made subject to the condition that the takeover will be authorized by the Cartel Office unconditionally.[103] In the event that the offeror accepts conditions imposed by such authorities, it is free to proceed by waiving the conditions to which it has made the offer subject.[104] Generally speaking, conditions concerning public authorities are admissible.[105]

Often, the offeror wants to acquire a certain shareholding in the target: for the conclusion of a control agreement and for the initiation of a squeeze-out procedure the offeror needs 75% or 95% of the shares of the target, respectively. It is admissible to make the offer dependent upon the condition that more than 75% or at least 95% of the shares of the target are offered to the bidder.[106] To permit the offer to be made subject to acquisition of a higher percentage beyond 95% would, however, defeat the objective that an offer should be binding. As it is quite unlikely that e.g. more than 99% of the target's shares would be offered to the bidder, the bidder could de facto withdraw the offer in practically all cases.[107] We are therefore of the opinion that an acceptance rate beyond 95% may not be used as a condition in a public offer.

A condition making the offer dependent upon the successful financing of the offer, is not admissible. The offeror must ensure the financing of the offer <u>before</u> the publication of the offer document.[108] The risk of failing to find

---

[100] § 17 Takeover Act.
[101] § 18 Takeover Act.
[102] Art. 7 para. 3 European Merger Control Regulation.
[103] Busch, AG 2002 p. 145, 146.
[104] § 21 para. 1 no. 4 Takeover Act.
[105] Explanatory Memorandum of the Federal Government on § 18 Takeover Act, BT-Drucks. 14/7034 of October 5, 2001, p. 47.
[106] Busch, AG 2002 p. 145, 146 et seq.; Explanatory Memorandum of the Federal Government on § 18 Takeover Act, BT-Drucks. 14/7034 of October 5, 2001, p. 47.
[107] Deutscher Anwaltsverein zum Referentenentwurf, NZG 2001 p. 420, 425.
[108] § 13 Takeover Act.

financing for the offer can, however, be covered by other means: the offeror should include a "Material Adverse Change" clause in the offer. By such a clause the offeror can cover risks of events outside the sphere of influence of any of the parties involved. Such clauses do not violate the provisions of the Takeover Act if the events upon which the effectiveness of the offer is dependent are precisely described in the offer document.[109] In contrast, a clause that leaves it to the discretion of the offeror to decide whether a material adverse change has occurred, would be an inadmissible condition, because the fulfillment of the condition would depend on the will of the offeror.[110]

Another risk with which the offeror is typically confronted is the fact that the management board of the target may initiate defensive measures.[111] As it is unreasonable for the offeror to acquire a corporation that is completely "restructured" by means of defensive measures after the publication of the offer document, it should be admissible to make the offer dependent upon the condition that certain defensive measures are not initiated.[112] A prerequisite is once again the precise description of the defensive measure that are prohibited.[113]

In the case of a share exchange, the offeror is also confronted with the risk that the price of the offeror's shares may rise after the publication of the offer document. Then the value of the consideration shares might be higher than the value of the target.[114] The most effective way to prevent such a development would be the subsequent adjustment of the offer price if the stock price of the offeror rises. The modification of an offer during the acceptance period, however, contradicts the binding character of an offer.[115] Therefore, an adjustment of the conversion ratio would require a new offer and the initiation of a new procedure. Hence the Takeover Act includes regulations that provide for the subsequent modification of the offer only as an exception to the general provisions.[116] Moreover, the wording of the Act permits only a subsequent increase in the consideration; not a subsequent lowering of the consideration.[117] Nevertheless, it should be admissible to include in the offer a clause which provides that the conversion ratio is to be adjusted to the current stock prices. The conversion ratio would de facto not be fixed by the number of shares delivered as consideration, but by the proportionate value of the companies ("fixed value" instead of the "fixed conversion ratio"), as long as the minimum price rules are complied with.[118]

---

[109] Busch, AG 2002 p. 145, 151; Hamann, ZIP 2001 p. 2249, 2253.
[110] § 18 para. 1 Takeover Act.
[111] § 33 Takeover Act; *see* in detail Ch. 4 no. 8 below.
[112] Explanatory Memorandum of the Federal Government on § 18 Takeover Act, BT-Drucks. 14/0734 of October 5, 2001, p. 47 et seq.
[113] Busch, AG 2002 p. 145, 149.
[114] Concerning similar problems *see* Ch. 4 no. 9. b (3) below.
[115] § 145 Civil Code; Palandt/Heinrichs, Bürgerliches Gesetzbuch, 61st ed., § 145 annot. 3.
[116] § 21 Takeover Act; Geibel/Süßmann/Thun, WpÜG § 21 annot. 22.
[117] § 21 para. 1 no. 1 Takeover Act.
[118] *See* also Ch. 4 no. 9. c. below.

6. Individual Steps in Making an Offer

(b) Prohibition of partial takeover offers

It should be noted that partial offers are not admissible[119] in the context of a takeover offer.[120] This contrasts with straightforward acquisition offers, which are not aimed at acquiring control. In the case of a takeover offer, the offer must apply to all shares and classes of shares of the target, i.e. all ordinary and preference shares, and the offeror must be prepared to acquire all shares which are offered to it. Each shareholder should have the opportunity to dispose of his or her shares and not be forced into a minority position.

(c) Content of the offer document

The offer must set out the subject matter of the acquisition (shares in the target) and the nature and amount of the consideration being offered, as well as information which is key to the acquisition (details of the offeror and target, conditions of the bid and the opening and closing dates of the acceptance period). In addition to these details, the Takeover Act[121] together with the Public Offer Regulation[122] also demand that information described as "additional information" should be provided in the offer document. All recipients of the offer should, as a result, be provided with all the relevant, substantiated information they require to be able to decide whether to accept the offer or not.[123] In particular, the offer document should include details of the following:

(i) details of how the offer will be financed and of how such financing will be secured;[124]
(ii) the effect of a successful offer on the assets, financial position and profitability of the offeror;[125] in this respect, it is expected that the Federal Supervisory Office will require a detailed projected comparison, supported by meaningful financial figures, of the offeror's financial situation for the two cases, firstly if the offer succeeds and, secondly, if the offer fails;
(iii) the offeror's intentions in relation to the future business of the target, in particular as to the use of its assets, the possible transfer of important facilities and the effects on the target's employees; and
(iv) any financial inducements made or promised to members of the management board or the supervisory board of the target.
(v) Details of the consideration which must be given are set out extensively in the Takeover Act. This reflects the important role which this infor-

---

[119] § 32 Takeover Act.
[120] Within the meaning of § 29 para. 1 Takeover Act.
[121] In detail: § 11 para. 2 clause 3 Takeover Act.
[122] § 11 para. 4 Takeover Act.
[123] *See* Schüppen, Die Wirtschaftsprüfung 2001 p. 958, 962.
[124] In addition a confirmation by a financial institution that the financing to perform the bid has been secured is part of the offer document, *see* Ch. 4 no. 6. b. (2) below.
[125] It is intended thereby to avoid a situation that the bidder gets into financial difficulty as a result of the takeover, which in turn could have adverse effects on the target. Certain financing techniques such as a leveraged buy-out, are also intended to be made more difficult thereby.

mation plays for the shareholders.[126] If shares are offered as consideration, the Act requires that information in respect of those shares should be given:[127] i.e. in the case of an offer by share exchange, the function of the offer document can be equated with that of a prospectus in an IPO and must comply with the requirements of the Prospectus Act. Making an offer by offering shares involves the public offer of shares. The shareholders in the target must be provided with the necessary information to enable them to make an accurate assessment of the issuer and of the shares offered.[128] In addition, the offeror must provide supporting evidence that the consideration proposed is adequate, and must provide details of the method of valuation used to calculate the consideration to be offered.

(2) Confirming how the offer is to be financed

Prior to the publication of the offer document, the offeror must take all necessary steps to ensure that the funds required to discharge the consideration are available.[129] If the consideration for the bid is intended to be in cash, the offer document must be accompanied by a statement of confirmation from an "investment services enterprise" independent of the offeror attesting that the offer is financially viable.[130] This confirmation must state that the offeror has taken the necessary measures to ensure that the required funds will be available at the point in time when the right of the target's shareholders to receive payment of the consideration arises. The confirmation of the financial institution need not be a guarantee; it is sufficient that the investment services enterprise confirms that, in its considered judgment, the offeror will be able to pay the consideration upon completion of the offer. The investment services enterprise is not obliged to pay deficiencies should the financing indeed fail because of unforeseen circumstances. Therefore, it is only liable if its judgment, at the time it is made, is inaccurate. We advise investment services enterprises to clearly state in the confirmation by means of a disclaimer that the confirmation may not be understood as a guarantee.

(3) Procedural steps

- Decision of the offeror to make an offer;
- Publication of the decision to make an offer;
- Preparation of the offer document;
- Presentation of the offer document to the Federal Supervisory Office;

---

[126] For the assessment of the consideration, *see* Ch. 4 no. 9. b. below.

[127] § 7 of the Prospectus Act and the Prospectus Regulation.

[128] § 1 Prospectus Act. This duty to provide information does not apply if a prospectus or company report was published less than 12 months prior to the publication of the offer document in Germany. In that case, reference to the prospectus and to how a copy of the prospectus might be obtained is adequate (§ 2 no. 2 Public Offer Regulation).

[129] § 13 Takeover Act.

[130] §§ 11 para. 2, 13 para. 1 Takeover Act.

- Examination and approval of the offer document by the Federal Supervisory Office;
- Publication of the offer document;
- Statement of the target's management board;
- "Takeover battle" in hostile cases;
- Acceptance of the offer by the target's shareholders; extension of the acceptance period and improvements of the bid (if any);
- Publication of the acceptance rate;
- Transfer of the shares and payment of the consideration.

The starting point of the takeover process is the publication of the offeror's decision to make an offer, as described above. The offeror is obliged[131] to send the offer document to the Federal Supervisory Office within four weeks of publication of the decision to make an offer.[132] The Federal Supervisory Office can extend this four-week period by up to a further four weeks, on the offeror's application, if the offeror is unable to comply with the initial four week period due to a cross-border offer or necessary capital measures which require a shareholders' resolution. In view of the short timeframe within which the offer document must be submitted to the Federal Supervisory Office and the legal consequence that the offer will automatically be prohibited by the Federal Supervisory Office if the timeframe is not adhered to,[133] the offer document should ideally be prepared when the offeror is considering whether to make a bid, as a precaution.

On receipt of the offer document, the Federal Supervisory Office will review the offer document to ensure that it complies with the requirements prescribed by the Takeover Act and the Public Offer Regulation. The Federal Supervisory Office has ten working days to carry out this review. This period can be extended by the Federal Supervisory Office by a further five working days to allow the offeror to revise the offer document if changes are necessary to comply with the statutory provisions and to avoid the offer being prohibited for reasons of non-compliance. If the Federal Supervisory Office approves the offer document or if the period for review expires without objection or prohibition from the Federal Supervisory Office,[134] the offeror must publish the offer document without delay.[135] The publication must be made on the Internet and in a national stock exchange gazette.[136] The offeror must also provide the target's management board with a copy of the offer document as soon as possible following publication. The management board must in turn pass the offer document on to the employees or the works

---

[131] § 14 para. 1 Takeover Act.
[132] Violation may result in a fine, § 61 para. 1 no. 2 a Takeover Act.
[133] § 15 para. 1 no. 3 Takeover Act.
[134] *See* § 15 Takeover Act.
[135] § 14 para. 2 Takeover Act.
[136] § 14 para. 3 Takeover Act. As an alternative to publication in a national stock exchange gazette, the offeror may make an announcement to the effect that the offer document is available free of charge at a certain location. Non-compliance with the obligation to publish and notify may result in a fine (§ 61 para. 1 no. 1 and 2 Takeover Act).

council, if any.[137] Together with the supervisory board, the target's management board must give its opinion on the takeover bid on the basis of the offer put forward in the offer document.[138]

The acceptance period for the takeover bid (which is stated in the offer document) begins to run on the date of publication of the offer document.[139]

(4) Liability for the content of the offer document and for the statement confirming how the offer is to be financed

Special liability provisions attach to both the offer document and the financing statement. As the offer document and the financing statement both represent key factors in the decision of the target's shareholders, the information contained in these documents must be accurate and complete.

The accuracy of certain information is not easy to assess, in particular if forecasts are involved: this applies particularly to information about the effect of a successful offer on the assets, financial position and profitability of the offeror.[140] In this respect the responsible persons are not liable for the truth of the information, but their *assessments* must be based on sound facts and have to be justifiable from a commercial point of view; caution is necessary,[141] and the statements should include meaningful language about the uncertainty of forward-looking statements. The information about the offeror's intentions in relation to the future business of the target, in particular as to the use of its assets, the possible transfer of important facilities and the effects on the target's employees[142] are of a special quality, because these forecasts depend on the will of the offeror itself. Nevertheless, this information must also be accurate[143] in order to protect the shareholders who must decide on the acceptance of the offer. On the other hand, the business discretion of the offeror cannot be substantially limited. The offeror must be able to react to changing circumstances without being bound by its statements in the offer document and the danger of liability. The offeror meets this prerequisite if it can prove that its intentions were justified at the point in time the offer document was published. The subsequent circumstances which caused the changing of the business plans must also be explained.[144]

Liability for the content of the offer document attaches to the parties who have issued the offer document or have accepted responsibility for it.[145] Those parties will be jointly and severally liable for any loss caused to the target's shareholders which results from them accepting the bid on the basis

---

[137] § 14 para. 4 Takeover Act.

[138] § 27 Takeover Act.

[139] § 16 para. 1 clause 2 Takeover Act.

[140] *See* Ch. 4 no. 6. b. (1) above.

[141] *See* cases to parallel problems concerning the legal liability for the statement made in prospectus: Federal Supreme Court, BGH WM 1982 p. 862, 865.

[142] § 11 para. 2 clause 3 no. 2 Takeover Act.

[143] Hamann, ZIP 2001 p. 2249, 2252.

[144] Hamann, ZIP 2001 p. 2249, 2252.

[145] They are to be stated in the offer document (§ 11 para. 3 Takeover Act).

of inaccurate or incomplete data in the offer document.[146] Such a claim may only be brought by those shareholders who have accepted the offer. The defects in the offer document must have led the claimant to accept the bid, and the claimant must not have known of the defect. In addition, liability is excluded if the persons responsible for the prospectus or the issuers of the offer document can prove that they were not aware of the inaccuracy or incompleteness of the offer document and that this unawareness was not the result of gross negligence, or if a correction was published prior to the offer being accepted. Further claims to be brought under provisions of the German Civil Code on the basis of contracts or intentional tort are admissible.[147] It should be noted that other claims, in particular claims for general prospectus liability, are excluded. Liability is therefore significantly limited.[148]

If the funds required to enable the cash consideration to be paid are not available to the offeror at the time when the right to payment of the consideration arises because the offeror has not taken the necessary steps to ensure that the funds are available, the investment services enterprise which issued the financing confirmation may be liable for loss caused by non- or part-performance by the offeror.[149] However, such liability arises only in the event that the non-availability of the funds results from the offeror not taking the necessary steps to ensure that the funds are available. The financial confirmation does not serve as a guarantee (see Ch. 4 no. 6. b. (2) above), and a claim against the investment services enterprise which issued the statement confirmation cannot succeed unless it is proved that it was aware of the inaccuracy of its confirmation or that it would have been so aware but for gross negligence.[150]

c) Acceptance Period; Changes to the Offer and Extension of the Acceptance Period

(1) Length of the acceptance period

The acceptance period for the offer begins with the publication of the offer document – as described above. The acceptance period must be between four and ten weeks.[151] It is fixed by the offeror and must be stated in the offer document. This period is intended to ensure (on the one hand) that the shareholders have adequate time to make a well-informed decision, and to ensure (on the other hand) that the business of the target is not subjected to continuing interference because of a pending public offer. The target should, however, also have sufficient time to consider what defensive measures it might take and to make the necessary preparations.

---

[146] § 12 para. 1 Takeover Act, which is based on the liability for a prospectus in §§ 45 et seq. Stock Exchange Act *("Börsengesetz");* Hamann, ZIP 2001 p. 2249, 2251.
[147] § 12 para. 6 Takeover Act.
[148] § 12 para. 6 Takeover Act.
[149] § 13 para. 2 Takeover Act.
[150] § 13 para. 3 Takeover Act makes reference to § 12 para. 2 to 6 Takeover Act.
[151] § 16 para. 1 Takeover Act.

(2) "Water-Level" announcements

During the acceptance period, the offeror must publish (i) the number of shares and the proportion of the voting rights in the target which it holds or is deemed to hold,[152] and (ii) the number of acceptances received (so-called **"water-level" announcements**).[153] These statements must be issued on a weekly basis during the acceptance period, and daily in the last week of the acceptance period. A final announcement should be made as soon as possible once the acceptance period has ended.

If the offer has been made subject to the approval of the offeror's shareholders' meeting, the shareholders' resolution must be passed no later than the 5th working day before the acceptance period expires.[154] This ensures that the shareholders are aware well in advance of the expiry of the acceptance period whether or not the takeover offer of the offeror has been carried.

(3) Amendments of the offer

The offeror may amend the takeover offer for the benefit of the target's shareholders. Any such amendment must be published in the same manner as the original offer document. Amendments are admissible up to one working day prior to the expiry of the acceptance period. The acceptance period is automatically extended by two weeks if the amendment is made within the last two weeks of the original acceptance period. This process can be repeated as often as desired, provided that the amendments are not made during the two week period immediately preceding the end of the original acceptance period. If an amendment is made within these final two weeks (triggering an extension of the acceptance period), any further amendment to the offer is inadmissible.[155] Only a limited range of amendments are allowed to be made:[156]

(i) the consideration may be increased;
(ii) a different type of consideration may be offered;
(iii) the minimum level of "uptake" stated in the offer can be reduced; or
(iv) conditions of the bid can be waived.

In the case of an amendment, shareholders who have accepted the offer prior to the publication of the amendment retain a legal right to withdraw their acceptance. This allows them to take advantage of the improved (amended) offer. Back-end loaded offers are therefore forbidden. By amending the bid, the offeror can react to circumstances which change during the period of acceptance (for example where a competing offer is launched). Likewise, the techniques of a low-ball offer or of planned revision can also (at least partly)[157] be employed depending on the acceptance among the shareholders.

---

[152] § 30 Takeover Act.
[153] § 23 para. 1 Takeover Act.
[154] § 25 Takeover Act.
[155] § 21 para. 6 Takeover Act.
[156] § 21 Takeover Act.
[157] Because of the provisions to be observed in relation to the structuring of the consideration, there is, however, only limited scope for variation.

(4) Extension of the acceptance period

An extension of the acceptance period may be triggered by various events:

(i) The acceptance period is extended to the legal maximum of ten weeks if (after the offer document is published) a general meeting of the target is called to discuss the offer, for example, with a view to deciding whether defensive measures should be taken.[158]

(ii) If the offeror publishes an amendment to the offer in the final two weeks of the acceptance period, the acceptance period is automatically extended by two weeks, irrespective of whether this exends the offer period beyond ten weeks.[159]

(iii) If a competing bid is made by a third party for the acquisition of the same shares during the acceptance period, the acceptance period for the first offer is extended up to the expiry of the acceptance period for the competing bid.[160] Theoretically, competing bids can be made as often as desired, and by any number of persons. Even competing bids which do not comply with the provisions of the Takeover Act or which are prohibited by the Federal Supervisory Office will have the effect of extending the acceptance period and may frustrate a speedy takeover. If shareholders have already accepted the first offeror's offer prior to the publication of the competing offer, they are legally entitled to withdraw their acceptance, provided they do so within the acceptance period. This allows them to accept the competing offer.

d) The Completion of the Takeover Process and Further Acceptance Period

The offer process ends, in principle, with the expiry of the acceptance period or its extensions. Immediately after the expiry of the acceptance period, the offeror must (as described above) inform the shareholders of the result of the offer and publish the number of shares and the proportion of voting rights in the target which it holds and is deemed to hold.[161]

On the expiry of the acceptance period in the case of a takeover offer[162] (as opposed to an ordinary public offer), a further acceptance period comes into effect.[163] This further two-week acceptance period begins with the publication of the number of shares and proportion of voting rights in the target held and acquired by the offeror as at the end of the acceptance period. Those shareholders who have not accepted the offer during the acceptance period may then decide to surrender their shares to the offeror. This so-called *"fence sitting provision"* („Zaunkönigregelung") is intended to release the shareholders from the pressure to accept the bid in order to avoid

---

[158] § 16 para. 3 Takeover Act.
[159] § 21 para. 5 Takeover Act.
[160] § 22 para. 2 Takeover Act.
[161] § 23 para. 1 clause 1 no. 2 Takeover Act.
[162] § 29 Takeover Act.
[163] § 16 para. 2 Takeover Act.

being in a minority shareholder position once the acceptance period has expired. The shareholders may await the outcome of the offer process and then sell their shares on the same conditions. The offeror should protect itself against the danger that it may still be required to buy shares after an unsuccessful takeover offer by making its takeover offer conditional on achieving a minimum percentage of voting shares. If this minimum threshold is not achieved during the acceptance period, no further acceptance period will be triggered.[164] On this basis, adopting a "wait and see" policy on the basis of the *Zaunkönigregelung* may backfire on hesitant shareholders: if a sufficient proportion of shareholders wait to see how fellow shareholders react to the offer, the offer may fail in any event for lack of acceptances.[165]

Where a further acceptance period is triggered, the takeover process ends with its expiry and the publication by the offeror of what proportion of the shares and voting rights it holds and is deemed to hold. The offeror must publish this information immediately following the expiry of the further acceptance period.[166]

Where in the case of a successful takeover offer or mandatory offer, the offeror (or persons acting in concert with it or its subsidiaries) acquires further shares in the target outside the offer procedure but within one year after the publication of the number of shares it had acquired by the expiry of the acceptance period,[167] the following applies: the offeror must publish such acquisitions and inform the Federal Supervisory Office without undue delay.[168]

e) Illegal Offensive Tactics

Since the 1980s, several types of unfair offensive tactics have been widely practiced, particularly in the U.S. Now, many of these tactics have been outlawed by applicable tender offer rules.

(1) Two-tier offers

A popular offensive strategy in the 1980s were the so-called "front-end loaded, two-tier tender offers." In such offers the bidder announces that it will purchase shares to obtain a controlling interest in the target ("first tier") at a certain price. After gaining control, it will acquire the remainder ("second tier") of the shares in a freeze-out transaction (e.g., an upstream merger of the target into the offeror) at a substantially lower price that might even fall far below the actual share price. Such offers have coercive power, as the target's shareholders, even if they deem the price of the first tier inadequate, will most likely accept the offer for fear of being squeezed out in the second tier, thereby receiving only the lower second tier price.

---

[164] § 16 para. 2 clause 2 Takeover Act.
[165] From a standpoint of economics, this regulatory scheme is questionable as it presents a classic "prisoners' dilemma" if the target's shares are widely held by small shareholders, none of whom has a significant influence on the success of the offer.
[166] § 23 para. 1 clause 1 no. 3 Takeover Act.
[167] § 23 para. 1 clause 1 no. 2 Takeover Act.
[168] § 23 para. 2 Takeover Act.

Case: Coercive Two-Tier Offers:[169]

Buccaneers Inc. has made a conditional $25 per share tender offer for 51 percent of Purity Corporation's shares. Buccaneers announces that the firms will be merged if the offer is successful and at least 51 percent of the shares are tendered. The shares not tendered in the first tier will receive a combination of bonds and preferred stock valued at only $22 per share when the merger is carried out. Analysts suggest that the shares are actually worth as much as $30 per share. Therefore, shareholder M would like the takeover to fail. We will assume that M is a small shareholder and, as such, does not affect the success or failure of the offer. M's payoffs in the event of the success or failure of the offer are the following:

	Value if M tenders	Value if M does not tender
Bid succeeds	$ 25/share	$ 22/share
Bid fails	$ 30/share	$ 30/share

As the above numbers indicate, M should tender his shares regardless of what he thinks they are worth. If the bid succeeds, M is better off having tendered. If the bid fails, M is indifferent as he keeps his shares whether or not he has tendered them.

As this case illustrates, two-tier offers can be coercive because they may force some shareholders to tender their shares at prices they believe are inadequate.

Two-tier offers were initially permitted in the U.S. Nowadays, coercive two-class offers are outlawed in most U.S. jurisdictions by fair price rules. The Model Business Corporation Act, e.g., provides that a shareholder dissenting from the second-tier freeze-out transaction is entitled to receive the "fair value" of his shares.[170]

Coercive two-class offers were never permissible under German law. German corporate law would not allow a majority shareholder to freeze minority shareholders out of the company at unfair prices in the second step of the two-tier offer. The different freeze-out tactics available under German law (as discussed in detail in Ch. 6) require the majority shareholder to offer fair consideration to the minority shareholders.[171] Minority shareholders may appeal the consideration in court if it falls short of a fair amount.

Moreover, the principle of equal treatment of shareholders as contained in the Takeover Act prohibits such two-tier offers,[172] as the same price has to be offered to all target shareholders.

---

[169] *See* Mark Grinblatt/Sheridan Titman, Financial Markets and Corporate Strategy, 1998, p. 698.

[170] § 13.02 of the Model Business Corporation Act (1984). It is not entirely clear how the fair value is to be determined. Most courts apply a combination of different valuation methods.

[171] §§ 320 b, 305 Stock Corporation Act.

[172] § 3 para. 1 Takeover Act; Explanatory Memorandum of the Federal Government on § 3 para. 1 Takeover Act (BT-Drucks. 14/7034 of October 5, 2001).

(2) Proxy fights

Another tactic popular in the U.S. is the systematic purchase of proxies for the voting rights in the shareholders' meeting (so-called "proxy fight"). In this way, the offeror may gain control over the target by influencing shareholders' resolutions relating, in particular, to the election of the board. In Germany, such buying of voting rights is an administrative offence for which the competent supervisory authority may impose fines.[173]

(3) Greenmailing

So-called "greenmailing" was a popular scheme in the U.S. until the legislator intervened. The greenmailer buys a minority interest in the target (usually on the markets), and then threatens to make a takeover offer unless the target repurchases the shares at a higher price. Greenmailing was very profitable for some time in the 1980s. An SEC study indicated that a total of $ 1 billion in profits was made from greenmailing between 1979 and 1984. Allegedly, $ 400 million in profits was obtained by the Bass Brothers of Fort Worth from one single greenmail scheme made in relation to Texaco.[174] Although greenmailing is ethically more than questionable, it was legal in the U.S. for quite some time, provided that the greenmail payments were fully disclosed.[175] This was because the provisions of the Williams Act were aimed at ensuring disclosure rather than at protecting the target's shareholders against selfish actions of the board.[176] However, for several reasons, greenmailing does not exist any more. Apart from anti-greenmailing statutes passed in some states, which provide for greenmail profits to be disgorged, Congress imposed an excise tax on greenmail profits, raising the effective capital gain tax on greenmail profits to 90%. Moreover, some courts decided that greenmailing payments were a breach of the target board's fiduciary duty to the target's shareholders.[177] The greenmailer itself was in some cases held liable for aiding and abetting such breach of fiduciary duties.

In Germany, courts would most probably deem greenmail payments a violation of sound business judgment and hold the directors liable for damages.[178] The reason why no such case has ever come before the courts is due to the strict limitations corporate law imposes on the purchase of its own shares by a corporation. It was only in 1998 that the legislator allowed a corporation to purchase its own shares as treasury shares in principle, if authorized by a shareholders' resolution. Such authorizations are now frequently adopted by most listed corporations; however, a corporation may not purchase more

---

[173] §§ 405 para. 3 no. 6 Stock Corporation Act, 36 Administrative Offence Act.

[174] Robert Prentice, Law of Business Organizations and Securities Regulation, 2nd ed., Ch. 23 p. 799.

[175] Sec. 10(b) and 14(e) of the Securities Exchange Act 1934.

[176] Robert Prentice, Law of Business Organizations and Securities Regulation, 2nd ed., Ch. 23 p. 799.

[177] Heckman v. Ahmanson, 214 Cal. Rptr. 177 (Cal. App. 1995); different opinion: Polk v. Good, 507 A.2d 531 (Del. 1986).

[178] A member of the management board has to observe the standard of care exercised by a diligent and prudent business executive, § 93 para. 2 Stock Corporation Act.

than 10% of its own issued share capital. Moreover, the repurchase may be carried out only by means of a public self-tender offer to *all* shareholders (in this event the Takeover Act will be applicable to the self-tender offer!) or on stock markets.[179] Therefore, the board may not buy the company's own shares at a price that exceeds the actual stock market price.[180] For these reasons, the board may not purchase the company's own shares from a greenmailer at an inflated price.

(4) Leveraged buyout

Another takeover technique is the leveraged buyout (LBO). In an LBO the purchase price for the target is financed with assets of the target. A loan is granted by the target or an outside bank to the purchaser, and secured by a pledge over the assets of the target. Up to 95% of the purchase price for the target can be financed so that the purchase price which must be paid with liquid funds amounts to no more than 5% of the target's value. This scheme enables relatively small purchasers to take over targets which are several times their own size. Moreover, as increasing the debt/asset ratio for the target up to 95% converts discretionary dividend payments into non-discretionary debt service, an LBO is an effective disciplinary action which incentivizes the management to increase the efficiency of the business operations in order to ensure stable cash flow. In the U.S., the market for leveraged buyouts reached its peak in the third quarter of 1999 with a volume of $ 24.9 billion,[181] with significantly reduced volumes ever since. Many LBOs are carried out by private equity buyout funds; Forstmann Little closed a buyout fund with a volume exceeding $ 6 billion in 2000. Often, those funds take the target private in the course of the LBO transaction, with the goal of later returning the target to public trading by way of an IPO, when the business has been restructured and the debt arising from the LBO has been reduced with cash flow generated by the business.

In Germany, LBOs are largely an unknown phenomenon. This is because financing the share purchase with the assets of the target (also called "financial assistance") conflicts with the rules on the maintenance of capital.[182] These rules prohibit a stock corporation from making payments to shareholders other than regular payments of dividends,[183] in order to protect the total assets of the corporation.[184] Also, these rules do not permit the use of the corporation's assets as collateral to finance a share purchase.[185] One way to accomplish an LBO under German law is to take the target private and convert it into a limited liability company („Gesellschaft mit beschränk-

---

[179] § 71 para. 1 clause 1 no. 8 and § 53 a Stock Corporation Act.

[180] Liebscher, ZIP 2001 p. 853, 869; Michalski AG 1997, p. 152, 162; Hauschka/Roth, AG 1988, p. 181, 194.

[181] Source: Securities Data Company, BUYOUTS.

[182] Becker, DStR 1998 p. 1429, 1430; Lutter/Wahlers, AG 1989 p. 1, 8.

[183] § 57 para. 1 clause 1 Stock Corporation Act.

[184] Arg. e §§ 58 para. 5, 59 Stock Corporation Act.

[185] § 71 a para. 1 clause 1 Stock Corporation Act.

ter Haftung," GmbH)[186] in order to leverage the GmbH vehicle. Although there are also maintenance of capital rules relating to a GmbH, these rules are less strict than those relating to stock corporations, in that the use of a GmbH's assets as security for financing share purchases is legally permissible as long as the nominal amount of the issued share capital (excluding additional paid-in capital) is fully covered by the net assets of the limited liability company,[187] under both a book value and true value approach.[188] However, even if the loan made to the shareholders or the use of the assets as security are in compliance with maintenance of capital rules, taxation problems may arise, if the resulting benefits to the shareholders are classified as "hidden profit distributions" with the result that the shareholders become liable to income tax.

(5) Bootstrap offer

Whereas an LBO is primarily a financing technique, the so-called bootstrap offer is a combination of this financing technique and a certain offensive tactic: the bidder offers to purchase a certain small percentage of shares in the target (say 10%). The size of this percentage is determined by two factors: first the offeror must be able to finance its offer completely from its own cash flow and secondly, the offeror must be able to offer an attractive price in order for the scheme to succeed. If the price offered for the small percentage of shares is relatively high, the offeror can expect that over 50% of the shares in the corporation will be tendered to the offeror in spite of the fact that the target's shareholders can expect to sell only part of their shares (since the purchase may well be made on a pro rata basis). In the event that the bidder has received or is certain that it will receive offers to purchase over 50% of the shares, it can request a loan from a bank. As over 50% of the shares have been tendered to it and the bidder is, therefore, in theory, able to take control of the target, it can offer the bank – as in the LBO – the assets of the target as security for the loan.

At first glance this tactic seems to be legally permitted under German law: the Takeover Act only specifies that the purchase of shares must be made on a pro rata basis and there is no provision which prohibits the bidder from purchasing all the shares offered to it despite having made only an offer for a limited number of shares. However, the bootstrap offer is in fact illegal for another reason: the pledging of the target's assets is contrary to the German maintenance of capital rules. The comments made on the maintenance of capital rules in the context of an LBO, therefore, also apply in this case.

---

[186] The Limited Liability Company is another legal form of a corporation.

[187] §§ 30, 31 GmbHG; Baumbach/Hueck/Fastrich, GmbHG, 17th ed., § 30 annot. 10.

[188] Baumbach/Hueck/Fastrich, GmbHG, 17th ed., § 30 annot. 12; Roth/Altmeppen, GmbHG, 3rd ed., § 30 annot. 7; Hachenburg/Goerdeler/Müller, GmbHG, 8th ed., § 30 annot. 42: § 30 GmbHG does not permit the lower of the net book value and the net true value to fall below the nominal value of the issued capital.

(6) Golden handshakes and parachutes

Initially, so-called "Golden Parachutes," i. e. provisions in managers' employment contracts granting enormous amounts of "severance" payments in the case of a hostile takeover, were used as shark repellants by potential targets as they make the takeover more expensive. These days, where deals have reached amazing volumes, even two-digit million parachutes are not really an efficient shark repellant any more.[189] Therefore, in the recent past, payments to executives of the target have been used more as an offensive tactic to obtain the approval of the target's management. One may very well take the view that the acceptance of such "Golden Handshakes" is a criminal offence for misappropriation of the target's funds; in any event, the Takeover Act also expressly outlaws such payments to the target's management beyond usual compensation schemes.[190]

7. Response of the Target

The principal duty of the management board of a target company facing a takeover offer is to maintain a neutral stance towards the offer:

a) Development of Law in the U.S.

The principle of maintaining neutrality has its roots in several U.S. court precedents. Originally, takeover bids and other takeover situations were barely regulated under U.S. securities law. The situation was such that, on the one hand, a variety of offensive – and yet legally permissible – tactics (including *prima facie* unfair practices such as coercive takeover bids) were at the disposal of a hostile bidder. On the other hand, the board of directors of the target company had an almost unfettered discretion to adopt whatever defensive strategy it felt appropriate. In assessing the legitimacy of such actions, the U.S. courts simply applied the Business Judgment Rule, which operated on the presumption that *"... the directors of a corporation acted on an informed basis, in good faith and in the honest belief that the action taken was in the best interests of the company."*[191] The essence of the Business Judgment Rule is that the courts will not interfere with the board's business judgment if the board's decision can be "attributed to any rational business purpose."[192]

In the 1980s, the U.S. courts recognized that, particularly in cases involving hostile takeovers, there was an "omnipresent specter that a board may be acting primarily in its own interests, rather than those of the corpo-

---

[189] Though not outlawed [*see*, e. g. International Insurance Co. v. Johns, 874 F. 2d 1447 (11th Cir. 1989)], golden parachute payments are subject to excise taxes in the U. S., discouraging the use of golden parachutes to a certain extent.
[190] § 33 para. 3 Takeover Act.
[191] Aronson v. Lewis, 473 A.2d 805, 812 (Del. 1984).
[192] Sinclair Oil Corp. v. Levien, 280 A.2d 717, 720 (Del. 1971).

ration and its shareholders."[193] As a consequence, the leading cases, *Unocal* and *Revlon,* set limits to the Business Judgment Rule as applied to takeover cases:

In *Unocal,*[194] the Delaware Supreme Court ruled in 1985 that the "directors must show that they had reasonable grounds for believing that a danger to corporate policy and effectiveness existed"[195] as a prerequisite to being able to take advantage of the court's presumption (under the Business Judgment Rule) that the board's defensive reaction to a takeover bid was in good faith and in the best interests of the company and its shareholders. The court pointed out that the board was, on the one hand, entitled, indeed obliged, to initiate defensive measures against unfair offers. On the other hand, however, those defensive tactics required the board first to determine that the offeror was employing unfair coercive offensive tactics which (for the benefit of the target company and its shareholders) it was in the target's best interests to resist. This flows from the fundamental principle of corporate law which provides that the directors have a duty to look after the interests of the shareholders.[196] Certainly, in the *Unocal* decision the board retained extensive discretion in determining whether unfair coercive tactics had been applied by the offeror and which appropriate defensive steps ought to be taken. However, the *Unocal* decision proved to be the first important step towards limiting the Business Judgment Rule in the context of takeover bids.

A year later, the same Court created what is known as the "Revlon Doctrine."[197] Under *Revlon,* the target company's board is prohibited from taking defensive measures if it becomes apparent that the sale of the target company is inevitable[198] and that the terms of the bid are not grossly inadequate. In this situation, the directors' role changes:

"from defenders of the corporate bastion to auctioneers charged with getting the best price for the stockholders at a sale of the company."[199]

The target company's management owes a fiduciary duty to its shareholders to maximize the company's value by urging the bidder to pay the highest possible purchase price or to solicit higher bids from other potential offerors.

---

[193] Unocal Corp. V. Mesa Petroleum Co., 493 A.2d 955. (Del. 1985).

[194] *Ibid.*

[195] *See* also Cheff v. Mathes, 199 A.2d 548 at 554 (Del. 1964).

[196] Ivanhoe Partners v. Newmont Min. Corp., 535 A.2d 1334, 1341 et seq. (Del. 1987); GAF Corp. v. Union Carbide Corp., 624 F. Supp. 1016, 1020 (S.D.N.Y. 1985).

[197] Revlon, Inc. v. MacAndrews & Forbes Holdings, Inc., 506 A.2d 173 (Del. 1986).

[198] Later decisions dealt with the definition when a sale of the target is inevitable, e. g. Paramount Communications v. Time, Inc. 571 A.2d 1140 (Del. 1989); Paramount Communications v. QVC Network Inc. 637 A.2d 34 (Del. 1994).

[199] Revlon loc.cit.

b) The Principle of Neutrality under German Law

The origins of the concept of neutrality under German law differ from the origins of the concept in the U.S.: in Germany, unfair coercive takeover bids are prohibited by law (see Ch. 4 no. 6. e. (1) above); those defense strategies permitted under the *Unocal* doctrine are, therefore, superfluous in Germany. Moreover, while U.S. courts consider shareholder value to be the major deciding factor in the stance adopted by the target's management when reacting to a takeover bid, German regulations require that a host of different interests should be taken into account, namely:[200]

(i) the interests of shareholders;
(ii) the interests of employees;
(iii) the interests of the company;
(iv) the public interest.

Of these four particular interests, none should take precedence over the others when the target's board deliberates on what approach to take.[201]

In the case of a takeover bid, the target's managing board could (in theory) justify taking defensive measures, claiming that these were in the best interests of its employees, whilst in fact acting in its own interests.[202] To avoid this specific situation arising in the case of a takeover bid, the legislature has created a principle of neutrality which is binding on the board of directors:

"after publication of the decision to make a bid..., the management board of the target company may not take measures that could prevent the success of the bid."[203]

But the aspect of increasing the consideration remains a goal at which managements facing a hostile takeover offer may aim under the new German regulations; indeed, in both the Mannesmann and FAG Kugelfischer cases, the boards of the target companies achieved a substantially improved bid notwithstanding the duty of neutrality under the then applicable Takeover Code. The *Revlon* doctrine, therefore, is paralleled by the "duty of neutrality" under German law. The target company's "duty of neutrality" is, therefore, not to be interpreted as a duty on the target's board to remain passive and inactive; it is merely a tool to prevent the target company's management from thwarting the offer, and to facilitate the shareholders (as owners of the enterprise) to decide for themselves whether or not to accept the

---

[200] Explanatory Memorandum of the Federal Government on § 3 para. 3 and § 27 para. 1 Takeover Act (BT-Drucks. 14/7034 of October 5, 2001); Hüffer, 4th ed., § 76 AktG annot. 12 et seq.; Mertens, Kölner Kommentar, § 76 AktG annot. 22; Schüppen, Die Wirtschaftsprüfung 2001 p. 958, 970; Wiese, DB 2001 p. 849, 850.

[201] Hüffer, 4th ed., § 76 AktG annot. 12; Mertens, Kölner Kommentar, § 76 AktG annot. 22.

[202] Schüppen, Die Wirtschaftsprüfung 2001 p. 958, 970.

[203] § 33 para. 1 Takeover Act.

bid.[204] This is consistent with the general principle that management may not decide on measures which adversely affect the shareholders' rights and their ownership of the enterprise.[205]

c) Exceptions to the Principle of Neutrality

The new German Takeover Act sets out a number of exceptions to the general principle of neutrality (possible defensive measures are discussed in detail in Ch. 4 no. 8 below).

(1) Shareholders' resolutions

Before a takeover bid is formally put forward, the shareholders of the target company may (in a shareholders' meeting) pass a "blocking" resolution, authorizing the board of the target company to initiate certain defensive measures in the event that an offer is made[206] (in detail see Ch. 4 no. 8. c. (3) (b) below). Once passed, this resolution remains valid for 18 months, after which time the resolution must be renewed, if required.[207] It requires a 75% majority.[208] The difficulty with this arrangement is that the shareholders revoke in advance their rights to consider the terms of any offer put forward during the 18-month duration of the "blocking" resolution, without knowing what those terms might be.[209] Conversely, the management board can use the resolution as an effective way of defending the target company, even if the majority of shareholders would have accepted a favorable bid from a hypothetical offeror. Therefore, it is rather advisable for the shareholders to decide on defensive steps at a shareholders' meeting called after the bid has been launched.[210] The problem in this respect is that it is within the due discretion of the management to call a shareholders' meeting pending a bid, and the board may decide to seek the approval of the supervisory board for defensive steps (see Ch. 4 no. 7. c. (2) below) rather than the approval of the shareholders. However, the German Corporate Governance Code of Best Practice,[211] which is binding for all publicly listed companies in the form of "comply or explain," requires that the board call an extraordi-

---

[204] Drygala, ZIP 2001 p. 1861, 1863. For this reason, some commentators think that the term "duty of neutrality" is misleading, e. g. Geibel/Süßmann/Schwennicke, WpÜG § 33 annot. 10; Möller/Pötzsch, ZIP 2001 p. 1256, 1259 fn. 20.

[205] Liebscher, ZIP 2001 p. 853, 866; Ebenroth/Daum, DB 1991 p. 1157, 1158; Hopt, ZGR 1993 p. 534, 548; Michalski, AG 1997 p. 152, 159.

[206] § 33 para. 2 clause 1 Takeover Act.

[207] § 33 para. 2 clause 2 Takeover Act.

[208] § 33 para. 2 clause 3 Takeover Act.

[209] Drygala, ZIP 2001 p. 1861, 1865.

[210] Ibid.

[211] Corporate Governance Codex passed by the Federal Government Commission on Corporate Governance, sec. III no. 7; this Codex is binding in that the boards must either comply with the provisions of the Code or explain to the shareholders that the company deviated from the provisions of the Code in specific cases, § 161 Stock Corporation Act.

nary shareholders' meeting in "appropriate cases" in order to discuss a tender offer, and to pass resolutions if necessary; the exact meaning of the term "appropriate cases" has yet to be clarified.

(2) Approval by the supervisory board

However, there is an even easier way for the target company's managing board to take a defensive stance: the board of directors only requires the approval of the supervisory board to undertake defense measures.[212] If the supervisory board agrees to the management board's proposal, no further approval of the shareholders' meeting is required. The only prerequisite is that the defensive steps fall within the responsibility of the management board under general corporate law. For example, the board can issue shares to a white knight only if the articles grant the board the general authority to issue shares.

This provision of the Takeover Act is supposedly intended to defuse the conflict between the principle of maintaining neutrality and the duty of the managing board to act in the interests of the target company.[213] However, if the principle of neutrality is to be compromised to such a great extent, can the original purpose of the law – the protection of shareholders' rights – be fulfilled?[214] This scheme is one of the major aspects of the Takeover Act that is not in compliance with the draft of the EU-Directive on corporate takeovers which recently failed to be passed by the European Parliament.

(3) Ongoing business operations

Faced with a takeover bid, the management board of the target may nonetheless fulfil its obligations under the terms of existing agreements, and may make whatever decisions and carry out whatever actions the management, acting prudently and conscientiously, would take if no takeover bid had been made, even where to do so effectively thwarts the offeror's bid (so-called "going-concern" exception).[215] The aim of the legislator was to allow the target's management board to continue the day-to-day running of the business and allow the company to pursue its business strategies, despite a pending takeover bid.[216] In the latter respect, the board is not limited to the scope of daily business operations, but may also take extraordinary steps to implement its business strategy.[217] It may, e.g., pursue a business acquisition even if such acquisition will cause antitrust and merger control impediments for the offeror.[218] This clearly exceeds the authority which U.S. courts would grant to the target's board under the *Revlon* doctrine. It contradicts

---

[212] § 33 para. 1 clause 2 Takeover Act.

[213] *See* Wiese, DB 2001 p. 849, 851; Mülbert/Birke, WM 2001 p. 705, 715.

[214] The reactions to this feature of the Takeover Act have been widely negative, e. g. Lutter, Handelsblatt of 20 December 2001, p. 10; Krause, AG 2000 p. 133, 137; other commentators took a more positive view, e.g., Schneider, AG 2002 p. 125, 129.

[215] § 33 para. 1 clause 2 Takeover Act.

[216] Explanatory Memorandum of the Federal Government on § 33 para. 1 clause 2 Takeover Act (BT-Drucks. 14/7034 of October 5, 2001).

[217] Geibel/Süßmann/Schwennicke, WpÜG § 33 annot. 45.

[218] Schneider, AG 2002 p. 125, 129.

the principle of neutrality and opens, to the management board, the door to obstruct offers by means of strategic moves which conflict with the planned business strategy of the offeror regarding the target's business. In the authors' opinion, the "going concern" exception should therefore be narrowly interpreted and should allow measures exceeding the daily business operations only if:[219]

- the strategic measure implements a business strategy that has already been pursued by the target company before the tender offer was published, and
- if the measure cannot be delayed until the end of the acceptance period without jeopardizing the pursued business strategy as a whole, or without doing substantial harm to the business of the target.

d) Statements of the Boards

The target company's management and supervisory boards are each required to publish statements relating to the offer, which statements must contain the following information:[220]

- statement on the amount and form of consideration offered;
- the expected consequences of a successful bid for the target company, its employees, work conditions, and the business locations of the target;
- the offeror's business objectives vis-à-vis the target company;
- whether, and to what extent, board members of the target company intend to accept the offer and surrender their own shares in the target company.

The statement is, however, by no means limited to these four items; the boards may include other aspects deemed important for the shareholders. Moreover, disclosure of personal interests of the board members and any agreements with board members in connection with the planned takeover should be included.[221] The boards should not discuss matters relating to trade secrets; while the general duty not to disclose trade secrets[222] might be reduced slightly in a takeover situation when there is a prevailing interest of the shareholders to obtain certain information, it will by no means be derogated by a tender offer.

The Act does not require the boards of the target company to make a recommendation to its shareholders. The shareholders may be provided with information on the four points outlined above and left to make an informed decision on the offer.

Both the management and supervisory boards must publish a statement. The two statements may be prepared and issued as a joint document or as two individual items. It is significant that both boards are required to give their views on the takeover bid. This allows the maximum amount of infor-

---

[219] *Compare*: Schneider, AG 2002 p. 125, 129.
[220] § 27 para. 1 Takeover Act.
[221] Geibel/Süßmann/Schwennicke/Grobys, WpÜG § 27 annot. 22; Thümmel, DB 2000 p. 461, 463 (relating to the Takeover Code).
[222] § 93 para. 1 clause 2 Stock Corporation Act.

mation to be disseminated to the shareholders. The management board usually has an in-depth, "hands-on" knowledge of the company's business, while the non-executive supervisory board, at more of a distance from the day-to-day workings of the company, might have a better overview of the company's global position. It should nevertheless be borne in mind that the two are interlinked in many ways: for instance, the members of the management board are nominated by the supervisory board, and the supervisory board is elected by the shareholders' meeting, which may in turn lead to its members being highly influenced by major shareholders with different priorities to those of the minority shareholders. The independence of the supervisory board and its statements should be assessed on a case-by-case basis as a question of fact.

For details regarding the statement as a means of a defense battle and the liability of the boards for inaccurate statements see Ch. 4 no. 8. c. below.

8. Defense Strategies

a) General

Defense strategies become relevant where the takeover of the target is hostile, i.e. where a takeover bid of an offeror is not supported by the target's management. Such situations are particularly prone to agency conflicts between the shareholders and management, as the bid is addressed to the shareholders who may or may not choose to sell their shares, but (as the shareholders are often a diverse body which is not usually in a position to take coordinated action vis-à-vis the offeror) it often falls to the target's management to take on the responsibility of negotiating with the offeror and of deciding on defensive tactics. In order to minimize the potential conflict between management and shareholders' interests, the takeover regulations attempt to create a "level playing field" with little or no leeway for unfair offensive tactics by the offeror on the one hand and narrow scope for defensive action by the target on the other. Although the Takeover Act permits the target to adopt a greater range of defensive measures than the draft of the EU Directive from which it partly originates,[223] the Act is nonetheless designed to promote an efficient takeover market in which takeovers can take place and hence provides only for a limited scope of defensive tactics.

In general, only **"ad-hoc" defensive measures** fall within the scope of the Takeover Act. So-called structural defense strategies[224] are not governed by the Takeover Act; in this regard, the general laws on corporations and corporate governance apply. Defensive corporate structuring is generally permitted by general corporate law and is not outlawed by the new Takeover Act.[225]

---

[223] 13th EU-Directive on Public Takeover Offers (Common Position adopted by the Council on June 19, 2000).

[224] E. g. staggered boards, authorized unissued capital, sale of own shares; *see* Ch. 4 no. 8. b. below.

[225] Geibel/Süßmann/Schwennicke, WpÜG § 33 annot. 33.

Nowadays, most public offers are successful, and hostile offers ultimately become friendly offers (as in the recent Vodafone/Mannesmann and INA/FAG Kugelfischer cases). Most cases where bids are not successful result from the success of a competing bid (such as the takeover of National Westminster Bank Plc. by Royal Bank of Scotland Group), or from the decision of the bidder to acquire a different target (such as the acquisition by BNP of Paribas instead of Société Generale S. A.). In most instances, defensive steps merely offer leverage for the target management in its negotiations with the bidder in order to obtain an improved bid. A professional management will generally not maintain opposition to an attractive offer as its reputation with institutional investors is at stake. Generally, a hostile bidder should allow for a potential (more or less modest – INA improved its bid by less than 10% from € 11 to € 12 per FAG share) improvement of the bid when determining the first offer price, as the target management needs to present a success story to its shareholders before it can convincingly step back from a defensive strategy.

b) Structural Defensive Tactics

Until recently, U.S. courts sanctioned the use of a number of different structural defense strategies.

(1) Poison pills

"Poison pills" (also called "shareholder rights plans"), are among the most potent defensive weapons available to a target. Many U.S. corporations have adopted poison pills in one form or another.[226] Once activated, all the shareholders of the target – other than the offeror – have the right to purchase further shares in the target company at a bargain price, thereby diluting the position of the offeror. Each of the following events would typically trigger the use of a poison pill:

- **Purchase of a certain level of control** (such as 30% or 50% of voting rights in the target) by an individual or entity.
- **Second-stage merger** initiated by the offeror after obtaining control in order to "squeeze out" the target's minority shareholders (usually at a discount to the true value of their shares). This triggering event is designed, in particular, to deter coercive two-tier bids.

The landmark U.S. case upholding preplanned poison pills was decided in Delaware in 1985.[227] Since then, poison pills have become a common structural means of defense. With the recent slump in the value of technology shares and with companies no longer able to rely on a high share price as an efficient shark repellant, poison pills have also become increasingly popular with technology companies. By 2001, about 1,600 U.S. firms adopted poison pills.

---

[226] Robert Prentice, Law of Business Organizations and Securities Regulation, 2nd ed., p. 804.
[227] Moran v. Household International, 500 A.2d 1346 (Del. 1985).

8. Defense Strategies

Selected Hostile Takeover Bids (Source: Securities Data Corporation)

Date	Offeror	Target	Value (US$ bn)	Acquisition Currency	Successful
14-Nov-1999	Vodafone AirTouch PLC	Mannesmann AG	202.8	Shares	Yes
04-Nov-1999	Pfizer Inc.	Warner-Lambert Co.	89.7	Shares	Yes
05-July-1999	Total Fina SA	Elf Aquitane	51.1	Shares	Yes
24-Sep-1999	Bank of Scotland PLC	National Westminster Bank PLC	38.8	Cash	No
29-Nov-1999	Royal Bank of Scotland Group	National Westminster Bank PLC	38.5	Shares/Cash	Yes
20-Feb-1999	Olivetti & Co. SpA	Telecom Italia SpA	24.8	Shares/Cash	Yes
02-May-2000	Unilever Plc.	Bestfoods	25.1	Cash	Yes
09-Mar-1999	BNP	Societe Generale	19.7	Shares	No
09-Mar-1999	BNP	Paribas SA	13.2	Shares	Yes
14-Sep-1999	Assicurazioni Generali SpA	INA	10.2	Cash	Yes
22-June-1999	Punch Taverns	Allied Domecq UK-Retailing	4.3	Cash	Yes
19-Feb-2001	Incentive Capital AG	Gebrüder Sulzer AG	2.2	Shares/Cash	No
21-Dec-2001	INA Vermögensverwaltungsges. mbH	FAG Kugelfischer Georg Schäfer AG	1.8	Cash	Yes
28-Aug-2000	OM Gruppen AB	London Stock Exchange	1.5	Shares	No
22-Nov-2000	WCM	Klöckner Werke	1.1	Shares/Cash	Yes
16-Nov-1999	SAAB AB	Celsius AB	0.6	Cash	Yes
16-Mar-1999	Unigate PLC.	Terranova Foods Plc	0.4	Cash	Yes

Case: Hilton Hotels Corp. adopted a rights plan as part of its merger with Promos Hotel Corp. on November 29, 1999. The rights agreement provided for one right per ordinary share in Hilton to be issued to its shareholders, in the form of a dividend of one preference share purchase right. Upon the occurrence of a triggering event, the rights entitled the holder to ordinary shares in Hilton at half price. This right did not, however, apply to the offeror. One shareholder challenged the rights plan in court, but without success. The court ruled that the Hilton rights plan had a structure similar to many other poison pill plans adopted since the Delaware 1985 Supreme Court ruling, and confirmed that poison pills were recognized in practically all jurisdictions in the U.S.[228]

The courts do, however, impose restrictions on the use of poison pills. The use of rights plans, particularly by the directors, is wholly subordinate to the directors' fiduciary duties; in other words, the target's response to a hostile takeover offer must ultimately be judged by the directors at the time of the bid:[229] on receipt of a bid, the directors must evaluate the offer and may only then decide whether it is in the best interests of the shareholders and whether or not the rights plan should, therefore, be used. Thus, so-called "dead-hand" and "no-hand" poison pills are not permitted. "Dead-hand" pills may only be removed by the directors who actually put them in place, and "no-hand" pills cannot be removed at all. No-hand pills are consistently declared invalid by U.S. courts[230] as they leave no room for exercise of the director's fiduciary duties when a hostile offer is received. The same applies to "dead-hand" pills:

Case: Mentor v. Quickturn:[231] Mentor had an interest in acquiring Quickturn, as some of Quickturn's patents were preventing Mentor from entering a growing, key strategic market. When Quickturn's share price plummeted from nearly $ 20 to below $10, Mentor launched an all-cash offer at $ 12.125, representing a premium of almost 50% over the pre-offer price (but a 20% discount on previous share price levels). Once initially accepted by the majority of Quickturn's shareholders, this offer would be followed by a second-step merger with the same cash value of $ 12.125 per share. On the advice of its financial advisers, Quickturn's board concluded that the offer was inadequate and adopted, inter alia, a dead-hand poison pill option as part of a rights plan. The rights plan included a deferred redemption provision under which a newly-elected board could remove the rights plan no earlier than six months after taking office, if removing the rights plan would (at that stage) facilitate a takeover transaction.

The Delaware Supreme Court declared the deferred redemption feature void as it would make it impossible for a newly-elected board to redeem the

---

[228] Leonard Loventhal Account v. Hilton Hotels Corp., 2000 Del. Ch. LEXIS 149, 2000 WL 1 528 909; affirmed: Delaware Supreme Court, September 06, 2001 (C. A. No. 17 803).

[229] Moran v. Household International, Inc., 490 A.2d at 1357 (Del. 1985).

[230] Carmody v. Toll Brothers, Inc., Del. Ch., C.A. No. 15 983 (1998); Bank of New York Co., Inc. v. Irving Bank Corp., 528 N.Y.S.2d 182 (N.Y. Sup. Ct. 1988).

[231] Delaware Supreme Court, No. 512, 1998, decided December 31, 1998.

poison pill at a future date if the board, pursuant to its fiduciary duty, considered the offer and the sale of the company to be in the best interests of the company and the shareholders at that time. Limiting the board's authority to exercise its fiduciary duties in relation to fundamental questions such as the sale of the company would contradict the founding principles of corporate law.

These court precedents reiterate that poison pills and their use by the board are only permissible to the extent that they are in the best interests of the shareholders. They must not be designed to deter takeovers in general; they may only be deployed to prevent unfair offensive tactics (such as two-tier offers) and under-priced offers. As soon as the shareholders are offered an attractive price, the management has a fiduciary duty to redeem the pill. It cannot circumvent its fiduciary duty by including no-hand and dead-hand pill features as part of the rights plan. Though poison pills are not legally permissible under German law (see below), this principle, developed by the U. S. courts, should have merit for Germany, i. e. the use of defense plans is subordinate to the board's fiduciary duty.

In **Germany**, the use of poison pills has never been permitted under general principles of corporate law.[232] Under German corporate law, the introduction of rights plans does not generally lie within the responsibilities of the board: it requires a shareholders' resolution. In addition, German law contains relatively strict protection against dilution measures; shareholders may only be excluded from the right to subscribe for new share issues in very limited circumstances, i.e. compelling reasons must be given to support the grounds for limiting shareholders' subscription rights.[233] This usually only occurs when new shares are issued as "acquisition currency" where a business is purchased by means of a share exchange transaction.[234] Defensive measures in takeover battles are not deemed to be in the company's best interests, relating instead to the shareholders' decision as to whether or not to dispose of their shares.[235]

This general principle, which has applied under German law until now, is consistent with the new (limited) "duty of neutrality" which has been expressly codified in the Takeover Act. The duty of neutrality prohibits the target's management from exercising a poison pill rights plan; exercising such a plan would impair the chances of the takeover offer succeeding and restrict the shareholders' freedom to decide whether or not to accept the offer.[236] (For limitations of the duty of neutrality see Ch. 4 no. 8. c. below).

---

[232] *See* Schanz, NZG 2000 p. 337, 343; Hauschka/Roth, AG 1988 p. 181, 190; Michalski, AG 1997 p. 152, 158.

[233] Federal Supreme Court, BGHZ 71 p. 40, 46; BGHZ 83 p. 319, 321; BGHZ 120 p. 141, 145; BGHZ 125 p. 239, 241.

[234] Federal Supreme Court, BGHZ 71 p. 40, 49; Lutter, Kölner Kommentar, § 186 AktG annot. 81.

[235] Hüffer, 4th ed., § 186 AktG annot. 32; Lutter, Kölner Kommentar, § 186 AktG annot. 74.

[236] Michalski, AG 1997 p. 152, 161.

(2) Staggered boards

The German two-tier board system[237] is one of the major deterrents to hostile takeovers because – aside from the 75% voting majority required to remove members of the supervisory board prior to the end of their term – large companies must have employee representatives on the supervisory boards.[238] These employee representatives cannot be removed by the shareholders.[239] Traditionally, employee representatives are opposed to takeovers, as takeovers usually entail job cuts. They are often also reluctant to appoint new directors proposed by a new majority shareholder on similar grounds.

This anti-takeover effect resulting from the two-tier board system can be further reinforced by staggering the terms of office of the supervisory board members.[240] This can be done in such a way as to prevent a purchaser from simply replacing the entire supervisory board (with the exception of the employee representatives, who may not be removed by the shareholders in any event) in a single stroke at the next available shareholders' meeting, unless the purchaser has a 75% voting majority. A staggered board is particularly effective for companies whose shares are held by a few, large shareholders who would be opposed to a takeover. This is the case for many family-founded companies, where the founding family keeps a relatively large shareholding in the company after going public, often maintaining a shareholding of between 25% and 50%. With a 25% share of the votes, a shareholder can (for example) veto an attempt to replace supervisory board members prior to the end of their terms of office. If, in addition, half of the target's supervisory board members are employee representatives, the purchaser must replace all shareholders' representatives on the supervisory board in order to acquire a voting majority on the supervisory board. This can be a tedious process if the appointments to the supervisory board are staggered.

---

[237] *See* Ch. 1 no. 1. a. above.

[238] Under the Shop Constitution Act 1952 (*"Betriebsverfassungsgesetz 1952"*), one-third of the members of the supervisory board of any stock corporation must be employee representatives. The Act does not apply to corporations with less than 500 employees. For corporations registered before August 10, 1994, this applies only if these corporations are family controlled (§ 76 para. 6 Shop Constitution Act). The Codetermination Act 1976 (*"Mitbestimmungsgesetz 1976"*) is applicable to all companies employing more than 2000 persons providing for equal representation of the shareholders and employees on the supervisory board. The Coal and Steel Codetermination Act (*"Montanmitbestimmungsgesetz"*) and the Supplementary Codetermination Act apply to corporations in the coal and steel producing industries employing more than 1000 persons. This Act also stipulates equal numbers of employee and shareholder representatives on the supervisory board. However, in the case of a stalemate on the supervisory board between shareholders' and employees' representatives, the Chairman of the supervisory board, who may be elected by the shareholders' representatives, has two votes.

[239] Schanz, NZG 2000 p. 337, 342; Peltzer, ZIP 1989 p. 69, 72; Hauschka/Roth, AG 1988, p. 181, 188.

[240] Schanz, NZG 2000 p. 337, 342; Hauschka/Roth, AG 1988 p. 181, 188.

8. Defense Strategies

Staggered boards are permissible under both general German corporate law and the Takeover Act, and have frequently been used in the past, not only as a defensive measure but also for corporate governance reasons, as they allow for a continuous, circulating turnover of supervisory board members.

(3) ESOPs

ESOPs (Employee Stock Option Plans)[241] may serve as a powerful structural defense strategy. By combining the shareholdings of the founders and other strategic investors with those of employees participating in ESOP's, substantial blocks of shareholdings whose holders are opposed to a takeover may be built up. 25% of the voting rights in shareholders' meetings gives rise to a number of minority rights, such as the ability to block the approval required to remove supervisory board members, the ability to block capital increases, and the ability to block the purchase of the company's own shares.

Under German law, the shareholders' meeting may authorize the management to issue shares under an ESOP up to a maximum of 10% of the issued share capital of the company.[242] Contrary to the position under U.S. law, however, those share options must be issued conditional on certain, defined targets being achieved, i.e., they are only exercisable when the established targets are reached. Such targets may relate to profits, share prices, etc;[243] the mere expiry of a certain period of service may not trigger the exercise of the stock options. This often makes it difficult for German companies to sell share option plans to employees of their U.S. subsidiaries: if share option plans for overseas subsidiaries grant options in respect of publicly traded shares in the German parent company, the terms of these ESOPs must comply with the requirements of German law. According to German conflict of laws rules, the law of the parent corporation's registered place of business is applicable to the ESOP. The "defined targets to be achieved" contained in the German-based ESOPs will often seem unreasonable to the U.S. employees.

(4) Cross-shareholdings of affiliated companies

Cross-shareholdings between affiliated corporations can be an efficient tool to deter hostile takeovers.[244] Such cross-shareholdings reduce the amount of free-floating shares, and the target is able to hold its own shares

---

[241] For an ESOP to be created under German law, a contingent capital increase (§ 192 Stock Corporation Act) is required. The contingent capital increase is carried out at that point of time and to the extent that rights holders exercise the stock warrants. In contrast to the ordinary capital increase (§ 186 Stock Corporation Act), preemptive rights of existing shareholders do not have to be observed. The stock warrants can be granted only to certain groups of persons, for instance to employees of the stock corporation.

[242] § 192 para. 2 no. 3, para. 3 Stock Corporation Act.

[243] Zeidler, NZG 1998 p. 789, 794; Kallmeyer, AG 1999 p. 97, 100; dissenting opinion: Hüffer, 5th ed., § 193 AktG annot. 9; Weiß, WM 1999 p. 353, 359.

[244] Klein, NJW 1997 p. 2085, 2089.

indirectly.[245] For example, if an affiliated corporation (F) purchases 25% of the shares in a potential takeover target (T) and T itself holds a 50% interest in F, then T holds (indirectly) 12.5% of its own shares without breaching maintenance of capital rules which prevent a German corporation from directly holding more than 10% of its own shares.[246]

Case (Southern Pacific Petroleum/Central Pacific Mining): An artificial cross-shareholding was established by an Australian company which had effectively divided itself into two companies: all the assets (in particular oil shale deposits) were held in two 50% blocks by each of two companies, Southern Pacific Petroleum (SPP) and Central Pacific Mining (CPM). Each company held 50% of each single asset and each had virtually identical financial statements, as well as the same board, management and personnel (employees being jointly employed by both companies). CPM owned 34% of SPP and SPP had a 30% stake in CPM.[247] This structure was originally chosen for tax purposes, but also served as a powerful defensive structure. As the "Oil Shale Twins" recently resolved to merge and unravel their 30-year-old dual structure, this protective feature no longer applies. Therefore, the new combined corporation plans to implement a two-year anti-takeover plan, preventing any one shareholder from owning more than 20% in the new combined corporation in order to establish a transition period from the previous structure. German corporate law would not allow such a cap on shareholdings.

The efficiency of such cross-shareholdings as a deterrent to poachers is, however, rather limited in Germany, as general corporate law imposes voting restrictions on cross-shareholdings. If the cross-shareholdings exceed 25% in both companies then one of the companies may not exercise more than 25% of the voting rights in the other company. If, in the above example, company F (knowing that T already owns a 50% stake in F) were to purchase additional shares in T (so that F's shareholding in T were to exceed 25%), F may not exercise more than 25% of the voting rights in T.[248] Of course, cross-shareholdings exceeding 25% may nevertheless assist in avoiding a takeover, since the number of free-floating shares will be reduced.[249]

Cross-shareholdings should not, however, exceed 50% in a company, because otherwise the controlled company may hold no more than 10% in the parent company.[250] Some scholars openly suggest that this 10% restriction

---

[245] Schanz, NZG 2000 p. 337, 346.

[246] § 71 para. 2 Stock Corporation Act; Marquardt, WiB 1994 p. 537, 541.

[247] As of September 2001.

[248] § 328 Stock Corporation Act. Generally, the company that reaches the 25% threshold first *and* notifies the other company accordingly may exercise all its voting rights while the other company is subject to the voting restriction.

[249] Assmann/Bozenhardt, ZGR Sonderheft 9 (1990) p. 1, 136.

[250] Schanz, NZG 2000 p. 337, 346; Klein, NJW 1997 p. 2085, 2089. A shareholding exceeding 50% in another company makes this company a subsidiary under corporate law and GAAP; therefore, shares in the parent company owned by the subsidiary are considered to be the parent company's own shares, and the amount thereof is limited to 10% of the issued shares of the parent company under German law (*see* § 71 d Stock Corporation Act).

should simply be disregarded if the associated companies consider this necessary as part of an effective defense structure.[251] Violation of the 10% limit is not (although it is a violation of corporate law) a regulatory offence,[252] and does not render the share acquisition and the cross shareholding structure legally invalid.[253] The authors disapprove of this approach.[254] Building defense strategies on illegal measures could severely impact on the confidence of the capital markets in the company.

(5) Authorized but unissued share capital – sale by a company of its own shares

As mentioned above (Ch. 4 no. 8. b. (1)), the management of a German corporation is, in principle, not entitled to issue new shares. Capital increases fall within the responsibility of the shareholders' meeting. However, the shareholders may authorize shares to be issued for use at the management's discretion.[255] It has been suggested that a sufficient amount of authorized unissued capital may be an efficient shark repellant since it allows the target's management to search for "white knights" and to grant shares to a white knight without difficulty,[256] whether before or after a hostile takeover offer has been launched. However, once a takeover offer has been made public, the target's management is under a duty to remain neutral, and that duty of neutrality may also limit the use of unissued capital by management.

Shares may also be issued to a white knight by selling the company's own shares (treasury shares). German law generally allows corporations to hold their own shares up to a maximum of 10% of the issued capital upon approval of the shareholders' meeting with a 75% voting majority.[257] Management may, therefore, gradually accumulate shares in the corporation to sell to a white knight later. However, once a takeover offer has been launched, it should be borne in mind that the target board's duty to remain neutral comes into play once again.

c) Ad-Hoc Defensive Tactics

As discussed above, the intention of the Takeover Act is to create a level playing field for corporate takeovers by operation of law so that the management of both the target and the offeror have little leeway or discretion as regards defensive and offensive tactics. As we have seen, under the Takeover Act and general corporate law principles, unfair offensive tactics such

---

[251] Schanz, NZG 2000 p. 337, 346.

[252] § 405 para. 1 no. 4 lit. a Stock Corporation Act.

[253] § 71 para. 4 clause 1 Stock Corporation Act.

[254] *See* also Marquardt, WiB 1994 p. 537, 542.

[255] §§ 202 et seq. Indeed, virtually all traded companies have authorized unissued capital available.

[256] Schanz NZG, 2000 p. 337, 343; Hauschka/Roth, AG 1988 p. 181, 193; Bungert, NJW 1998 p. 488, 492.

[257] § 71 para. 1 clause 1 no. 8 Stock Corporation Act.

as two-tier front-loaded offers are not allowed; as a counterpart, poison pills designed to deter unfair offers are not permissible under German law. Nevertheless, a natural imbalance between the power of the "attacker" and the "victim" remains in terms of timing. While the offeror has plenty of time to choose a target, determine an appropriate price and prepare its "advertising campaign," the target may be surprised by the offer and unable to counter the ambush efficiently and effectively. In the U. S., this power imbalance has frequently been used by offerors launching surprise hostile takeover offers, perhaps by making a bid public late on a Friday afternoon (the so-called **"Saturday Night Special"**), setting the acceptance period for the target's shareholders at only a week or 10 days,[258] so that the time within which the target's management can react is reduced to a minimum.

Such abusive practices have been banned by the Williams Act in the U.S. (which requires that the offer is held open for no less than 20 working days).[259] The previous German Takeover Code required the offeror to hold open a bid for a minimum of 28 calendar days,[260] while under the new Takeover Act an offeror must hold open the offer for a minimum period of four weeks and a maximum of 10 weeks.[261] The target may nevertheless be under time pressure to put together a defensive strategy. Extensive advance planning (together with a long-term strategy and structural defensive measures) is essential for companies which are susceptible to hostile takeovers. Such companies should keep a so-called "Pearl Harbor File" detailing potential defense strategies and collecting relevant materials to ensure that they are prepared for action in the event of a hostile takeover offer.

Notwithstanding the target management's general duty to remain neutral when faced with a takeover offer, the Takeover Act (presumably recognizing this natural imbalance between the offeror's advantageous and the target's disadvantageous position in terms of time and preparation) permits the target to employ a limited number of ad-hoc defensive measures.

(1) Public relations activities

The most obvious defensive strategy is a well-managed advertising campaign. Neither the Takeover Code which applied previously, nor the Takeover Act now in force, have ever disputed the fact that the target is entitled to attack the offer in publications and advertisements.

(a) Official statements of the target's boards ("Defense Document")

An important public relations tool are the mandatory statements of the target's management and supervisory boards which must be published as a response to the tender offer (often called the "defense document").[262] Under the

---

[258] *See* Robert Prentice, Law of Business Organizations and Securities Regulation, 2nd ed., p. 795, 796.

[259] Regulation 14E, Rule 14 e-1 (a), 17 C.F.R. 240.14 e-1(a).

[260] Art. 11 Takeover Code; the maximum acceptance period shall be 60 calendar days.

[261] § 16 para. 1 Takeover Act.

[262] Land/Hasselbach, DB 2000 p. 1747, 1749.

previous Takeover Code, the target had to publish the statement within two weeks of the publication of the offer.[263] This deadline was considered too short. For instance, in the FAG Kugelfischer/INA Holding case, the target (FAG Kugelfischer) published a 26-page statement – poorly drafted and unstructured, containing a muddle of charts and tables the purpose of which was not clear – and which had obviously been produced under great time pressure. The Takeover Act does not contain a fixed deadline, but the target must now publish the statement "without undue delay."[264] The interpretation of this term will depend on the circumstances of each single case: in large, difficult transactions the statement might be more voluminous than might be the case in relation to smaller offers; on the other hand, the larger target might have more powerful resources, including professional advisers (investment banks, lawyers and consultants), to assist in expeditious drafting of the statement. In any event, the statement should be published early enough to allow the target shareholders enough time to make their decision. The statement should be published sooner rather than later, as the possible impact of the statement will diminish the later it is published.

In friendly takeover bids, it was legally permissible (and in compliance with past practice) to publish the target's statement at the same time as – and together with – the offer. The Federal Supervisory Office has indicated that it will not accept this practice under the Takeover Act; the target's statement needs to be published separately from, and after, the offer.

The target's official statement must include details of the following items:

- form and amount of the consideration offered;
- the expected consequences of a successful offer for:
  - the target;
  - the target's employees and the works council;
  - working conditions; and
  - the business locations of the target;
- opinion on the offeror's objectives in putting forward the takeover offer;
- whether or not the target's board members intend to accept the offer in relation to their own personal shares.

The target's statement is not a prospectus entailing strict liability vis-à-vis a target's shareholders.[265]

Nonetheless, the target's boards certainly have a general duty of care[266] when preparing the official statement, as this statement may be one of the main sources of information upon which the shareholders base their decision.

According to a long line of legal precedents, violations of the general fiduciary duty of the board give rise to the board being liable to the corpora-

---

[263] Art. 18 Takeover Code.

[264] § 27 Takeover Act.

[265] § 12 Takeover Act provides for strict liability for inaccurate statements made in the offer document; the Takeover Act does not contain a corresponding liability provision for the statement of the target.

[266] § 93 Stock Corporation Act; Winter/Harbarth, ZIP 2002 p. 1, 16.

tion, not, however, to the shareholders. Correspondingly, claims by the corporation for damages against the management board are asserted by the supervisory (non-executive) board. In the event of a misrepresentation in the official statement, the shareholders' only remedy is to urge the supervisory board to pursue liability claims against the management board members in the name of the corporation.[267]

There is, thus, a substantial gap in the remedies available to shareholders in the event that the target's management board makes inaccurate statements. The shareholders may only urge the supervisory board to file a damages claim against the management board; however, the supervisory board may only claim damages suffered by the target company, not damages suffered by the shareholders. The shareholders have a direct cause of action against the management board only in the event that intentional misrepresentations have been made to them.[268] For details on the shareholders' remedies see no. Ch. 4 no. 8. c. (5) below.

(b) Advertising campaigns

Along with the official statement to be published, the target's board may conduct a general advertising campaign against the offer, notwithstanding its duty of neutrality. This was generally accepted under the Takeover Code and is also permitted by the Takeover Act.[269] However, the Federal Supervisory Office may take action against abusive advertising behavior.[270] The Takeover Act does not define the term "abusive advertising."

Case: Mannesmann/Vodafone:[271] The costs of the public relations campaign in the Mannesmann/Vodafone case (which were estimated at DEM 700 million) were widely criticized.[272] One Mannesmann shareholder applied to the competent court for an interim injunction to prevent Mannesmann's management from continuing the press campaign. The court dismissed the application. However, the court did not expressly discuss the question of abusive advertising. It explained that advertising in a takeover situation is an ordinary management responsibility, and the shareholders have no remedy to prevent the management from performing certain mana-

---

[267] § 147 para. 1 Stock Corporation Act: the supervisory board must assert claims against the management board, if the shareholders' meeting so resolves with a simple voting majority, or if a minority representing at least 10% of the company's capital submits the relevant demand to the supervisory board.

[268] § 826 BGB; *see* Geibel/Süßmann/Schwennicke, WpÜG § 33 annot. 90. § 823 para. 2 Civil Code contains a general private cause of action in the event of a violation of statutes and regulations that are specifically designed to protect individual rights. § 12 Takeover Act is, however, not a statutory ground for such a private cause of action, arg. e. § 12 para. 6 Takeover Act, *see* Geibel/Süßmann/Schwennicke, WpÜG § 33 annot. 88; Krause, AG 2000 p. 217. Some scholars take the opposite view.

[269] Drygala, ZIP 2001 p. 1861, 1863; Körner, DB 2001 p. 367, 368; Grunewald, AG 2001 p. 288.

[270] § 28 Takeover Act.

[271] Regional Court of Düsseldorf, LG Düsseldorf, AG 2000 p. 233.

[272] Körner, DB 2001 p. 367, 369; Hopt: Festschrift für Lutter 2000, p. 1361, 1382; Kort, Festschrift für Lutter 2000, p. 1421, 1439; Altmeppen, ZIP 2001 p. 1073, 1076.

gerial activities. This corresponds to the principle of German corporate law that the shareholders in general have no direct remedy for violations of management duties, and that management owes fiduciary duties only to the corporation as its principal, rather than to the shareholders. The shareholders' rights are limited to the exercise of their voting rights in shareholders' meetings, and as a rule it is beyond the competence of the shareholders' meeting to vote on management actions. Under the so-called "Holzmüller doctrine," exceptions apply only in cases where managerial actions have a fundamental structural impact on the corporation and the shareholders' rights;[273] in Holzmüller cases, the shareholders have a right to demand that the management call a shareholders' meeting. The shareholders may then vote on the planned management action. In the Vodafone/Mannesmann case, the court declined to recognize a takeover offer situation as one in which the Holzmüller doctrine would apply,[274] as the takeover offer was addressed to the shareholders, and it was exclusively the decision of the shareholders to accept or decline the offer. The only responsibility of the management board is to provide information to the shareholders.

The legal situation is no different under the Takeover Act, save that the Federal Supervisory Office may intervene in cases of abusive advertising. However, the Act, following the court decision in the Mannesmann/Vodafone case above, does not grant any means to the shareholders to prevent management from carrying out excessive advertising.[275]

It is as yet unclear in what circumstances the Federal Supervisory Office may decide to take steps to prevent abusive advertising. In our opinion, two distinct cases should be distinguished:

- **Unjustifiable Expenses**: Advertising campaigns are abusive if the amount spent is excessive in relation to the value of the transaction itself. In our opinion, this was clearly not the case in the Mannesmann takeover battle – notwithstanding general criticism of the advertising campaign. Given that the takeover transaction was the largest takeover ever (involving an offer by Vodafone in excess of € 200 billion), Mannesmann's advertising costs of less than € 0,4 billion represented some 0.02% of the transaction volume. This was money well spent from the point of view of Mannesmann's shareholders,[276] as the share conversion ratio was raised from 53.7 to 58.9646 Vodafone shares for each Mannesmann share. As a consequence, Mannesmann shareholders forced Vodafone's offer higher and received as a result of Mannesman's advertising

---

[273] Federal Supreme Court, BGHZ 83 p. 122; examples in Lutter/Leinekugelm, ZIP 1998 p. 806: acquisition and alienation of essential parts of the enterprise; admission of new shareholders into a former 100% subsidiary that constitutes an essential part of the company's business; going public; delisting (Appeal Court of München, OLG München, ZIP 2001 p. 700 – "Macrotron").

[274] Agreeing: Körner, DB 2001 p. 367, 369; Krause, AG 2000 p. 217, 221; dissenting: Mülbert, IStR 1999 p. 83, 88 et seq.

[275] Geibel/Süßmann/Schwennicke, WpÜG § 28 annot. 8.

[276] Drygala, ZIP 2001 p. 1861, 1863; Grunewald, AG 2001 p. 288, considers the extent of the Mannesmann campaign to be "the limit of what is legally permissible."

campaign altogether a conversion ratio 9.8% higher than previously offered. This improvement of the bid is even more drastic if the share price movements during the acceptance period are taken into account: Vodafone's first offer was based on a share price of € 240 per Mannesmann share whereas the last offer was based on a share price of € 350.50.[277] Mannesmann shareholders received an additional premium of 46.04% for their shares. This accords entirely with the "Revlon doctrine" (see Ch. 4 no. 7. a. above) which requires the target's management to attempt to achieve the highest possible share price for the target's shareholders.

- **Inaccurate Information**: In our view, the second case where an abuse of advertising practices can be said to have taken place is when advertising contains inaccurate or misleading information.[278] On the one hand, the target's management should be allowed to express its opinion and give clear recommendations against (or in favor) of the offer. This is also expressly provided for the U. S. in **Regulation 14E**, which gives the target a choice between (i) recommending acceptance of the offer, (ii) recommending rejection of the offer (iii) expressing no opinion, or (iv) stating that it is unable to evaluate the takeover offer.[279] However, the target's management may not make misrepresentations to the shareholders. There is a fine line between expressing a negative *opinion* on the merger (which is admissible) and giving inaccurate or misleading *factual information* (which is illegal). The target's management board would be well-advised in these circumstances to state clearly that it is giving its own opinion as such, and take the utmost care to include (in particular in forward looking statements regarding the future business of the corporation) cautionary language which clearly indicates the uncertainty and risks involved in making such predictions.[280] The management should also seek to present information in as complete and well-balanced a manner as possible; omitting certain facts may lead to a statement being grossly misleading, even if the facts presented are true as such.

Other cases of abusive advertising (besides unjustifiable expenses and inaccurate information) may relate to the means of communication (e.g., unsolicited e-mails or faxes to target shareholders) or to the tone of the advertising (e.g., emotional advertising with no other substantial content).[281]

---

[277] From November 18, 1999 (announcement of the first offer with a conversion ratio of 53.7 shares) to February 3, 2000 (announcement of the improved offer with a conversion ratio of 58.9646), Vodafone's share price increased from € 4.50 to over € 6; however, in the following days, the share price sharply fell (supposedly on the basis of the improved bid).

[278] *See* Geibel/Süßmann/Schwennicke, WpÜG § 28 annot. 14; Winter/Harbarth, ZIP 2002 p. 1, 16.

[279] 17 CFR 240.14 e-2 (a).

[280] U. S. courts have developed the so-called "Bespeaks Doctrine" which provides for a safe harbor if a statement of projected business is accompanied by clear cautionary language. According to some courts this doctrine should even apply when cautionary language does not cover the specific risk factors in question, Harris v. Ivax Corp. (11th Cir. 1999).

[281] *See* Geibel/Süßmann/Schwennicke, WpÜG § 28 annot. 13, 14.

(2) Search for a "White Knight"

Faced with a hostile takeover offer, the target's board may look for another offeror to make a competing "friendly" takeover offer. When a competing takeover offer is launched before the expiry of the acceptance period for the first offer, those shareholders who have already accepted the first bid may revoke their acceptance and accept the later offer.[282] Additionally, the acceptance period for the first offer automatically runs parallel with the competing bid so that the shareholders can freely choose between the competing offers.

However, the target management may not directly issue shares to a white knight (unless expressly authorized by the shareholders meeting, see Ch. 4 no. 8. c. (3) below), enter into an exclusivity agreement with a white knight, or agree on "goodbye fees" with the white knight, as this would impair the right of the target's shareholders to freely decide whether or not to accept either one of the competing offers. Moreover, the target company may not financially support the white knight's competing bids, for example by making advances or granting loans to the white knight.

(3) Approval by the shareholders' meeting

The target's management may also take defensive steps which have been approved by the target's shareholders. The shareholders may approve defensive steps either in the abstract *before* an offer has actually been made, or in a shareholders' meeting called *after* the publication of a particular offer.

(a) Shareholders' meeting after publication of an offer

The target's management may call an extraordinary shareholders' meeting after publication of a takeover offer.[283] In this case, the usual notice period of one month which is required for a shareholders' meeting[284] may be reduced to two weeks.[285] When management calls an extraordinary shareholders' meeting, the acceptance period for the takeover offer is automatically extended to ten weeks, even if a shorter acceptance period is stated in the terms of the offer.[286]

The shareholders may authorize management to take defensive steps by a simple majority of votes cast, unless the articles of association or general corporate law specify that a greater majority is required.[287]

---

[282] § 22 para. 3 Takeover Act.
[283] § 119 para. 2 Stock Corporation Act.
[284] § 123 para. 1 Stock Corporation Act.
[285] § 16 para. 4 clause 1 Takeover Act.
[286] § 16 para. 3 clause 1 Takeover Act.
[287] The bidder has full voting rigths if it has already acquired shares in the target prior to the offer (Winter/Harbarth, ZIP 2002 p. 1, 14). Note: e.g., if the shareholders want to authorize the management to issue shares, then a simple voting majority is sufficient only if a general authorization to issue shares already exists. Otherwise, such authorization requires a 75% voting majority under the Stock Corporation Act (§§ 202 para. 2, 179 para. 2).

The Takeover Act does not list specific measures which the shareholders may approve; thus, the scope of admissible measures is governed by general corporate law, and the following defensive actions are permitted:

- **Purchase of its own shares by the target:** The purchase by the target of its own shares is generally limited to 10% of the company's issued share capital,[288] unless a greater number of shares must be purchased to fend off immediate and serious threats to the well-being of the company.[289] It is unclear whether a hostile takeover offer constitutes a serious threat in this sense.[290] In our view, as the Takeover Act contains a dense network of provisions for the protection of the target and its shareholders, there is a presumption that a hostile takeover offer does not pose a threat to justify purchases exceeding the regular 10% limit. However, special circumstances might refute this presumption, such as when a competitor makes the hostile bid in order to break up the target.[291]
- **Issue of New Shares:** The shareholders may approve the issue of new shares in the target. The issue of new shares will make the offer substantially more expensive as more shares will need to be taken up by the offeror. Further, if shares are issued to a friendly company ("white knight") or to existing shareholders opposed to the takeover, the offer may successfully be obstructed. However, specific problems arise in this regard. Generally, new shares may be issued only in the form of a rights issue, entitling all shareholders to participate in the issue on a pro rata basis in order to prevent the dilution of their existing shareholdings. The pre-emption rights of the shareholders may only be overridden in special circumstances where the overwhelming interests of the company outweigh the protection of the shareholders against dilution of their voting rights. The acquisition of a business using shares as acquisition currency is usually considered to be such a compelling interest, if the company has a strong strategic interest in the acquisition. The question is whether, in the context of a takeover, fending off a hostile takeover is, in itself, sufficient justification for excluding the pre-emption rights of the shareholders. In our opinion, this is not necessarily the case.[292] Shareholders may still need protection against dilution of their voting rights if a hostile takeover offer is made. Therefore, an issue of new shares to a white knight without pro rata subscription rights for existing shareholders is only permitted if the participation of the white knight has strategic advantages for the target, over and above the purpose of resisting the hostile bid. If this is the case, the board must submit a report to the shareholders' meeting with de-

---

[288] § 71 para. 1 clause 1 no. 8 Stock Corporation Act.

[289] § 71 para. 1 clause 1 no. 1 Stock Corporation Act.

[290] Consenting: Barz, Großkommentar, § 71 AktG annot. 7; dissenting: Lutter, Kölner Kommentar, § 71 AktG annot. 24; Aha, AG 1992 p. 218, 220.

[291] Federal Supreme Court, BGHZ 33 p. 175, 186; Hüffer, 4th ed., § 71 AktG annot. 9; Geßler/Hefermehl/Bungeroth, § 71 AktG annot. 56.

[292] Assmann/Bozenhardt, ZGR Sonderheft 9 p. 129; Marquardt, WiB 1994 p. 537, 541; different view: Geibel/Süßmann/Schwennicke, WpÜG § 33 annot. 59; Schanz, NZG 2000 p. 337, 343.

tailed reasons for the exclusion of the shareholders' pre-emptive rights.[293] This shows once again that the Takeover Act does not erode shareholder protection features that apply under general corporate law principles.

The question remains whether the power of the shareholders' meeting – despite the legal limits detailed above – is subject to additional limitations or is completely free to decide upon defensive measures. Generally, shareholders have unfettered discretion in passing resolutions; as long as shareholders' resolutions are in compliance with general legal requirements (such as the protection of the shareholders against dilution of their shares as explained above), they are not subject to judicial review. The same should apply in a takeover context; as the law leaves it to the shareholders to decide on defensive measures, their decision should not be restricted except within the limits of general corporate law.[294]

(b) Shareholders' resolutions <u>before</u> publication of an offer

The shareholders may authorize the management board to take defensive steps against hostile bids before a bid has actually been published.[295] Such resolutions require a 75% voting majority and are valid for a maximum of 18 months.[296] The resolution must determine the kind of defensive measures the board may take in the event of a hostile takeover offer, e.g. purchase of the company's own shares, issue of new shares or sale of assets. It is questionable whether the shareholders' resolution must specify assets (e.g. certain strategic parts of the business) that the board might sell. According to some commentators, this is not necessary.[297] In our view this is problematic as it gives the board a broad discretion to sell even core assets, the sale of which might severely damage the target's business,[298] in order to frustrate potential offers. On the other hand, a shareholders' resolution which is too detailed would enable the hostile offeror to prepare itself for the defensive steps specified in the resolution of the target's shareholders.[299]

The question remains whether such precautionary resolutions are a carte blanche for the management to frustrate any takeover bids. If so, the shareholders would be ill-advised to pass such resolutions, as an established management could make use of the authority to obstruct takeover bids in its own interests rather than for the benefit of the shareholders. In our opinion, the management must still exercise its due discretion when making use of an authorization given by the shareholders to conduct a defense battle. This is in accordance with the general principle that the board does not breach its fiduciary duties by merely carrying out instructions given to it by sharehold-

---

[293] § 16 para. 4 clause 4 Takeover Act; § 186 para. 4 clause 2 Stock Corporation Act.
[294] Geibel/Süßmann/Schwennicke, WpÜG § 33 annot. 58.
[295] „Vorratsbeschlüsse" (Pre-prepared Resolutions).
[296] § 33 para. 2 Takeover Act. The articles of association may prescribe an even greater voting majority; however, a minimum voting majority of 75% is required.
[297] Geibel/Süßmann/Schwennicke, WpÜG § 33 annot. 76.
[298] Theater, NZG 2001 p. 789, 790, even requires that the shareholders' resolution determines the conditions of the sale, in particular the consideration for the assets to be sold.
[299] Geibel/Süßmann/Schennicke, WpÜG § 33 annot. 76.

ers' resolutions, as is expressly stated in the Stock Corporation Act.[300] This principle applies only if the shareholders' resolution *requires* the board to take specific action.[301] It does not apply in the case of a mere general *authorization* not connected to a specific hostile offer.[302] Therefore, even if the board is generally authorized to take defensive actions, it should first determine that it has reason to believe that the offer is not in the best interests of the target company and its shareholders, and only then exercise its authority to take defensive steps.[303] Indeed, if the board does reach the conclusion that defensive steps are required, it may be obliged, pursuant to its fiduciary duties, to exercise that authority.

The use by the board of the shareholders' authorization is subject to a concurrent consent of the **supervisory board**.[304] In this respect, the relationship between the decision of the management board to act, and of the supervisory board to approve, is unclear. In particular, may the management board rely on a consent to taking defensive steps given by the supervisory board and then take the defensive steps without exercising its own judgment? This should not be possible since consent to actions of the management board by the supervisory board does not release the management board from its responsibility or liability.[305]

The last open question is that of the criteria which apply to the decision of the supervisory board approving the defensive actions of the management board. In our view, the supervisory board should be subject to the same duties of care as the management board when approving defensive actions. Problems may arise in this respect where representatives of the employees are elected to the supervisory board,[306] as employee representatives will generally be opposed to hostile takeovers, and it is extremely unlikely that such members, who are elected to represent the interests of the employees, will act primarily to increase shareholder value.

(4) Approval by the supervisory board

Even with no corresponding shareholders' resolution, the management board may undertake defensive steps, if the supervisory board approves of such actions. However, in this case, the scope of possible actions the management board can take is limited to actions which the board may take independently of the takeover bid under general corporate law principles. Thus,

---

[300] § 93 para. 4 clause 1 Stock Corporation Act.

[301] Geßler/Hefermehl § 93 AktG annot. 50; Mertens, Kölner Kommentar, AktG § 93 annot. 114.

[302] *See* Geibel/Süßmann/Schwennicke, WpÜG § 33 annot. 80.

[303] The principles developed by the Delaware Supreme Court in *Unocal* (Fn. 113) could apply accordingly.

[304] § 33 para. 2 sentence 4 Takeover Act; the statutory requirement of a consent given by the supervisory board supports our view that the management board has to exercise due discretion within the scope of the shareholders' authorization, which discretion needs to be controlled by the supervisory board, *see* Geibel/Süßmann/Schwennicke, WpÜG § 33 annot. 80.

[305] § 93 para. 4 sentence 2 Stock Corporation Act.

[306] *See* Fn. 238.

the board may issue new shares (for example, to a white knight) only if it has unissued capital available, already authorized by the shareholders' meeting. Therefore, approval of defensive steps by the supervisory board merely suspends the duty to neutrality which is imposed upon the management board when a takeover offer is made; however, the management board can only take such action as would, in any event, be available to it, if it were not for the duty of neutrality.

The applicable standard regarding exercise of the discretion and the duty of care is as discussed above, i.e. both the supervisory board and the management board must act in the best interests of the company and its shareholders.[307] In general, the board, will be well-advised to call an extraordinary shareholders' meeting in order to obtain the approval of the shareholders (see no. Ch. 4 no. 8. c. (3) (a) above). This might even be the case if the shareholders' meeting has already passed a resolution on defensive steps before an offer is made (see Ch. 4 no. 8c. (3) (b)). Shareholders may have challenged such resolution in court so that a decision on the validity of the resolution might be pending at the time the offer is launched. Should the resolution ultimately be declared void by the court then management will be grateful to have its defensive steps supported by a second resolution passed after the offer is made, expressly authorizing the specific defensive action in relation to the bid.[308]

(5) Remedies of the shareholders

(a) Remedies for breach of fiduciary duties

The Takeover Act contains no specific provisions regarding the liability of the target's board for breach of its fiduciary duties when responding to a takeover offer. While the Act expressly provides that the offeror's board is liable to the target's shareholders for the accuracy of the offer document,[309] no such liability is provided for in the event of misconduct by the target's board. Therefore, general principles which determine the liability of the target's board apply.

U.S. courts have consistently allowed shareholders to sue board members for breach of fiduciary duties. Most of these lawsuits are so-called "derivative actions," where the shareholders do not sue on their own behalf but rather for the benefit of the corporation.[310] However, in many circumstances, shareholders may sue the board on their own behalf, in particular in the event of a breach of corporate disclosure requirements.[311] In addition, U.S. courts have allowed actions by shareholders of the target against the target for damage caused by wrongful defensive measures taken by its board

---

[307] Geibel/Süßmann/Schwennicke, WpÜG § 33 annot. 49.

[308] *See* § 93 para. 4 clause 1 Stock Corporation Act; Winter/Harbath, ZIP 2002 p. 1, 13.

[309] § 12 para. 1 Takeover Act.

[310] E. g. Zapata Corp. v. Maldonado, 430 A.2d 779 (Delaware 1981).

[311] Herman & MacLean v. Huddleston, 459 U.S. 375 (1983) allows an implied private cause of action for violation of disclosure rules (Section 10(b) of the Securities Exchange Act 1934).

and have granted injunctive relief. For example, in the *Hilton* case,[312] a shareholder of Hilton Hotels sucessfully sued the company because of the adoption of a poison pill rights plan.

Under **German law**, shareholders do not generally have a cause of action against the company or the board, whether by way of derivative or direct action. The board owes fiduciary duties only to the corporation rather than to the shareholders. Action in respect of breaches of fiduciary duties by directors can thus only be taken by the corporation.[313] In the case of a breach of fiduciary duties by the management board, it is the responsibility of the supervisory board to sue the relevant directors on behalf of the corporation,[314] and individual shareholders do not have a legal lever to urge the supervisory board to pursue claims against the management board, unless demanded by either the shareholders' meeting or a minority of the shareholders who hold an interest of not less than 10% or one million Euro in the issued share capital of the corporation.[315]

Consequently, the shareholders of the target will not generally have a cause of action for **breach of fiduciary duties** against the board or the target itself in the event that inaccurate statements are made in the defense document or advertising campaigns, or in the event that wrongful defensive tactics against a takeover offer are employed.

(b) Claims in tort

The question remains whether shareholders have a claim in tort for breach of disclosure duties in the event that inaccurate or misleading information is given in the defense document or in advertising campaigns, or in the event of other wrongful defensive measures.

German courts have consistently stated that general notification and disclosure duties[316] do not give rise to a cause of action by the shareholders, as these duties are designed to protect the public interest in efficient capital markets rather than individual shareholders' interests.[317] Only in very limited circumstances may shareholders have a private cause of action, i.e. if the board *knowingly* makes wrong disclosures for the purpose of manipulating share prices.[318] However, as incorrect disclosures and illegal defensive actions in the course of takeover situations will generally not have the manipulation of share prices as their aim, shareholders of the target will generally have no remedy available in such cases.[319]

---

[312] Leonard Loventhal Account v. Hilton Corp., 2000 Del. Ch. LEXIS 149, 2000 WL 1528909; *see* Ch. 4 no. 8.b. (1) above.

[313] Hüffer, 5th ed., § 93 AktG annot. 19; Regional Appeal Court of Düsseldorf, AG 1991 p. 70, 71.

[314] § 112 Stock Corporation Act.

[315] § 147 para. 1 Stock Corporation Act.

[316] § 15 Securities Trading Act.

[317] *See* § 15 para. 6 Securities Trading Act; AG München, DB 2001 p. 2336.

[318] §§ 88 para. 1 no. 1 Stock Exchange Act, § 823 para. 2 Civil Code; Regional Appeal Court of Augsburg, WM 2001 p. 1944, 1945 – "Infomatec."

[319] *See* Geibel/Süßmann/Schwennicke, WpÜG § 33 annot. 90; Krause, AG 2000 p. 217; Winter/Harbarth, ZIP 2002 p. 1, 16 et seq.; Thümmel, DB 2000 p. 461, 464,

(c) Amount of damages

Damages to be claimed by the target *company* in the event of illegal defensive measures should mainly relate to the expenses incurred by such illegal steps and to disadvantages in the case that the offer fails; the latter may mainly consist of lost synergies and strategic advantages anticipated from a successful takeover.[320]

The *shareholders' loss* (in the limited circumstances in which shareholders do have a direct cause of action, see Ch. 4 no. 8. c. (5) (a) and (b) above) will mainly consist in the lost premium if the bid fails. Share price declines following the failure of the offer should generally mirror the loss suffered by the target through loss of synergies and strategic opportunities. If both the company *and* the shareholders could claim damages, then the claim would be duplicated; therefore, the target company's claim for damages has priority over compensation for the shareholders' losses.[321] Only if the target company's claim fails (e.g., because it is unable to prove a specific amount of damages) should the shareholders be entitled to demand compensation for a share price decline.[322]

(6) Remedies of the bidder

Generally, the bidder has no remedies available against defensive steps of the target, as the takeover rules in this respect are designed solely for the protection of the target and its shareholders.[323]

(7) A practical note

The duty of neutrality severely limits the choice of defensive steps; public relations measures are almost the only means of defense in a hostile takeover situation. Other defensive measures based on authorization obtained by

---

takes a different view: illegal defensive steps which are not authorized by the shareholders' meeting are a violation of the shareholders' rights giving rise to a tort claim under § 823 para. 1 Civil Code; *see* also Thaeter, NZG 2001 p. 789, 791. Some scholars differentiate between damages and injunctive relief; while they do not see a cause of action for damages, they favor the right of the shareholders to injunctive relief against illegal defense actions; e.g.: Winter/Harbarth, ZIP 2002 p. 1, 17; in the Mannesmann/Vodafone case, the Regional Court of Düsseldorf took the opposite view, *see* Ch. 4 no. 8. c. (1) (b) above.

[320] Thümmel, DB 2000 p. 461.

[321] Hüffer, 5th ed., § 93 AktG annot. 19; Appeal Court of Düsseldorf, OLG Düsseldorf, AG 1997 p. 231, 236 – "Arag/Garmenbeck;" Geibel/Süßmann/Schwennicke, WpÜG § 33 annot. 91.

[322] Some authors are of the opinion that the shareholders too might have difficulties proving a specific amount of loss as stock price movements after the failure of an offer may have a variety of causes that may not exactly be identifiable with the failure of the offer (e. g., Thümmel, DB 2000 p. 461, 464); we take the opposite view, as stock price movements upon the launch or failure of an offer are usually very sudden, so that such sudden fluctuations should be a sufficient indication of the losses suffered by the shareholders.

[323] Geibel/Süßmann/Schwennicke, WpÜG § 33 annot. 92; *see* also Thümmel, DB 2000 p. 461, 464; Thaeter, NZG 2001 p. 789, 791.

shareholders' resolutions (see Ch. 4 no. 8. c. (3) above) might not become widely popular in Germany for the following reasons:

Shareholders' resolutions passed before an actual takeover offer is made are valid for a maximum of 18 months and thus need to be renewed at every annual shareholders' meeting. Moreover, they require a voting majority of 75%; particularly in companies with a large number of free-floating shares such majority will be hard to achieve because the target's shareholders generally receive a sizeable premium for their shares in a takeover transaction and will, therefore, be reluctant to authorize the board to obstruct takeover offers, especially since such authorization may be abused to further the personal interests of the board members. Further, the share price might react negatively to such a shareholders' resolution.

We foresee that the **supervisory board** too will be reluctant to approve defensive measures; the members of the supervisory board (approximately comparable with "outside directors" of large U.S. corporations) are generally not involved in the active business management and do not have large portions of their personal wealth at stake in the corporation. In addition, they have a professional reputation to lose if they avoid hostile takeover offers which would involve payment of a premium to the shareholders. Also, although board members are generally not liable to the shareholders (see Ch. 4 no. 8. c. (5) above), they might very well be liable vis-à-vis the corporation if they prevent a takeover to the detriment of the target, for example, if an affiliation with the offeror would have been strategically advantageous for the target.

Furthermore, the **scope of possible defensive activities** is narrow even with the approval of the shareholders. Purchases by the target of its own shares are limited to 10% of the issued share capital (see Ch. 4 no. 8. c. (3) (a) above). The only other admissible and practically feasible defensive step is the issue of new shares to a white knight. Apart from the fact that such action is subject to certain corporate law requirements (see Ch. 4 no. 8. c. (3) (a) above), the target might not be able to find a white knight in the short period of time available. For example, when INA Holding made its offer for FAG Kugelfischer, the latter was not able to secure the support of a white knight, although it had been reported to be in negotiations with several financial and strategic investors; FAG favored a partnership with NTN which would supposedly have generated synergies of € 3 to € 4 per share.[324]

Therefore, the main efforts of the target's management should, and will, be focused on **improving the consideration** for the shareholders as was the case in both the Vodafone/Mannesmann and INA Holding/FAG Kugelfischer takeovers.[325] Skilful advertising and limited self-tender offers or purchases by the target of its own shares appear to be the most valuable tools.

---

[324] FAG defense document p. 18; FAG blamed the September 11th events for the failure to attract a white knight.

[325] In the INA Holding/FAG Kugelfischer case, the consideration was improved from € 11 to € 12 per share; Vodafone increased its bid from 53.7 to 58.9646 Vodafone shares per Mannesmann share.

The design of a corporate **structure** (staggered boards, ESOPs, composition of the shareholders) is the most promising way to withstand hostile takeover offers. Nevertheless, the introduction of a "takeover safe structure" will always be a fairly unpredictable matter, since the capital markets may punish such companies with a discount. Therefore, such structural defensive measures should be designed very carefully.

9. Consideration

The Takeover Act contains detailed price regulations both as to the value and the form of the consideration to be offered to the target's shareholders. Applicability of these price rules has three prerequisites:
- the bid aims at the acquisition of a **controlling interest,** i.e. a stake of no less than 30% of the voting rights in the target;[326]
- the target is **publicly traded;**[327]
- the bid is made to all shareholders of the target (**public offer**).

a) Form of Consideration

The offeror may offer actively traded shares or Euro denominated cash as consideration. Other kinds of consideration are permitted only if the target's shareholders have a choice to replace such other consideration for cash or liquid shares.

(1) Consideration in liquid shares

In a share exchange transaction, the target's shareholders will usually be offered shares in the bidder which might offer treasury shares or use newly issued shares. However, this is not necessarily the case; the bidder may very well offer shares in third companies. This will usually be the case where the bidder is not itself publicly quoted but has a publicly listed parent or subsidiary company.[328]

The shares offered must be "liquid" so that the shareholders can immediately convert them into cash. Therefore, the shares must be so actively traded that one can assume that the target's shareholders can sell the shares without the increased amounts of shares offered in the market leading to a significant stock-price decline.[329]

It is not required that the shares offered by the bidder are already registered and traded at the time the offer is published. It is rather sufficient that the shares are quoted at the time they have to be transferred to the target's shareholders under the terms of the offer.[330] A yet unresolved question arises when the registration and listing of the shares offered unexpectedly

---

[326] § 29 Takeover Act.
[327] § 31 para. 1 Takeover Act.
[328] Geibel/Süßmann/Thun, WpÜG § 31 para. 31 annot. 9.
[329] *See* Krause, NZG 2000 p. 905, 909; Riehmer/Schröder, NZG 2000 p. 820, 822.
[330] Explanatory Memorandum of the Federal Government on § 31 Takeover Act, BT-Drucks. 14/7034 of October 5, 2001; Krause, NZG 2000 p. 905, 909.

fails. In this case, the bidder should be obliged to pay the anticipated value of the shares in cash as damages since the bidder is in breach of the terms of its offer. Moreover, the target's shareholders should have a right to rescind their acceptance of the bid and to demand the return of the shares surrendered to the bidder, in particular in the event that the bidder is not able to pay the damages.[331]

If the target's shares confer voting rights, then the bidder too must offer shares with voting rights. Preference shares may only be offered in exchange for preference shares in the target company.[332]

(2) Cash consideration

Apart from actively traded shares, the bidder may only offer Euro denominated cash to the target's shareholders.

In the recent public takeover of FAG Kugelfischer, the offeror INA Holding had to offer cash to the stockholders of FAG because INA Holding is not publicly quoted, so that it was not able to offer liquid shares.

In the case that the offeror purchased **"toe holds"** in the target, i.e. shares purchased on stock markets before the public offer is made, the offeror is under an obligation to offer cash to the target's shareholders in the following circumstances:[333]

- the "toe holds" amount to at least **5% of the shares** or voting rights in the target;[334]
- those shares were acquired **for cash**,
- **within three months** before the decision to make a bid was published.[335]

The same applies if shares amounting to no less than 1% of the shares in the target were acquired by the offeror for cash pending the offer, i.e. between the publication of the decision to make a bid and the expiry of the acceptance period.[336]

Toe holds, which are popular in order to decrease the average acquisition price as no control premium need be paid on shares purchased step-by-step in the open market, might boomerang on the offeror. This becomes in particular relevant when the offeror reaches the control threshold of 30% by purchasing shares for cash, which gives rise to a mandatory offer (see Ch. 4 no. 10. below) so that the acquirer might find itself in a position where it must acquire 70% of the shares of the target in cash, whether or not it has the necessary funds available. This situation might be particularly precarious since the financing of stock acquisitions in lev-

---

[331] §§ 323, 325 Civil Code.

[332] § 31 para. 2 clause 2 Takeover Act.

[333] § 31 para. 3 no. 1 Takeover Act.

[334] This 5% limit corresponds to the threshold where a shareholder has to report its shareholding to the Federal Supervisory Office (§ 21 para. 1 Securities Trading Act).

[335] It is sufficient that the 5% threshold is reached at any point in time during the three-month period, even if the percentage is later reduced, e. g. by dilution because of the issuance of new shares in the target; *see* Geibel/Süßmann/Thun, WpÜG § 31 annot. 31.

[336] § 31 para. 3 no. 2 Takeover Act.

eraged transactions is rather difficult under German corporate law, as financial assistance[337] is generally prohibited (see in more detail Ch. 4 no. 6. e. (4) above).[338]

It should be noted that the acquisition of toe holds may be part of an overall plan to acquire the target with an acquisition of shares in the public stock market as a first step and a subsequent public bid as a second step. In such a case, the bidder has already made the decision to launch a public offer at the time the toe holds are acquired; therefore, the bidder needs to publish a notice that it intends to make a bid[339] *before* the toe holds are acquired.

(3) Other forms of consideration

The bidder may offer other forms of consideration only as an alternative at the target's shareholders' choice. Therefore, the target's shareholders must always have the option to receive the entire consideration in Euro denominated cash and/or liquid shares.[340]

b) Amount of Consideration

(1) Average-price rule

The amount of consideration offered in a public takeover offer may not fall below the weighted average of public stock quotes for a period of three months preceding the publication of the decision to make a bid, if the target's stock is listed on a *German* stock exchange.[341] The average is weighed according to the Euro volume of the trades.[342] In the case of a stock exchange offer, the average-price calculation applies accordingly to the determination of the offeror's share price.[343]

If the target's shares are *exclusively* traded on one or several *foreign* stock exchanges,[344] then the weighted average must be determined on the basis of the trades on the foreign stock exchange with the largest volume of trades in the target's shares.[345]

(2) Income/DCF approach – thinly traded stocks

The average-price rule does not apply if the target's stock is so thinly traded that quotes were announced on less than one third of the trading days

---

[337] "Financial Assistance" refers to using the target's assets to finance the acquisition of its shares.

[338] §§ 57, 71 a Stock Corporation Act expressly prohibit an acquirer from using the target corporation's assets for financing the share purchase.

[339] § 10 para. 1 clause 1 Takeover Act.

[340] Liebscher, ZIP 2001 p. 853, 864; Thaeter/Barth, NZG 2001 p. 545, 547; Land/Hasselbach, DB 2000 p. 1745, 1750.

[341] § 5 para. 1 Public Offer Regulation.

[342] § 5 para. 3 Public Offer Regulation, § 9 Securities Trading Act.

[343] § 7 Public Offer Regulation.

[344] In Europe, otherwise the Takeover Act will not apply.

[345] § 6 para. 1 Public Offer Regulation.

and if several subsequent quotes differ from each other by more than 5%.³⁴⁶ In this case, the offeror must provide for a regular valuation of the target's business in order to determine a fair price for the target's stock. The regulations do not call for a particular valuation method. Following a long line of court precedents, the "true value" should be determined under an income or discounted cash flow (DCF) approach³⁴⁷ (see in more detail Ch. 5 no. 5. a. (2) below).

However, in this situation, the offeror may not have adequate information on the basis of which to conduct a proper valuation of the target, and the management of the target is generally neither obliged nor entitled to forward to the offeror any information that is not publicly available, or to allow a **due diligence exercise**; management is under a strict obligation of confidentiality as to trade secrets,³⁴⁸ and this obligation also applies vis-à-vis the offeror. It is an unresolved question whether a confidentiality agreement between the offeror and the target might put the target's management in a position to forward information to a potential offeror. In our view, this depends on the circumstances of each single case; the financial and/or strategic interest of the target and its shareholders in the (potential) bid should be weighed against the danger of secret information becoming available to the offeror or the public.³⁴⁹ At least, the management of the target should insist that the confidentiality agreement be easily and strictly enforceable, e.g. by means of a penalty clause or liquidated damages, though even with such safeguards it is problematic to forward sensitive information to an offeror which is a competitor of the target. In case of doubt, the target's management should rather not forward information to the offeror and rely on its confidentiality obligations, as in no circumstances is there an *obligation* to disclose any information to the offeror,³⁵⁰ and in hostile cases the target's management will, of course, take good care that the bidder receives no information on the target whatsoever.

(3) Problems of the average-price rule

According to the Public Offer Regulation, the average price rule applies mandatorily³⁵¹ (except for thinly traded stocks).³⁵² No other exception is

---

[346] § 5 para. 4 Public Offer Regulation.

[347] Appeal Court of Celle, OLG Celle, AG 1999 p. 128, 129; Appeal Court of Zweibrücken, OLG Zweibrücken, AG 1995 p. 421; Appeal Court of Düsseldorf, OLG Düsseldorf, AG 1990 p. 397, 398; Hüffer, 5ᵗʰ ed., § 305 AktG annot. 19; Koppensteiner, Kölner Kommentar, 2ⁿᵈ ed. 1987, § 305 AktG annot. 35.

[348] § 93 para. 1 clause 2 Stock Corporation Act; Ziemons, AG 1999 p. 492, 495.

[349] *See* Oechsler, NZG 2001 p. 817, 819; Ziemons, AG 1999 p. 492, 495; Mertens, AG 1997 p. 541; Werner, ZIP 2000 p. 989, 991; Ziegler, DStR 2000 p. 249, 253; in general a due diligence exercise should be permissible if the target has a compelling strategic interest in an acquisition of its shares by the bidder, Lutter, ZIP 1997 p. 613, 617.

[350] Rosen/Seifert/Schander, Die Übernahme börsennotierter Unternehmen, 1999, p. 341, 347; Ziegler, DStR 2000 p. 249, 253.

[351] § 3 Public Offer Regulation.

[352] § 5 para. 4 Public Offer Regulation.

allowed. This price scheme might pose serious problems in the case of target corporations in financial distress or with stock prices falling abruptly because of extraordinary events, such as a filing for bankruptcy proceedings.

Case: Teldafax AG: This problem is illustrated by the case of Teldafax AG, a German telecom stock corporation whose financial position sharply deteriorated in a short period of time, so that Teldafax voluntarily filed for bankruptcy on 1 June 2001; within six months, the stock price had fallen from € 2.60 (January 2, 2001) to € 0.38 (June 2, 2001). The following table illustrates the premium a potential offeror would have had to pay under the average price rule. A public takeover offer published in April 2001 for Teldafax shares would have required a premium of more than 400% on the actual Teldafax stock price.

Date	Share price	90-day average	Required premium
27 Dec. 00	€ 2.30	€ 5.90	**157%**
01 March 01	€ 1.50	€ 3.90	**160%**
03 March 01	€ 0.49	€ 2.80	**470%**

In order to allow more flexibility in such cases, we recommend that the regulations be amended to the effect that the Federal Supervisory Office may grant an exemption from the average price rule in appropriate circumstances. A similar exception in restructuring cases is already available in respect of mandatory offers: the Federal Supervisory Office may, in its considered discretion, exempt an acquirer from making a mandatory offer if the target is in financial distress[353] (see Ch. 4 no. 10. c. below). It should likewise be in the Office's discretion to exempt an offeror from the average price rule where its application would have unreasonable consequences; also, in connection with an exemption from the average price rule it should be possible to grant a shortening of the acceptance period (under current law the minimum acceptance period is four weeks),[354] as a takeover of a company in financial distress generally needs to be accomplished in a rather short period of time.

c) "Variable Consideration"

In the course of the acceptance period, the stock price of the offeror may move substantially so that, in the case of a share exchange plan the value of the consideration changes; if the tendency is negative, the offeror may, until the last business day prior to the expiration of the acceptance period, increase the consideration in order to make the offer more attractive for the target's shareholders.[355] If, on the other hand, the stock price of the offeror moves upwards, the Takeover Act does not, in principle, allow the offeror to

---

[353] § 9 no. 3 Public Offer Regulation.
[354] § 16 para. 1 Takeover Act.
[355] § 21 para. 1 no. 1 Takeover Act.

adjust the conversion ratio in order to reduce the value of the consideration to the previous level. However, the offeror may make the offer contingent on a certain maximum price of its stock not being exceeded at the end of the acceptance period.[356] Also, the offeror may fix a certain *value* of the consideration rather than a firm conversion ratio, i.e. a certain value for each target share to be paid in shares of the offeror based on the stock price at the end of the acceptance period. However, for reasons of transparency, such consideration scheme must be clearly explained and easily understandable in the offer document.[357] Moreover, such variable conversion ratio may not, in any circumstances, fall below the conversion ratio based on the three-month average of both the offeror's and target's shares before the publication of the intention to make a bid.[358]

d) "Most Favored Status of a Bid" and Improved Bids

Besides the average price rule, the new regulations contain minimum price requirements in the case that the offeror acquires shares in the target

- within three months before (pre-offer acquisitions), or
- pending the public offer (parallel acquisitions), or
- within one year after a public offer (post-offer acquisitions).

(1) Pre-offer acquisition

In the first case, any purchase of shares within three months before the publication of the decision to make a bid sets a minimum reference price.[359] The actual acquisition and *transfer* of the shares to the bidder need not take place in this three-month reference period; it is sufficient that the bidder has agreed to acquire shares at a higher price within the three-month period.[360]

The acquisition of (call) **options** by the offeror in the three-month reference period is likewise sufficient.[361] In principle, the minimum reference price set by the purchase of options is the *exercise* price of the option. Some commentators, however, are of the opinion that the relevant basis is the sum of the exercise price and the option price.[362] We do not follow this view. The minimum reference price refers to the value of the *shares* in the target that is represented by the exercise price. The option price reflects the value of the option right as such, as a sum of the time premium of the option and the intrinsic value of the option;[363] when calculating the reference price,

---

[356] Busch, AG 2002 p. 145, 152.

[357] Busch, AG 2002 p. 145, 152, is of the opinion that a variable conversion ratio is not permissible for reasons of transparency.

[358] This follows from the average price rule, § 5 para. 1, § 7 Public Offer Regulation.

[359] § 4 Public Offer Regulation.

[360] Geibel/Süßmann/Thun, WpÜG § 31 annot. 82.

[361] § 31 para. 6 clause 1 Takeover Act; put options do not fall under § 31 para. 6 clause 1 Takeover Act.

[362] Geibel/Süßmann/Thun, WpÜG § 31 annot. 70.

[363] Defined as the difference between the exercise price and the actual stock price.

only the intrinsic value of the option should be accounted for, the time premium must not be taken into consideration. Therefore, the correct reference price should correspond to the exercise price, plus or minus the (positive or negative) intrinsic value of the option (at the time the option is purchased); this corresponds to the exercise price as if the option were *at the money* when purchased.[364]

Previous drafts of the Public Offer Regulation permitted the price for the public offer to be 15% below such reference price, if the offeror had purchased the relevant shares in the target in a private transaction. Thus, a premium of up to 15% would have been permissible in privately negotiated transactions. Under the version of the Public Offer Regulation which actually came into force on January 1, 2002, any pre-acquisition of shares in the target sets a minimum reference price, whether the shares were pre-acquired publicly or in privately negotiated transactions. Therefore, **no premium whatsoever may be paid within three months before the publication** of the decision to make a bid. This regulatory scheme leads to harsh consequences, in particular, in the case of target corporations with large controlling shareholders. No control premium may be paid to such shareholders within the reference period. Moreover, it is not possible to circumvent these rules by launching the public offer outside the three-month reference period if the offeror acquires a controlling interest in the target prior to the bid; in this case, the offeror must make a mandatory public offer within four weeks after the acquisition of the controlling interest.[365]

(2) Acquisitions pending the offer

If the offeror acquires shares after the publication of the offer document, and before the publication of the acceptance rate, for a higher consideration than stated in the offer, then the consideration to be offered to the target's shareholders is automatically adjusted in value.[366] In this respect, the situation is similar as with pre-offer acquisitions.

The offeror has to publish a notice of any acquisitions of the target's shares pending the offer.[367]

(3) Post-offer acquisition of shares

Moreover, the offeror is required to improve its bid in the case of further acquisitions of shares in the target within one year after completion of the bid,[368] unless such additional shares are acquired on a stock exchange. In

---

[364] In even more sophisticated models, payment of dividends becomes also a factor in option valuation; for a detailed description of option valuation models *see* Reilly/Brown, Investment Analysis and Portfolio Management, 6th ed. 2000, Ch. 11 and 23.

[365] Exactly: four weeks after the publication of the notice that the offeror achieved control of the target, which publication must take place no later than seven calendar days after the acquisition of the controlling interest, § 35 para. 2 clause 1 Takeover Act.

[366] § 31 para. 4 Takeover Act.

[367] § 23 para. 2 Takeover Act.

[368] Exactly: within one year after the publication of the acceptance proportion, §§ 31 para. 5, 23 para. 1 clause 1 no. 2 Takeover Act.

this respect, the acquisition of one single share for a price higher than the public offer price is sufficient to raise the price for *all* target shareholders who have accepted the offer. This mandatory improvement of the consideration might have unfair consequences where the higher price paid after completion of the bid is caused by synergies or other contributions (such as infusion of new capital by the offeror, generation of new business for the target based on the business relationships of the offeror, or other strategic advantages) attributable to the offeror rather than the target. In this event, the previous shareholders of the target benefit from a value created by the offeror and therefore might receive "windfall profits."

As with pre-offer and parallel acquisitions, a post-offer acquisition giving rise to an improvement of the bid does not require that the shares actually vest in the offeror within the one-year postoffer period. It is sufficient that the offeror obtains a right to acquire additional shares in the target,[369] such as a calloption or a share-purchase agreement to be fulfilled outside the one year's deadline.[370] It is, therefore, hardly possible to circumvent the regulations on improved bids by designing post-offer acquisitions with options or other creative agreements.

The offeror must publish a notice of any post-offer acquisitions of shares in the target within the one-year post-offer period.[371]

The price improvement rules do not, however, apply when the offeror has paid a higher consideration based on a legal obligation to pay a fair compensation to minority shareholders for their shares.[372] This may be the case if the controlling shareholder initiates a "squeeze-out"[373] of the minority shareholders after the takeover or effects an integration,[374] an up-stream merger, or a control and profit transfer agreement with the controlled target company.

(4) Form of the price improvement

(a) Pre-offer acquisitions

In the case of pre-offer acquisitions, the consideration offered in the offer document may not, *in value,* fall short of the price paid for pre-offer acquisitions. In the case of share exchange plans, the conversion ratio based on the three-month weighted average of the share prices must not be less than the cash price paid by the offeror for pre-offer acquisitions, unless pre-acquisitions in cash exceed 5% of the shares in the target (see Ch. 4 no. 9. a. (2) above).

---

[369] § 31 para. 6 clause 1 Takeover Act.

[370] Explanatory Memorandum of the Federal Government on § 31 para. 6 Takeover Act (BT-Drucks. 14/7034 of October 5, 2001).

[371] § 23 para. 2 Takeover Act.

[372] Federal Supreme Court, BGH DB 2001 p. 2705; Appeal Court of München, OLG München, DB 2001 p. 1297 (regarding Art. 15 Takeover Code).

[373] Which requires a 95% shareholding in the target, § 327 a Stock Corporation Act; *see* in detail Ch. 6.

[374] §§ 319, 320 b Stock Corporation Act.

(b) Acquisitions pending a public offer

In the case of parallel acquisitions for a higher price, the consideration in the public offer is, by operation of law, adjusted *in value*. Therefore, if the public offer is made in the form of a share exchange plan while the parallel acquisition was in cash, then the conversion ratio will be adjusted accordingly, rather than adding an additional cash payment, and *vice versa*.

In the case of a share exchange plan, the adjustment is calculated on the basis of the value of the offeror's shares according to the weighted average within the three months before publication of the decision to make a bid. Therefore, price movements in the offeror's shares since that publication are not taken into account for purposes of the calculation of the price adjustment.

(c) Post-offer acquisitions

The bidder must pay the difference between the consideration offered in the public offer document and the price paid in post-offer acquisitions in *cash* to the target's shareholders who have accepted the offer, whether the acquisition consideration in the public offer was cash or liquid shares.

This cash compensation is immediately due when the event takes place which triggers the increased consideration, i.e. the actual acquisition of the shares, the agreement on the acquisition, or the purchase of a call option, whichever happens earlier. A later due date or deferral of the payment of the purchase price for the post-offer acquisition is irrelevant.[375] In the case of an option acquired by the bidder, the increased consideration is due at the time the option is purchased while the exercise date is irrelevant; therefore, it is likewise irrelevant whether or not the bidder exercises the option at all.[376]

e) Legal Consequences and Remedies for Non-compliance

The Takeover Act provides for several legal consequences, when the consideration offered in a public bid does not comply with the price rules discussed above:

(1) Remedies of the Federal Supervisory Office

- Should the price fall below the average-price rule or below a reference price set by pre-bid acquisitions, then the Federal Supervisory Office *must* prohibit the offeror from publishing the offer.[377]
- Should the offeror publish the bid although the Federal Supervisory Office has prohibited it, then all transactions in connection with the bid are null and void.[378]

According to the wording of the Takeover Act, the aforementioned remedies are only applicable if the infringement of the Act or Regulation is *obvious* to the Federal Supervisory Office. The scope of scrutiny under this "obviousness standard" is not yet clarified. Generally, the legal term of

---

[375] Geibel/Süßmann/Thun, WpÜG § 31 annot. 62.
[376] Geibel/Süßmann/Thun, WpÜG § 31 annot. 70.
[377] § 15 para. 1 no. 2 Takeover Act.
[378] § 15 para. 3 clause 2 Takeover Act.

"obviousness" under German law is interpreted restrictively, i.e., an obvious violation is one beyond any serious doubt.[379] We are of the opinion that such a narrow interpretation will certainly further an expeditious processing of offers by the Office. On the other hand, the legislative objective of the Takeover Act is to foster an efficient and reliable market for corporate takeovers (see Ch. 3 above), which objective would be obstructed by insufficient supervision. Therefore, we are in favor of a bifurcated interpretation: the Federal Supervisory Office should strictly enforce the Act in its *legal* aspects, but it should be released from deep *factual* investigations. Thus, the Office should generally not conduct an in-depth review of the price calculation under the average price rule.

(2) Private cause of action

The protection of the target's shareholders is effectively guaranteed by a private cause of action in the event of a violation of pricing rules.

The offer document is a prospectus-like document with a relatively broad liability on the bidder and other responsible persons for its accuracy (see Ch. 4 no. 6. b. (4) above). Consequently, as the amount of consideration offered and the principles applied for its determination, are mandatory items of the offer document,[380] the latter contains an implied assertion that the calculation of the consideration is in compliance with the minimum price rules. Should this assertion prove to be wrong then the target shareholders have a private cause of action for damages for misrepresentation in the offer document:[381]

- **Shareholders who accepted the bid** can claim any deficiency of the consideration received in the public offer compared to the minimum price allowed under applicable pricing provisions, whether or not the shareholders had positive knowledge of the violation. They should not, however, be entitled to rescind their acceptance of the bid.
- **Shareholders who did not accept the bid** should be entitled to make a late acceptance of the offer at the (hypothetical) minimum price that would have been allowed under applicable pricing rules. Should they have already disposed of their shares otherwise they may claim money damages if they have sold their shares at a price lower than the minimum price required by the pricing rules.

---

[379] Regarding the term "obviousness" within the scope of § 16 para. 3 Reorganization Act: Appeal Court of Frankfurt, OLG Frankfurt, ZIP 1997 p. 1291; Appeal Court of Düsseldorf, OLG Düsseldorf, NZG 2002 p. 191, 192.

[380] § 11 para. 2. no. 4 Takeover Act, § 2 no. 3 Public Offer Regulation.

[381] § 12 Takeover Act; the bidder and other responsible persons are released from their liability if they prove that they are not guilty of *gross* negligence (§ 12 para. 2 Takeover Act); however, as compliance with minimum price rules can be assured by simple calculations of average stock prices, such proof is hardly possible.

10. Mandatory Bids

a) General Principles

The Takeover Act[382] requires a shareholder to make a mandatory bid where that shareholder has acquired a controlling interest (for a definition of a controlling interest see Ch. 4 no. 10. b. below) in the target. This mandatory bid is an essential feature of protection afforded to the target's minority shareholders.

The mandatory bid provision offers minority shareholders a smooth exit from the target. The minority shareholders are bought out at a fair price. This avoids conflicts with controlling shareholders, and prevents bidders from carrying on unfair practices, for instance, making a two-tier front-end loaded bid. A two-tier bid would typically consist of a bid for a controlling stake in the target as a first step, followed by a second bid for the shares held by the remaining minority shareholders at a substantially lower consideration. Such an offer can be unfairly coercive since it forces the target's shareholders to accept the first stage of the bid: to refuse and be left as minority shareholders, they would face either discrimination by the controlling shareholder or be required to part with their shares at a reduced price.[383] Such two-tier offers were a common takeover practice in the U.S. but have been banned by state regulations in most states.

Though the concept of mandatory bids was incorporated into the Takeover Code which was used previously,[384] mandatory bids have never had statutory authority in Germany prior to the coming into force of the Takeover Act on January 1, 2002.

b) Triggering Events – Controlling Interest

A mandatory bid is generally triggered by the acquisition of a controlling interest in the target, that is to say, where any one shareholder acquires (directly or indirectly)[385] a shareholding carrying 30% or more of the voting rights in the target.[386] No mandatory bid is required where a shareholder who already has a controlling interest wishes to purchase further shares to extend that interest.

The way in which the controlling interest is acquired is, largely, irrelevant. It may, for example, be acquired in the following ways:

---

[382] § 35 Takeover Act.
[383] Such two-tier offers are a typical example of a "Prisoners' Dilemma" or "Tragedy of the Commons" where an uncoordinated mass of people (free float shareholders) are forced to act in their personal best interest but ultimately compromise their interests by achieving an outcome which is not ideal for the shareholding body as a whole; *see* in more detail Ch. 4 no. 6. e. (1).
[384] Art. 16 – 17 Takeover Code.
[385] § 30 Takeover Act; regarding the calculation of the percentage of the voting rights *see* Ch. 4 no. 2. b. above.
[386] § 29 para. 2 Takeover Act.

- by purchasing shares on public stock markets;
- by purchasing privately held shares;
- by inheritance.

A critical issue in this respect is that of controlling interests arising in a **merger transaction**,[387] i.e., where two companies merge on the basis of shareholder resolutions in both companies, with a majority of 75% or more. In this case, the target is either merged into the bidder, i.e., the bidder acquires all the assets of the target and the target's shareholders receive a number of shares in the bidder in proportion to the equity values of the bidder and the target ("upstream merger").[388] Alternatively, a new company ("NewCo") may be established. In this case, the assets of the two merging companies transfer to the NewCo and the shareholders of each of the two merging companies receive shares in the NewCo in direct proportion to their previous shareholdings in the two merging companies.[389] Such a merger would not generally be viewed as a takeover bid which would fall within the remit of the Takeover Act. A merger is governed by shareholder resolutions of the merging companies as opposed to a purchase of shares; the roles of bidder and target may be almost indiscernible. Tax and/or accounting considerations are often a decisive factor in determining the merger structure.

Although not governed by the Takeover Act as such, a merger might nonetheless create new controlling interests and give rise to mandatory bids. This topic was broadly discussed in the case of the cross-border merger between Bank Austria and HypoVereinsbank AG:

Case 1: "Bank Austria/HypoVereinsbank": The merger was carried out in three stages: Bank Austria (BA) first transferred all its assets to a 100% subsidiary (BAS). It then contributed this 100% shareholding in BAS to HypoVereinsbank (HVB) in return for the issue of new shares in HVB (giving BA 21% of the aggregate shareholding in HVB). As a result, BAS became a 100% subsidiary of HVB. Finally, BA was merged into BAS (in doing so, BA was closed down as a legal entity), and the BA shareholders received BA's 21% shareholding in HVB. The transaction resulted in a change of control, with HVB taking over the business operations of what was previously BA.

Case 2: B, a public stock corporation, with an equity value of 100, was owned 60% by a majority shareholder M, with the remaining 40% of the shares owned by free-floating shareholders. T was also a publicly quoted stock corporation with an equity value of 50. B's and T's shareholders decided (at their respective general meetings) to merge. After the merger, M owned 40% of the combined BT Newco, with B's former minority shareholders owning 26.7% of the BT NewCo, and T's former minority shareholders owning 33.3% of the shares in the BT NewCo. The change in the balance of control resulted in M becoming the new majority shareholder vis-à-vis the former shareholders of T.

---

[387] *See* in detail Ch. 5.
[388] § 2 no. 1 Reorganization Act *(„Umwandlungsgesetz")*.
[389] § 2 no. 2 Reorganization Act.

In the **BA/HVB** case, the question was raised as to whether or not HBV needed to make a mandatory cash bid to BA's shareholders under the Austrian Takeover Act.[390] Although some commentators are of the opinion that a mandatory cash bid should be made in these circumstances,[391] the authors are of the opinion that corporate mergers (as opposed to acquisitions) do not trigger mandatory bids. The rationale for this is that corporate mergers are based on shareholder resolutions where a considerable majority (75% of the shareholders entitled to vote) must consent to the motion in hand before it can be validly passed.[392] The laws on corporate mergers include several safeguards to protect dissenting shareholders, particularly with regard to the ratio which is used to exchange the old shares for new. Under German law, BA's shareholders could have voted against the merger with HVB and (if the merger had in any event been carried with the required 75% majority) challenged the conversion ratio applied to the shares in a special court proceeding[393] where the court would have been required to determine the "fair value" of the BA shares.[394] No further protection for the shareholders of the merging entity is needed under the Takeover Act.

Case 2 is less clear: it would appear that the minority shareholders of company B had no right to receive a mandatory bid from M, as M was already a majority shareholder in B before the merger. However, for T's shareholders, a clear change of control took place when M became the new controlling shareholder of the combined entity. There is a strong argument to suggest that M (and not B, which is the essential difference between the present case and the BA/HVB case) should have been required to make a mandatory bid to T's shareholders.[395] This would, however, have resulted in T's shareholders being treated differently from B's shareholders, despite the fact that they both became shareholders in the same (BT NewCo) entity. Such different treatment would contradict the principle of all shareholders being treated equally.[396] This inconsistency illustrates that mergers are transactions *sui generis* which do not fit within the framework of the mandatory bid rules. It has been suggested that two cases should be differentiated, (i) where two entities are consolidated into a newly established vehicle (NewCo), the provisions on mandatory bids should not apply; however, a merger may very well give rise to a mandatory bid (ii) where one company with a controlling shareholder is merged into the surviving entity without establishing a NewCo.[397] Therefore, in our Case 2 (see above), the neccessity of a mandatory bid would depend on the merger structure: M would be required to make a mandatory offer to T's shareholders if B were merged

---

[390] § 22 of the Austrian Takeover Act corresponds to § 35 of the German Takeover Act.

[391] Karollus/Geist, NZG 2000 p. 1145 et seq.; Kalss/Winner, ÖBA 2000 p. 51 et seq.

[392] § 65 para. 1 Reorganization Act.

[393] So-called „*Spruchstellenverfahren.*"

[394] §§ 15, 29, 305 et seq. Reorganization Act *("Spruchstellenverfahren")*.

[395] Kalss/Winner, ÖBA 2000 p. 51 et seq.

[396] § 53 a Stock Corporation Act.

[397] Technau, AG 2002 p. 260, 263 et seq.

into T as surviving entity. The opposite would be the case if a NewCo as merger vehicle were established with both B and T being consolidated into NewCo. In an economic sense, however, there is no material difference between the two merger structures; therefore we do not follow this differentiated approach.

Result: In our view, corporate mergers are not governed by the Takeover Act and do not trigger mandatory bids.[398] **The rules applicable to corporate mergers offer sufficient minority protection.**

The practice of the Federal Supervisory Office on this issue is not clear as yet. However, the Office has indicated that it might take a different view, holding that merger transactions may trigger mandatory bids. Investors and advisors should, therefore, be alert on this topic.

Moreover, a mandatory bid is, of course, required in the event of a merger between two entities which both hold shares in the same third company, i.e., in cases where the target is not itself involved in the merger.

Example: Companies A and B, wholly unconnected companies, each hold a 15% shareholding in company C. A and B decide to merge. Therefore, the new combined AB NewCo entity now owns a 30% stake in C. As AB NewCo has acquired control of C other than by means of a public bid, it must make a mandatory bid to the remaining 70% of company C's shareholders, who now have a new controlling shareholder (AB NewCo) following the merger of A and B.[399]

c) Exemptions from the Requirement to make a Mandatory Bid

The Takeover Act contains several exemptions from the requirement to make a mandatory bid:

- Where a controlling interest was obtained prior to January 1, 2002:

  A controlling shareholder need not make a mandatory bid where the controlling interest was acquired before the effective date of the Takeover Act (January 1, 2002).[400] This is a logical consequence of the fact that statutes may not be applied with retrospective effect under the German Federal Constitution. Inconsistencies may still arise where one shareholder has a 30% (or higher) interest prior to January 1, 2002 and a second shareholder acquires a controlling interest after January 1, 2002, by purchasing the target's shares on the public stock market. In this scenario, the new controlling shareholder would need to make a mandatory bid to the shareholders, including the existing "30% plus" shareholder. In an extreme case, it could be conceived that the more recent 30% shareholder would be required to make a mandatory bid to an existing 70% shareholder. In this case, however, the Federal Supervisory Office may grant an exemption.[401] The crite-

---

[398] Weber-Rey/Schütz, AG 2001 p. 325, 329; Nowotny, RdW 2000 p. 330; dissenting with respect to the Austrian Takeover Law: Karollus/Geist, NZG 2000 p. 1145 et seq.; Kalss/Winner, ÖBA 2000 p. 51 et seq.

[399] *See* Altmeppen, ZIP 2001 p. 1073, 1081.

[400] Explanatory Memorandum of the Federal Government on § 35 Takeover Act (BT-Drucks. 14/7034 of October 5, 2001).

[401] § 9 para. 2 no. 1 Public Offer Regulation; Harbarth, ZIP 2002 p. 321, 331.

ria for this discretionary decision of the Federal Supervisory Office have not yet been clarified.[402]

- Where a controlling interest is obtained by means of a public offer:

  There is no duty to make a mandatory bid if the control is acquired by a public offer made to all shareholders.[403] This is explained by the fact that partial takeover bids are not permitted: where an offeror makes a bid with the aim of taking control of the target company, that offer may be accepted by <u>all</u> shareholders of the target.[404] As a result, the shareholders of the target have an equal "shot" at the public bid, and no further minority protection is needed.

- Where "control" is ostensible and not actual:

  In some cases, an interest of between 30% and 50%, though exceeding the formal control limit of the Takeover Act,[405] may not actually give the shareholder with that interest effective control of the target, where an exceptionally high proportion of shareholders attend shareholders' meetings.[406] Where the shareholder (with what appears to be the controlling interest) can prove – by reference to the three previous ordinary shareholders' meetings – that this situation is an ongoing state of affairs and that he has, in fact, only ostensibly a controlling stake, the Federal Supervisory Office may grant an exemption. Such an exemption should generally be granted on a temporary basis only.[407]

- Where treasury stock is being purchased:

  The Federal Supervisory Office may grant an exemption where the 30% control threshold is exceeded as a result of a reduction of the total voting rights in the target pursuant to a purchase of treasury stock. Under German law, voting rights are suspended for treasury stock.[408] In these circumstances, the control limit may inadvertently be exceeded by a shareholder holding just short of 30% of the target's shares, without there being any actual intention to exercise or intensify control over the company.

  The Federal Supervisory Office may grant the exemption on the condition that the shareholder who inadvertently reaches the 30% controlling

---

[402] Altmeppen, ZIP 2001 p. 1082, takes the view that a discretionary exemption is not sufficient in this case.

[403] § 35 para. 3 Takeover Act.

[404] § 32 Takeover Act.

[405] § 29 para. 2 Takeover Act.

[406] It is long-standing practice of the German courts to determine "control" based on the relation between voting rights and the attendance at shareholders' meetings, *see:* Federal Supreme Court, BGHZ 69 p. 334, 347 ("Veba/Gelsenberg"); BGHZ 135 p. 107, 114 ("Volkswagen"); Regional Court of Berlin, AG 1996 p. 230, 231 and AG 1997 p. 183, 184 ("Brau und Brunnen").

[407] § 9 para. 2 no. 2 Public Offer Regulation; Explanatory Memorandum of the Federal Government on § 9 Public Offer Regulation (BT-Drucks. 14/7034 of October 5, 2001).

[408] § 71 b Stock Corporation Act.

threshold, disposes of those shares which take him over the 30% threshold in a fair and even-handed manner.[409]

- Where the company is undergoing restructuring:
  An exemption may be granted if the controlling interest is acquired in connection with a corporate restructuring of a company in financial distress.[410]

- Other exemptions:
  For various other exemptions, please refer to the Public Offer Regulation (§ 9) in Appendix 2 (e.g. cases of inheritance, bequests, gifts, etc.).

d) Consideration

The consideration to be offered to the minority shareholders as part of the mandatory bid is to be assessed by applying the same principles that apply to public takeover bids.[411] Please refer to the discussion in no. 9 of this Chapter 4 for further details.

e) Sanctions

The Takeover Act imposes the following punitive measures where a controlling shareholder fails to comply with the requirement to make a mandatory bid:

(i) The minority shareholders shall earn interest on the proposed consideration, at a rate of 5% above the basic interest rate applicable at that time („*Basiszinssatz*").[412]

(ii) The voting rights of the controlling shareholder in the target are suspended, and the controlling shareholder forfeits the rights which would otherwise attach to its shares in the event of liquidation or profit announcements made during that period, unless the shareholder can demonstrate that it did not withhold the mandatory bid in bad faith, and makes the required bid without further delay.[413]

(iii) The Federal Supervisory Office may impose a fine of up to € 1 million on the controlling shareholder.[414]

(iv) Though this is not expressly stated in the Takeover Act, the authors are of the opinion that the Federal Supervisory Office would be within its general supervisory powers[415] if it issued administrative decrees ordering that a mandatory bid be made.

---

[409] Explanatory Memorandum of the Federal Government on § 9 para. 1 no. 5 Public Offer Regulation (BT-Drucks. 14/7034 of October 5, 2001).
[410] § 9 para. 1 no. 3 Public Offer Regulation.
[411] §§ 39, 31 Takeover Act.
[412] § 38 Takeover Act, § 247 Civil Code.
[413] § 60 Takeover Act.
[414] §§ 61 para. 1 no. 1 a, 35 Takeover Act.
[415] § 4 para. 1 clause 3 Takeover Act.

(v) It is questionable and as yet unclear whether or not the minority shareholders of a target would have a **private cause of action** against a controlling shareholder which violates an obligation to make a mandatory bid. The Takeover Act does not expressly make provision for such a private cause of action. Additionally, there is no contractual relationship between the shareholders which could serve as a basis for a private cause of action. However, since mandatory bids are a central protective feature designed to prevent discrimination against minority shareholders, it might be argued that an implied right to a private cause of action exists.[416] The duty to make a mandatory bid should be construed broadly, so as to ensure that minority shareholders' rights are effectively protected. Minority protection rights are a distinctive feature of efficient capital markets (see the discussion in Ch. 3). The authors approve of the concept of an implied private cause of action for minority shareholders, which would ideally include the right to claim both injunctive relief and pecuniary damages.

11. Supervision by the Federal Supervisory Office[417]

Contrary to the situation under the Takeover Code, the provisions of the Takeover Act may be enforced by the Federal Supervisory Office. For this purpose, the Federal Supervisory Office has broad authority to investigate and to issue decrees.

a) Responsibilities of the Federal Supervisory Office

The most important areas for the exercise of the Federal Supervisory Office's responsibilities are the following:

(i) Publication Duties:

The Office supervises the proper performance of publication duties, such as the announcement of a bid.[418]

(ii) Mandatory Offer:

The Office supervises the due fulfillment of obligations regarding mandatory offers, in particular the publication of the acquisition of a controlling interest, and of a mandatory offer, if applicable.[419]

---

[416] § 823 para. 2 Civil Code contains a general private cause of action in the event of a violation of statutes and regulations that are specifically designed to protect individual rights.
[417] *"Bundesanstalt für Finanzdienstleistungsaufsicht."*
[418] § 10 para. 1 clause 1 Takeover Act.
[419] § 35 para. 2 clause 1 Takeover Act.

(iii) Restraining Orders against Illegal Offers:

The most powerful responsibility of the Federal Supervisory Office is that of prohibiting the publication of illegal offers.[420] Before the offeror may publish a bid, it must submit the offer document to the Federal Supervisory Office.[421] The latter may prohibit the publication of the bid within ten working days, and grant a further "grace period" of five working days to the offeror in order to remedy any legal defects in the offer document.[422] For example, in May 2002, the Office prohibited SPS GmbH from publishing a mandatory offer for the shares of Adori AG because, inter alia, a proper financing statement was missing.

(iv) Abusive Advertising Practices:

The Federal Supervisory Office may prohibit abusive advertising practises in hostile takeover battles (see Ch. 4 no. 8. c. (1) (b) above).[423]

Within its responsibilities the Federal Supervisory Office may issue decrees ordering compliance with provisions of the Takeover Act, and may impose fines in various circumstances.[424] Moreover, the Federal Supervisory Office has broad authority to investigate and may demand information and submission of documents.[425] It may enforce such investigational inquiries by means of fines and other compulsory action.[426]

b) Other Sanctions

The responsibilities of the Federal Supervisory Office are supplemented by other sanctions in various respects:

(i) In the event that the acquisition of a controlling interest has not been published, or a duty to make a mandatory offer has not been duly fulfilled, all rights attached to the acquired shares are suspended[427] (see also Ch. 4 no. 10. e. above), i. e. the right to receive dividends, pre-emptive rights in the case of an issue of new shares, and the voting rights.[428] Moreover, the minimum consideration that would have to be offered in the context of a mandatory offer bears interest until the mandatory offer is actually launched.[429]

(ii) In the event that the Federal Supervisory Office prohibits the publication of an offer because the offer document or the terms of the offer are not in compliance with the Takeover Act, the offeror may not publish an of-

---

[420] § 15 Takeover Act.
[421] § 14 para. 1 Takeover Act.
[422] § 14 para. 2 Takeover Act.
[423] § 28 Takeover Act.
[424] *See* in detail § 61 Takeover Act.
[425] § 40 Takeover Act.
[426] § 47 Takeover Act in conjunction with the Administration Enforcement Act *("Verwaltungsvollstreckungsgesetz")*.
[427] § 59 Takeover Act.
[428] Geibel/Süßmann, WpÜG, § 59 annot. 50.
[429] §§ 35, 38 Takeover Act.

fer for the securities of the same target within one year.[430] However, the Federal Supervisory Office may grant an exemption, provided the target company approves such exemption.

c) Remedies

Decrees of the Federal Supervisory Office may be appealed against by the persons affected by such decrees. In the first instance, the Federal Supervisory Office itself renders a decision on the appeal; for this purpose, a special "Appeals Committee"[431] is formed at the Federal Supervisory Office.[432] Against the decision of the Appeals Committee a further appeal may be filed with the Court of Appeal *("Oberlandesgericht")* in Frankfurt/Main that has exclusive jurisdiction over decrees issued by the Federal Supervisory Office.[433]

---

[430] § 26 Takeover Act.
[431] *"Widerspruchsausschuss."*
[432] § 41 Takeover Act in conjunction with §§ 68–73 Administrative Court Procedure Act *("Verwaltungsgerichtsordnung")*.
[433] § 48 Takeover Act.

Chapter 5. Merger of Equals

1. Introduction

The most common form of business combinations besides a transfer of shares are mergers with the effect of integrating the target company into the acquiring company. To give a brief overview, the following summarizes the legal requirements and procedure of a merger which is, however, a very complex legal structure under German law. Mergers are dealt with in the Reorganization Act. The Reorganization Act defines merger as the transfer of the entire assets of one or more legal persons to another legal person in return for shares or membership in the acquiring entity, and without liquidation of the legal person concerned, i.e. two entities are legally consolidated.

Takeovers and mergers differ in the decision making process: the merger requires a resolution of the shareholders' meeting of each company; i.e. the shareholders decide about the merger using their voting rights. The takeover involves an offer to the shareholders of the target company; i.e. each shareholder decides on the alienation of his own shares within the scope of his ownership rights. The consequences for the differing processes are as follows:

A friendly business combination in the form of a merger requires a majority of 75% of the voting rights of both shareholders' meetings. In contrast, a friendly takeover requires only the consent of the management of both companies. In this case, the success of the business combination depends on the takeover offer. If the offer is attractive, the shareholders of the target will accept it. A takeover offer may be problematic if both companies are equal in strength, because neither of them may be able to finance an attractive offer. Under these circumstances a merger is the better option.

An unfriendly business combination in the form of a merger presents itself if the attacker already owns more than 75% of the shares in the target, so that it has the required voting majority in the target in order to pass the merger resolution. For all other unfriendly business combinations a takeover offer would usually be the better opportunity.

A special case of a merger is the so-called "upstream merger:" a 100% subsidiary is merged into its parent company. An upstream merger suggests itself as a second step following a successful takeover offer.[1] In most cases, however, a squeeze-out would be necessary in advance, because this procedure is basically the only way to exclude the minority shareholders and to acquire 100% of the shares.[2]

---

[1] Note that an upstream merger lifts the corporate veil between the two companies; i.e. the parent company will become fully liable for all risks of the subsidiary; therefore, in many circumstances the subsidiary should be kept as a separate legal entity.

[2] *See* for details Ch. 6.

2. Relationship of the Reorganization Act with the Takeover Act

The relationship between the Reorganization Act and the Takeover Act is not finally settled. In this respect the practice to be adopted by the Federal Supervisory Office[3] has still to be determined. In general, the Takeover Act should not be applicable to merger transactions since the Reorganization Act contains a detailed and self-contained procedure for merger transactions which does not fit underneath the umbrella of the Takeover Act.[4] Some commentators, however, discuss an application of the provisions for mandatory offers[5] to merger transactions, in that the controlling shareholders of the combined entity would have to make an offer to the minority shareholders in certain circumstances.[6] Along with other scholars,[7] we reject this approach, while the Federal Supervisory Office has indicated that it might very well take the view that merger transactions can give rise to mandatory offers (see in detail Ch. 4 no. 10. b. below).

3. Forms of Merger under the Reorganization Act

A merger can take place in two ways: either as a merger by takeover or by the formation of a new entity:

- In the case of a **merger by takeover**,[8] the assets of one or more legal entities (transferring entity) are transferred to an already existing (and surviving) entity;
- In the case of a **merger by the formation of a new entity**, two or more entities transfer their assets to a new entity, formed at the same time.

Both forms of merger involve the extinction of the transferring entity or entities.[9]

A merger by the formation of a new entity is procedurally more complex than a merger by takeover, as the formation procedure is additional to the merger procedure. A further disadvantage is the increased cost (e.g. additional notarial costs based on the assets of both entities). In addition, the necessity of transferring the real estate of both entities to the new entity often arises, incurring Real Estate Transfer Tax on the real estate of both entities

---

[3] "Bundesanstalt für Finanzdienstleistungsaufsicht."

[4] Geibel/Süßmann/Angerer, WpÜG § 1 annot. 106; Explanatory Memorandum of the Federal Government, BT-Drucks. 14/7034 of 5. 10. 2001, p. 31.

[5] § 35 Takeover Act.

[6] Technau, AG 2002 p. 260; for a detailed discussion *see* Ch. 4 no. 10. b.

[7] Geibel/Süßmann/Angerer, WpÜG § 1 annot. 105, Weber-Rey/Schütz, AG 2001 p. 325, 328.

[8] A merger by takeover can still be a merger of equals; the term "takeover" in this context refers to the legal structure which does not necessarily reflect the economic situation: sometimes the smaller player, in a legal sense, takes over the larger player, for tax purposes or other legal reasons.

[9] §§ 20 para. 1 clause 1 and 2, 36 para. 1 Reorganization Act.

(3.5% of the market value of the real estate transferred). A further disadvantage is that within the first two years of formation, the management board of newly formed stock corporations must obtain approval by the shareholders' meeting for transactions with the founders or substantial shareholders (more than 10%) if such transaction exceeds a certain volume (more than 10% of the issued capital).[10] In spite of the disadvantages described above, psychological (e.g. if two equal corporations cannot agree on which of them is to act as transferring entity) and tactical aspects may favor a merger by the formation of a new entity. A significant legal advantage is that the merger can be expeditiously completed in the case of a formation of a new entity, because the possibility of challenging the merger, as such, on the basis of an inadequate conversion ratio does not arise. While an "action to set aside"[11] the merger resolution of the *transferring* entity cannot be based on the claim that the exchange ratio between shares of the old entity for those of the new entity is not adequate,[12] such a ground can indeed be availed of in challenging the merger resolution of the *receiving* entity. For the shareholders of the *transferring* entity, the German legislature has provided a special "compensation assessment procedure" („*Spruchstellenverfahren"*), which can result only in rights to compensation payments, but not prevent the completion of the merger itself.[13]

The merger by means of a newly formed entity has one further advantage: if, simultaneously with the merger, a certain legal form of the combined entity is intended which is different from that of the participating entities, both objectives can be achieved in one step by the new formation, the so-called "merger with change of legal form."

4. Merger and Anti-Trust Law

The concentration of market dominance created by the merger of two companies can adversely influence competition, and a merger may, therefore, be problematic under anti-trust law.

a) German Merger Control

Mergers must be notified to the Federal Cartel Office before completion, if the participating entities had a combined turnover in the preceding financial year of more than € 500 million, and at least one participating entity

---

[10] § 52 Stock Corporation Act; however, § 52 Stock Corporation Act does not apply to transactions in the ordinary course of business, § 52 para. 9 Stock Corporation Act. The restriction of § 52 Stock Corporation Act cannot be circumvented by using an already existing shelf company as acquiring entity since the two-year period starts on the day on which the shelf company was converted into an operating entity; Pentz, Münchener Kommentar zum Aktiengesetz, § 52 annot. 5.
[11] For a definition *see* Glossary.
[12] § 14 para. 2 Reorganization Act.
[13] §§ 305 et seq. Reorganization Act.

had a domestic turnover of more than € 25 million.[14] A merger which is subject to notification is to be prohibited by the Federal Cartel Office if the merger would create or strengthen a market dominance,[15] which is assumed if a company enjoys a market share of one third.[16] However, if the entities involved in the merger prove that competition will be improved by the merger and that this outweighs the disadvantages of market dominance, the merger will not be prohibited.

The Federal Cartel Office has one month from the filing of the notification[17] to decide whether the merger is free to go ahead or whether the main examination proceedings[18] will be initiated. If no notification is received from the Federal Cartel Office within the month to the effect that main examination proceedings will be commenced, the merger may be completed.[19] If the main examination proceeding is commenced, the Federal Cartel Office has four months from the filing of the notification to decide whether the merger is free to go ahead or will be prohibited.

b) European Merger Control

Mergers may also be subject to the European Merger Control Regulation, which is applicable if the merger has a community-wide significance.[20] Such a significance exists if the participating entities have a combined world-wide turnover of more than € 5 billion, and at least two participating entities have a community turnover each of more than € 250 million. This does not, however, apply if the entities participating in the merger each achieve more than two thirds of their community turnover in the same member state.[21] If the merger reaches one of these thresholds, it has to be notified to the European Commission at the latest one week after the conclusion of the merger contract.[22] If the merger gives ground for serious reservations, the European Commission initiates the procedure.[23] The decision about the initiation of the procedure will be issued, as a rule, within a period of one month or six weeks.[24] The European Commission prohibits the merger if it creates or strengthens a position of market dominance.[25] The German merger supervision does not apply to mergers which are subject to the European procedure.[26]

---

[14] § 35 para. 1 Anti-trust Act.
[15] § 36 para. 1 Anti-trust Act.
[16] § 19 para. 3 clause 1 Anti-trust Act.
[17] § 39 para. 2 Anti-trust Act.
[18] „Hauptprüfverfahren."
[19] § 40 para. 1 Anti-trust Act.
[20] Art. 1 European Merger Control Regulation.
[21] Art. 1 para. 3 European Merger Control Regulation.
[22] Art. 4 para. 1 European Merger Control Regulation.
[23] Art. 6 para. 1 c) European Merger Control Regulation.
[24] Art. 10 para. 1 European Merger Control Regulation.
[25] Art. 2 para. 2 European Merger Control Regulation.
[26] § 35 para. 3 Anti-trust Act.

5. Steps in a Merger under German Law

The legal processing of a merger takes place over the following stages:

- **audit** of the valuations and conversion ratio by independent auditors;
- conclusion of a **merger agreement** (contingent upon approval by the shareholders' meetings);
- submission of a detailed and comprehensive **merger report** to the shareholders of the participating entities;
- approval of the merger by the **shareholders' meetings;**
- **registration** of the merger in the commercial register of the participating entities;
- issuance (and stock exchange registration, if necessary) **of new shares** by the surviving or newly formed entity.

The co-ordination of the process demands complex project management, involving both entities as well as appraisers and legal and financial advisors.

a) The Decision on the Exchange Ratio

The process of determining an exchange ratio is the one central element in the transaction. Stated simply, the objective is that the shareholders who lose their shares in the transferring entity, are afterwards in possession of the same wealth as before, in the form of shares in the surviving or newly formed entity.

The exchange ratio must be calculated so that the value of the shareholding in the new combined entity equals the previous shareholding in the transferring entity. For the purposes of this calculation, the participating entities must be accurately valued.

(1) Intrinsic and extrinsic value

In general there are two fundamentally different methods of valuing shares: one determines the intrinsic and the other the extrinsic value. The intrinsic value can be determined by application of income methods (capitalized earnings, discounted cash flow; see Ch. 5 no. 4. a. (2) below). The extrinsic value can be determined by application of market valuation methods (share prices, comparable multiple valuation, comparable transaction method).

Financial theory and practice usually applied valuation methods based on income or cash flow to determine the value of merging entities with no regard to extrinsic values. Following a decision of the Federal Supreme Court, the application of income methods to merger cases has to be reviewed: the famous case of **"DAT/Altana"**[27] dealt with a **control and profit transfer agreement** between a parent company and its subsidiary, and the mandatory compensation and takeover offer that under German law has to be made to

---

[27] Federal Supreme Court, BGH DB 2001 p. 969 et seq.

the minority shareholders of the subsidiary. The Federal Supreme Court held that the public share price before the conditions of the mandatory compensation and takeover offer had become public, determines the minimum amount of compensation to be offered to the minority shareholders. The Federal Supreme Court did not, however, expressly decide whether, and in what circumstances, the stock exchange price should also influence the valuations of entities in a **merger** case. This question is highly disputed, scholars argue in both directions:

Some scholars argue that the principles of *DAT/Altana* should also be applied in merger cases: for the calculation of the cash compensation in the case of company agreements (control and profit transfer agreements, such as in the *DAT/Altana* case), the relative value of the entities is relevant if the minority shareholders receive shares as compensation (share exchange).[28] The same applies to mergers where the relative value of the merging entities determines the conversion ratio. It should therefore make no difference whether such relative valuation is carried out in merger cases or against other backgrounds such as control and profit transfer agreements.[29] The legislature expresses that it places as much importance on the protection of the (minority) shareholders in the case of company agreements as in the case of mergers.[30]

This view, however, overlooks the fact that in merger cases the minority shareholders of the *receiving* (surviving) entity must also be protected:[31] if, for example, the intrinsic value of the transferring entity's shares is below the stock exchange price, while the intrinsic value of the receiving entity corresponds to its stock exchange value, the shareholders of the *transferring* entity obtain a gain as the receiving entity receives only the lower intrinsic value, because the shares of the transferring entity (and its extrinsic value) are extinguished by the merger.[32] While shareholders of the transferring entity benefit, the shareholdings in the receiving entity will be diluted.

Moreover, the argument of the Federal Supreme Court in *DAT/Altana*, that the shareholder should receive as much as in the case of a free disposal of the investment, does not apply if the compensation consists of shares in the receiving entity. In that case, the shareholder retains his investment in the form of shares in the combined entity. The stock exchange price can, therefore, only be the lower limit if the shareholders are offered compensation in cash.[33]

In view of the above, the *DAT/Altana* principles are not transferrable to non-dominated mergers of equals: the negotiation process is an adequate safeguard to ensure the determination of a fair conversion ratio. Therefore, the courts should only intervene where the conversion ratio is due to a gross failure of the negotiation process, and is obviously not based on a sound and

---

[28] §§ 305 para. 3 clause 1; 320b para. 1 clause 4 Stock Corporation Act.
[29] *See* Behnke, NZG 1999 p. 934; Vetter, AG 1999 p. 572; Vetter ZIP 2000, p. 566.
[30] Erb, DB 2001 p. 523, 524.
[31] Bungert, BB 2001 p. 1163, 1166.
[32] Riegger, DB 1999 p. 1889, 1890.
[33] §§ 29, 207 Reorganization Act; Wilm, NZG 2000 p. 234, 237.

reasonable (relative) valuation of the merging entities. No single valuation method should be used, but rather a combination of methods based on income/cash flow and market valuation methods should be applied. Note that the pricing rules of the Takeover Act (see Ch. 4 no. 9) are not applicable to merger transactions.

(2) Determination of the intrinsic value of an enterprise

Since the stock exchange value does not play a decisive (at least, not an exclusive) part in the case of non-dominated mergers, the question arises as to how the intrinsic value of a corporation should be determined.

In contrast to the position in the U.S., where fairness opinions on the valuation are obtained from investment banks and recognized as the basis for the determination of the conversion ratio, the valuations under German law are usually carried out by CPA firms, engaged by each of the participants to value the other. Although there are detailed and comprehensive professional recommendations for CPA firms on carrying out company valuations,[34] some basic legal questions remain controversial.

Several methods of valuation have been developed in practice, and, of these, the capitalized earnings method and the discounted cash flow method are most accepted. In the case of the latter, future cash flow to equity holders discounted to the valuation day, rather than future accounting profits, is taken as a basis.[35]

However, the valuation practice of German CPA firms is based most frequently on the capitalized earnings method, which assumes that the value of an enterprise is represented by its future success, which is understood to be the discounted surplus of its future income over its outgoings.[36] The calculation is usually based on the profits of the past 3 to 5 years, adjusted for special items.[37] However, past results cannot simply be projected into the future. Future developments within the enterprise and in the market are to be estimated, and taken into account. The projections are usually divided into several phases. The first phase is based on detailed business planning. The length of this phase differs in accordance with the size, structure and business area of the enterprise.[38] In accordance with some court judgments, this phase may be as short as one year, in a particular case.[39] For the second and,

---

[34] IdW, Principles for the Carrying out of Company Valuations, Die Wirtschaftsprüfung 2000 p. 825.

[35] Mayer, Widmann/Mayer, Umwandlungsgesetz, 61st supplementary delivery 2001, § 5 annot. 100.1; Bula/Schlösser in Sagasser/Bula/Brünger, Umwandlungen, J annot. 49 et seq; for details on the DCF method: Pratt/Reilly/Schweihs, Valuing a Business, 4th ed. 2000, Chapter 9.

[36] Bula/Schlösser in Sagasser/Bula/Brünger, Umwandlungen, J 37; as the accounting profits are adjusted for special items, in most cases the results of the DCF method and capitalized earning method do not differ substantially.

[37] Engelmeyer, Die Spaltung von Aktiengesellschaften, p. 109.

[38] IdW, Principles for the Carrying out of Company Valuations, Die Wirtschaftsprüfung 2000 p. 825, 832.

[39] Supreme Appeal Court of Bavaria, BayObLG, DB 2002 p. 36, 37.

possibly, a third phase, the surpluses can only be approximately estimated, taking into account general economic indicators and data from the industrial sector concerned.[40] The last phase (second or third phase, respectively), represents the so-called "terminal value" which is determined as perpetuity. The total value derived from the two or three phases is then discounted to the valuation date.

(3) Relative valuation of the merging entities

As explained above, the stock exchange value does not play a crucial role in the case of so-called "non-dominated" mergers. The opposite is the case in dominated mergers,[41] especially in the case of "upstream mergers," in which a subsidiary is merged with its parent. In such cases, there is no equal negotiating position from which agreement on reasonable consideration could be secured. Minority shareholders are, therefore, in need of protection exactly as in the case of contracts of domination. The principles developed in the *DAT/Altana* judgment should be applied correspondingly.[42] For ascertaining the value of the dominated company, the stock exchange value is to be regarded as the minimum value. If the "intrinsic value" arrived at by the general valuation methods is higher, this must, in accordance with the *DAT/Altana* principles, apply. In the event of dispute, this value can be proved by an expert report. With regard to the valuation of the shares of the "dominating" or "controlling" company, the minority shareholders do not, according to the *DAT/Altana* judgment, have a right to insist on the stock exchange value as a maximum.[43] However, the stock exchange value is generally presumed to be reasonable. In the exceptional case where the stock exchange value of a dominating company does not correspond to its market value, this has to be proved. An expert report, in which the company is valued in accordance with the usual valuation methods, is not, as such, sufficient in this respect. The reasons why the stock exchange price does not, in the actual case, reflect the value of the company, must specifically be explained. A possible explanation could be that the stock markets in general are weak at that time. This would have to be proved by means of the share prices of all significant indices.[44]

It is questionable, however, whether the company values of the merging entities can reasonably be compared if the stock exchange value cannot be taken into account in an individual case. Four possible problematic instances may apply:

---

[40] IdW, Principles for the Carrying out of Company Valuations, Die Wirtschaftsprüfung 2000 p. 825, 833.

[41] A dominated merger arises if a company can, at its decision, force the other company to merge. As both companies require a resolution of their shareholders' meetings with a 75% majority, a dominated merger exits if one company holds more than 75% of the shares in the other company. Wilsing/Kruse, DStR 2001 p. 991, 996.

[42] Wilsing/Kruse, DStR 2001 p. 991, 996.

[43] DAT/Altana: Federal Constitutional Court, BVerfG ZIP 1999 p. 1442; Federal Supreme Court, BGH DB 2001 p. 969, 972.

[44] Federal Supreme Court, DB 2001 p. 969, 972 et seq.

1. for the dominated company, an estimated intrinsic value is given which is in excess of the stock exchange value,
2. proof is successfully provided that the market value of the dominating company is, as an exception, higher than the stock exchange value,
3. the stock exchange value cannot be taken into account in the case of *one* of the companies, because trade in the stocks is either too thin or a company is not at all traded on the stock exchange,
4. both the dominating and the dominated company are valued without reference to the share price, because of one of the reasons 1–3 above.

Case 4 is the easiest to resolve. Here it is only necessary to ensure that the same valuation method is applied to both companies, i.e. either the capitalized earnings method or the DCF method.[45]

In cases 1–3, the principles of the DAT/Altana judgment lead to the situation that differing methods of valuation must be applied to each company. This conflicts with the prevailing opinion regarding mergers, namely, that application of the same method of valuation is required in all cases.[46] As the valuation methods are based on projections and are not, therefore, exact, a satisfactory result would only be achieved if the two companies are compared to each other. Thereby, projection errors would affect both companies and would be balanced out. This is, however, only possible if the same valuation method is applied to both companies.[47] In addition, a criticism is voiced that the application of the DAT/Altana principles favors the shareholders of the transferring company.[48] The latter argument is not entirely sustainable. If the intrinsic value of the *dominating* company is, in an individual case, higher than its stock exchange value, the fact that the stock exchange value does not constitute a maximum favors the shareholders of the dominating company. An unreasonable advantage in favor of the dominated company does not, therefore, arise. If the application of differing valuation methods does actually lead to imprecision, this is acceptable, in the opinion of the authors, so that a fair exchange ratio is established in cases in which the stock exchange value of one company is the fair value, and the intrinsic value is the fair valuation of the other company.

(4) Synergy effects – stand-alone basis

According to a long line of court precedents, the merging companies must be valued on a **stand-alone basis,** i.e. future synergies arising from the merger must not be accounted for.[49] If synergy effects which arise within the merged enterprise were to be taken into account for the benefit of the

---

[45] Lutter, Umwandlungsgesetz, 2nd ed., § 5 annot. 23 c.
[46] Bermel/Hannappel, Goutier/Knopf/Tulloch, Kommentar zum Umwandlungsrecht, § 5 annot. 23 et seq., Mayer, Widmann/Mayer, Umwandlungsgesetz, 61st supplementary delivery, § 5 annot. 101; Lutter Umwandlungsgesetz, 2nd ed., § 5 annot. 19 et seq.
[47] Lutter, Umwandlungsgesetz, 2nd ed., § 5 annot. 19 et seq.
[48] Bunger/Eckert, BB 2000 p. 1845, 1847; Wilsing/Kruse, DStR 2001 p. 991, 994.
[49] Appeal Court of Celle, OLG Celle, AG 1999 p. 128, 130; BayObLG, AG 1996 p. 176, 177; Appeal Court of Hamburg, OLG Hamburg AG 1980 p. 163, 165.

102   *Chapter 5. Merger of Equals*

transferring entity, those shareholders would not only be compensated, they would be placed in an improved position. Without the merger the shares would not have benefited from the synergy effect.[50] Moreover, the shareholders of the transferring entity will become shareholders in the surviving entity, and will thereby benefit fully from the synergy effect anyway.[51] If, however, increased value were to be attributed to the shares in the transferring entity because of the anticipated synergy effect in the merged entity, the shareholders of the transferring entity would benefit from the synergy effect twice over. The shareholders of the transferring entity would thereby have preferential treatment, in breach of the corporate law principle of equal treatment.[52] Furthermore, it is, in practice, impossible to evaluate the effect of synergy exactly, and to apportion it correctly between the merging entities.[53]

Some scholars take the opposite view, based on the argument that a shareholder freely selling would obtain a price which would reflect the achievable synergies. This is based on the management theory that the value of an object is determined not by its characteristics, but by the subjective appreciation of its usefulness.[54] According thereto, the synergy effect should be estimated and apportioned between the participating entities.[55] This view has, however, not found broad agreement among either courts or scholars. The merging entities should therefore be valued on a stand-alone basis.

There is, however, agreement that the value assessed must not be less than the price which would be achievable if each asset item were sold separately (liquidation value).[56]

(5) The valuation date

The Reorganization Act does not fix a date for the valuation. However, the same date must be fixed for the valuation of all merging entities.[57] In general, the parties have a relatively broad discretion to decide on a valuation date.[58] However, a valuation which is no longer relevant to the situation at the time of the merger must be avoided. It is, therefore, necessary to inform the shareholders at the time of the merger resolution of relevant developments after the date of the valuation and to supplement the merger report accordingly.[59] This leads in practice to a "stand still period" between the

---

[50] District Court of Dortmund, LG Dortmund AG 1981 p. 236, 23.
[51] Mertens, AG 1992 p. 321, 331.
[52] Mertens, AG 1992 p. 321, 331.
[53] Koppensteiner, Kölner Kommentar, 2nd ed. 1987, § 305 AktG annot. 34.
[54] Sieben/Schildbach, DStR 1979 p. 455.
[55] Walther Busse von Colbe, ZGR 1994 p. 595, 605.
[56] Mayer, Widmann/Mayer, Umwandlungsgesetz, 61st supplementary delivery, § 5 annot. 101.
[57] *See* Sagasser/Ködderitzsch, Sagasser/Bula/Brünger, Umwandlungen, J annot. 29; *see* Lutter, Umwandlungsgesetz, 2nd ed. 2000, § 5 annot. 21.
[58] Appeal Court of Bremen, OLG Bremen, DB 1992, p. 671; Lutter, Umwandlungsgesetz, 2nd ed., § 5 annot. 21; Kraft, Kölner Kommentar, 2nd ed. 1990, § 340b AktG annot. 11; dissenting opinion: Mayer, Widmann/Mayer, Umwandlungsgesetz, 61st supplementary delivery, § 5 annot. 131.
[59] Marsch-Barner, Kallmeyer, Umwandlungsgesetz, 2nd ed. 2001, § 8 annot. 21.

publication of the merger report and the shareholders' meeting, as regards transactions which would influence the valuation, because at the time of the shareholders' meeting any change in the merger report is hardly practicable because the periods for making the report available *("Auslegungsfristen")* are already running.

b) Merger Agreement

The merger is accomplished by a merger agreement.[60]

(1) Minimum content of the merger agreement

The required minimum content of the merger agreement is fixed by law.[61] The minimum content includes, inter alia:

- Reference to the **agreement to transfer the assets** of the transferring entity as a whole in return for consideration in the form of shares or membership in the receiving entity.[62] In consequence of the merger a full legal succession takes place, i.e. all rights and duties of the transferring entity pass to the receiving entity.
- The **exchange ratio**. Information must be given about the class or type of the shares granted as consideration. These details are important because the shareholder who loses preference shares in the transferring entity has the right to receive preference shares in the combined entity as consideration.[63] If this is not possible in an individual case, e.g. because of lack of disposal over the shares in the receiving entity, there is a right to compensation.[64]
- The point at which **participation in profits** of the combined entity arises and the effective date of the merger; the latter is the date on which the merger becomes *financially* effective, in particular, the taking over of the accountancy procedures.[65] The merger comes into *legal* effect only on entry in the commercial register.[66]
- Granting of **specific rights to single shareholders** or third parties; this may be the case, e.g., if specific shareholders are to have the right to appoint a certain number of members of the supervisory board.[67] Furthermore, all advantages for board members in connection with the merger have to be specified as far as they exceed their rights out of their existing employment contracts.

---

[60] § 4 para. 1 Reorganization Act.
[61] § 5 para. 1 Reorganization Act.
[62] § 5 para. 1 no. 2 Reorganization Act.
[63] Lutter, Umwandlungsgesetz, 2nd ed., § 5 annot. 10.
[64] § 29 Reorganization Act.
[65] Bula/Schlösser, Sagasser/Bula/Brünger, Umwandlungen, J annot. 63.
[66] § 20 para. 1 Reorganization Act.
[67] It is possible for up to one third of the members of the supervisory board to be elected by the shareholders' meeting, § 101 para. 2 Stock Corporation Act ("Golden Shares").

- The **compensation** in cash to be offered if two different forms of legal entities are be merged, or if the new shares offered to the shareholders of the transferring entity are not freely transferable. Shareholders may claim such compensation if they object to the merger ("dissenters' rights").[68]
- The merger agreement must further include a statement about the consequences of the planned merger for the **employees** and their representation within the enterprise.[69] The purpose of this is to inform the employees about the planned merger at any early stage, and by giving this information, to enable their representatives to pave the way for a socially "digestible" arrangement of the merger.[70]

Consequences of a merger for employees are:

(i) Dismissal protection

The receiving entity takes over all employment contracts of the transferring entity by operation of law. Therefore, a dismissal based on the merger itself is invalid.[71] But dismissals due to operational requirements are still possible, i.e. if employees become redundant because of the merger's effects.[72]

(ii) Binding collective bargaining agreements

Collective bargaining agreements[73] of the transferring entity may, under certain circumstances, be effective and binding on the receiving entity.

If there is no collective bargaining agreement applicable to the receiving entity, the German Civil Code provides that the regulations of the collective bargaining agreement of the transferring entity become a part of the employment contract of each employee of the transferring entity. The regulations are incorporated into the contracts of employment by operation of law.[74] These regulations stay in effect for at least one year after the registration of the merger. Before this point in time the employment contracts may not be modified to the disadvantage of the employees.[75]

Works bargaining agreements[76] generally stay in effect after the merger. A conflict may arise when the receiving entity also has established works agreements. In such cases, the works agreement of the receiving entity is applicable and in principle supercedes the works agreement of the transferring entity even if the overidden works agreement was more favorable for the employees.[77]

---

[68] § 29 Reorganization Act.
[69] § 5 para. 1 no. 9 Reorganization Act.
[70] Lutter, Umwandlungsgesetz, 2nd ed., § 5 annot. 39.
[71] § 324 Reorganization Act and § 613a para. 1 Civil Code.
[72] Bermel/Hannappel, Goutier/Knopf/Tulloch, Kommentar zum Umwandlungsrecht, 1st ed. 1996, § 5 annot. 72.
[73] „Tarifvertrag," for a definition *see* Glossary.
[74] § 613a para. 1 clause 2 Civil Code.
[75] § 613a para. 1 clause 2 Civil Code.
[76] „Betriebsvereinbarungen," for a definition *see* Glossary.
[77] Bermel/Hannappel, Goutier/Knopf/Tulloch, Kommentar zum Umwandlungsrecht, § 5 annot. 76.

(iii) Employee representation

While the merger agreement has *legal* consequences, the *organization* at the works floor level is not necessarily affected. Hence the members of the works councils remain in office.[78] If a joint works council existed in the transferring entity, it is dissolved. Nevertheless, it may be necessary to establish a joint works council in the combined entity if the receiving entity had only one works council prior to the merger and by the merger acquires at least one more.[79] Regarding the codetermination on the supervisory board,[80] a distinction must be made: since the transferring entity is dissolved by the merger, its corporate organs (including its supervisory board) are dissolved. The corporate organs of the receiving company stay in office. In case the number of employees rises over a certain threshold, a supervisory board may have to be formed according to the Codetermination Act or other applicable rules of codetermination.[81]

(2) Form of the merger agreement

The merger agreement, along with all side agreements, must be notarized. The notarization can take place after the merger resolution.[82]

(3) Presentation of the merger agreement to the works council

The merger agreement is to be passed to the relevant works council of the participating entities one month prior to the shareholders' meetings which vote on the merger.[83] The purpose of this provision is to ensure that the employees' representatives are informed in good time as to the consequences for the employees.[84] The works council, however, has no right to object, alter or amend the agreement.

The merger will not be registered and become effective if these information rights of the works council are not observed. Nevertheless, the works council itself cannot prevent the merger from becoming effective. If, how-

---

[78] Lutter, Umwandlungsgesetz, 2nd ed., § 5 annot. 48.

[79] Mayer in Widmann/Mayer, Umwandlungsgesetz, 61st supplementary delivery, § 5 annot. 196.

[80] Under the *Shop Constitution Act* one third of the members of the supervisory board of any stock corporation must be employee representatives. The Shop Constitution Act does not apply to corporations with less than 500 employees. For corporations that were registered before August 10, 1994 this is valid only if these corporations are family controlled (§ 76 para. 6 Shop Constitution Act). The *Codetermination Act* is applicable to all companies that employ more than 2000 persons. The supervisory board is composed of an odd number of shareholders and employee representatives. The *Coal and Steel Codetermination Act* and the Supplementary Codetermination Act apply to corporations in the coal and iron producing industrial sector employing more than 1000 persons. These Acts stipulate equal numbers of employee and shareholder representatives on the supervisory board.

[81] Bermel/Hannappel, Goutier/Knopf/Tulloch, Kommentar zum Umwandlungsrecht, § 5 annot. 95.

[82] § 4 para. 4 Reorganization Act.

[83] § 5 para. 3 Reorganization Act.

[84] § 5 para. 1 no. 9 Reorganization Act.

ever, the merger causes changes in the organization of the works, the works council negotiates with the management of the transferring entity about adequate compensation for employees who are adversely affected by such changes.[85]

c) Merger Audit

The merger agreement of stock corporations must be reviewed by an expert to be appointed by the competent court.[86] A joint audit expert for both merging entities may be appointed. The purpose of this is to ensure the reasonableness of the exchange ratio. That does not mean that the expert must revalue the company; the expert must, however, check into the reasonableness of the parameters of the valuation (in particular: correct application of the specific valuation method; reasonableness of the income projections and discount rate).

d) Merger Report

The boards of the merging entities must each prepare a detailed report on the merger and submit it to the shareholders.[87] The merger report must include a full description of all relevant aspects of the merger.[88] Minority shareholders often meticulously look for mistakes or omissions in the merger report in order to challenge the merger in court. It is therefore, advisable that considerable care is exercised to ensure that the merger report is absolutely "watertight."

(1) The scope of the report obligation

The purpose of the merger report is to place the shareholders in a position to review the proposed merger as to its plausibility. The shareholders decide on the merger and must therefore be in a position to take a view on the financial soundness of the proposal.[89] However, the report need not be so detailed as to recount all particulars of the process.[90] The shareholders need to know the basic economic factors such as area of activity, turnover and market share of the merging entities, so that they obtain an idea of the potential merger partner and its subsidiaries.[91] The **synergy effects,** and where it is expected they may be achieved, must also be explained (e.g. stronger bargaining position as purchaser, increased use of capacity, etc.). It is not necessary that the effects be quantified and justified in detail.[92] On the

---

[85] § 112 Shop Constitution Act; Gaul, DB 1995 p. 2265, 2267.
[86] § 9 Reorganization Act.
[87] § 8 Reorganization Act.
[88] Lutter, Umwandlungsgesetz, 2nd ed., § 8 annot. 13.
[89] Federal Supreme Court, BGHZ 107 p. 296, 303.
[90] Appeal Court of Hamm, OLG Hamm ZIP 1999 p. 798.
[91] Lutter, Umwandlungsgesetz, 2nd ed., § 8 annot. 15 et seq.
[92] Appeal Court of Hamm, OLG Hamm NZG 1999 p. 562; Appeal Court of Düsseldorf, OLG Düsseldorf NZG 1999 p. 567.

other hand, negative effects such as redundancies, integration costs and the possible loss of qualified employees must be included.[93] Finally, advantages and disadvantages of the merger are to be weighed against each other.[94]

The core of the merger report is the explanation of the calculation of the **exchange ratio** and of the cash compensation to be paid to dissenters in certain circumstances.[95]

As far as the **method of valuation** is concerned, reference to and a short explanation of the capitalized earnings method is usually sufficient as this is the generally accepted valuation method. Only if another valuation method has been chosen is it necessary to provide a justification.[96] In view of the fact that in similar valuation cases the Federal Supreme Court has regarded the stock exchange price as the lower limit, and the fact that the application of this principle to mergers is not yet judicially clarified (see Ch. 5 no. 4. a. (1) above), it is recommended that at least for comparison purposes the stock exchange value on the basis of the weighted price of the past three months should be given.[97] Also, the discount rate along with a short explanation should be given.

In principle, the past financial figures and the projections upon which the valuation of the enterprise is based must be stated in the report. However, the reasonable interests of the participating entities in maintaining confidentiality must also be observed. The overall annual figures in each case are therefore sufficient; further explanation (e. g. as to net results of certain product segments) is not necessary.[98] The confidentiality issues are, of course, important if two competitors wish to merge and it seems possible that the merger could be rejected in the shareholders' meeting.

The Reorganization Act expressly specifies some other special issues: **particular difficulties in valuing the enterprises** must be mentioned.[99] This includes circumstances which may render projections highly uncertain. Either circumstances within the enterprise itself (corporate restructuring requirements) or external circumstances (in particular, dangers or opportunities in regard to market developments) must be discussed.[100] Typical cases in this respect are companies in financial distress; if the financial projections predict a "turn around" for such companies then the corresponding restructuring measures need to be explained in detail.

Furthermore, the report must mention the **effects on the shareholding structure**.[101] This requirement is aimed at instances in which a shareholder

---

[93] Lutter, Umwandlungsgesetz, 2nd ed., § 8 annot. 17.

[94] Mayer, Widmann/Mayer, Umwandlungsgesetz, 61st supplementary delivery, § 8 annot. 22.

[95] Bermel, Goutier/Knopf/Tulloch, Kommentar zum Umwandlungsrecht, § 8 annot. 17.

[96] Court of Mannheim, OLG Mannheim AG 1988 p. 248, 249; Appeal Court of Karlsruhe, OLG Karlsruhe ZIP 1989 p. 988, 990.

[97] Lutter, Umwandlungsgesetz, 2nd ed., § 8 annot. 21.

[98] Court of Mannheim, OLG Mannheim AG 1988 p. 248, 250.

[99] § 8 para. 1 clause 2 Reorganization Act.

[100] Lutter, Umwandlungsgesetz, 2nd ed., § 8 annot. 29.

[101] § 8 para. 1 clause 3 Reorganization Act.

achieves or indeed loses an important position (blocking minority, majority) in the merged enterprise or loses such a position in the transferring enterprise.[102]

The report must mention **affiliated companies** (both parent companies and subsidiaries of the merging entities).[103] These are, in the first place, companies in which a majority shareholding is held (those companies are usually consolidated in the financial statements) and secondly, those with which an even closer relationship exists, for example, in the form of a company agreement (in particular, control and profit transfer agreement).[104] If a *parent company* participates in a merger, the report must include references to the subsidiaries which are of significance to the business of the parent company. If the value of a subsidiary amounts to more than 10% of the assets of the parent company or if a subsidiary contributes more than 10% of the annual profit of the parent company, the financial position of the parent is significantly influenced by the subsidiary. Past annual financial figures as well as projections are to be reported for the subsidiary in the same manner as those of the parent company.[105] If a *subsidiary* is to be merged, the annual results of the parent generally do not influence the results of the subsidiary. In such case it is sufficient to give the name of the parent company and the manner in which the companies are related.[106]

(2) **Confidentiality requirements**

Confidentiality requirements might set limits to the reporting obligation.[107] Facts (in particular trade secrets) the disclosure of which could cause significant damage to one of the participating entities or an associated company need not be mentioned in the merger report. Instead, the reasons for their not being mentioned are to be explained. The shareholders must be in a position to assess, on the basis of the information given, whether the non-disclosure is justified.[108]

e) **Merger Resolution**

The merger agreement is only effective when the shareholders of the merging entities have approved it by resolutions in shareholder's meetings.[109] If a merger agreement has not legally been concluded, the draft thereof can be voted on.[110]

---

[102] Mayer, Widmann/Mayer, Umwandlungsgesetz, 61st supplementary delivery, § 8 annot. 41.
[103] § 8 para. 1 clause 3 Reorganization Act.
[104] § 15 Stock Corporation Act.
[105] Lutter, Umwandlungsgesetz, 2nd ed., § 8 annot. 41.
[106] Lutter, Umwandlungsgesetz, 2nd ed., § 8 annot. 42.
[107] § 8 para. 2 clause 1 Reorganization Act.
[108] Mayer, Widmann/Mayer, Umwandlungsgesetz, 61st supplementary delivery, § 8 annot. 52.
[109] § 13 para. 1 Reorganization Act.
[110] Bermel, Goutier/Knopf/Tulloch, Kommentar zum Umwandlungsrecht, § 13 annot. 14; Zimmermann, Kallmeyer, Umwandlungsgesetz, 2nd ed., § 13 annot. 7.

In the case of a corporation as merging entity, a 75% majority of the votes cast is required for the approval of the merger.[111] The Articles of Association of the relevant entity may, however, provide for an even greater majority. If the Articles of Association require a larger voting majority for an amendment of the Articles, then this majority requirement is applicable to mergers as well, even if the case of a merger is not expressly mentioned in the Articles in this respect.[112]

The merger comes into effect on registration in the commercial register of the receiving entity. Legally binding effects can, however, arise from the merger resolution as such. Internally the shareholders are bound by their resolution. Externally, the resolutions of the participating entities will be binding on each other.[113]

f) Capital Increase at the Receiving Entity

The shareholders of the transferring entity will, by virtue of the merger, become shareholders of the new consolidated entity. This requires that the receiving entity has unissued shares available which can be issued to the new shareholders. If this is not the case, such shares can be created by means of a capital increase.

g) Notification of the Merger to the Register

In order to become effective, the merger must be entered in the commercial register of the receiving entity.[114] This requires an application to the competent register court which, in addition to checking the completeness of the documents filed,[115] reviews to a certain extent substantive law issues connected with the effectiveness of the merger, for example, the possible invalidity of the merger agreement due to the absence of mandatory information.[116]

h) Legal Protection of Shareholders

Every shareholder – even if holding only one single share – may challenge the merger resolution in court.[117] If such a law suit is pending, the

---

[111] Lutter, Umwandlungsgesetz, 2nd ed., § 13 annot. 21.

[112] Lutter, Umwandlungsgesetz, 2nd ed., § 13 annot. 21; Heckschen, Widmann/Mayer, Umwandlungsgesetz, 61st supplementary delivery, § 13 annot. 70; Zimmermann, Kallmeyer, Umwandlungsgesetz, 2nd ed., § 13 annot. 11; see Weber/Volhard, Arbeitshandbuch für Unternehmensübernahmen, § 17 annot. 229; dissenting opinion: Sagasser/Ködderitzsch, Sagasser/Brula/Brünger, Umwandlungen, J annot. 122.

[113] § 145 Civil Code.

[114] § 20 para. 1 Reorganization Act.

[115] § 17 Reorganization Act.

[116] See for more details Sagasser/Ködderitzsch, Sagasser/Bula/Brünger, Umwandlungen, J. annot. 142.

[117] §§ 243, 246 Stock Corporation Act.

merger cannot be registered and therefore cannot become effective.[118] In view of the duration of the legal proceedings connected with such challenges, possibly through several instances, this means that any shareholder can block a merger for a virtually indefinite period and, if the merger is, due to the passage of time, deprived of its financial advantage, often prevent it altogether.[119]

An "action to set aside" therefore provides a means of blackmail and is often instituted with the sole objective of achieving share redemptions. The following case illustrates the potential extent of blackmail if the planned merger requires major capital, and if particular time pressure is involved:

Case: Aachener-Münchner/Freitag[120]

At the beginning of 1987, the Aachener-Münchner Insurance Company acquired the majority in a bank for a price of 1.9 billion DM. The purchase contract required the approval of its shareholders. In order to obtain the funds necessary for the acquisition, a capital increase was required, which also required approval by the shareholders' meeting. The shareholders' meeting was called for March 9, 1987. On the agenda all points which required approval were stated. In addition, it had been made known to the press that the purchase price was due on June 1, 1987, and that all transactions were subject to the approval of the shareholders. One person thereupon bought three shares. Shortly before the conclusion of the shareholders' meeting, he objected to the resolutions so that he could institute an action to set aside and block the acquisition.[121] After the shareholders' meeting, he threatened to file an action to set aside the resolution within one month. This objection was soon well-known in the public. The leader of the bank consortium then demanded the return of the subscription form which it had already issued to the Aachener-Münchner. By returning this subscription form, the Aachener-Münchner would have lost the financing opportunity for the acquisition. The payment of the purchase price due on June 1, 1987 was therefore in danger. Negotiations took place with the challenging shareholder concerning the withdrawal of his objections. It was finally agreed that he would withdraw his objection in return for 1.5 million DM though such payment is actually not allowed under applicable stock corporation law as no shareholder may receive special advantages according to the principle of equal treatment. Although the Aachener-Münchner case concerned an acquisition rather than a merger, the blackmail potential is equally existent in the case of a merger.

In order to reduce this blackmail potential, the new Reorganization Act provides that an action by a shareholder of the *transferring* entity to set aside the merger resolution cannot any longer be based on a claim that

---

[118] § 16 para. 2 clause 1 Stock Corporation Act.
[119] Bermel, Goutier/Knopf/Tulloch, Kommentar zum Umwandlungsrecht, § 16 annot. 35.
[120] Federal Supreme Court, BGH ZIP 1988 p. 1497.
[121] § 245 no. 1 Stock Corporation Act.

the exchange ratio has been incorrectly calculated.[122] For such claim the shareholders are referred to a special compensation assessment procedure *("Spruchstellenverfahren")*.[123] This procedure can result only in an adjustment of the exchange ratio, but cannot delay or prevent the merger as such. The same applies in the case that the merger report contains insufficient information in connection with the determination of the exchange ratio.[124] Shareholders of the *receiving* entity are not, however, restricted in their right to file an action to set aside on the basis that the exchange ratio is incorrect. The reason for that, given by the legislature, is the fact that a capital increase is necessary at the receiving entity in order to carry through the share exchange, which capital increase must remain subject to challenge. Any other solution would be too radical an interference with the rights of the shareholders. This legal situation might be a valuable argument for structuring the merger by formation of a new entity, as in this case the restriction on actions to set aside applies to the shareholders of both merging entities.

If a shareholder files an action to set aside,[125] a clearance procedure *("Unbedenklichkeitsverfahren")*[126] provides a possibility of lifting the block on registration.[127] This procedure is of particular importance where actions to set aside are in the nature of blackmail. In this procedure, the court can clear the registration of the merger if the action to set aside is frivolous or unfounded,[128] or if the completion of the merger appears to have priority, weighing the seriousness of the alleged infringement of the law against the damage which is threatened to the participating entities (e.g., the loss of synergies).[129] In particular, on this basis, lawsuits which allege only insignificant defects can be excluded.

6. Cross-Border Corporate Mergers

In recent years cross-border corporate mergers have become more frequent as a consequence of the globalization of the economy and the integration of the national economic systems in Europe.

---

[122] § 14 para. 2 Reorganization Act.

[123] §§ 305 et seq. Reorganization Act.

[124] *See* Federal Supreme Court, BGH ZIP 2001 p. 199; Heckschen, Widmann/Mayer, Umwandlungsrecht, 61st supplementary delivery, § 14 annot. 42; opposite view: Schmitt/Hörtnagl/Stratz, 3 d. ed., § 14 UmwG annot. 21.

[125] For other reasons than an inappropriate conversion ratio if filed by the transferring entity's shareholders.

[126] § 16 para. 3 Reorganization Act.

[127] Explanatory Memorandum of the Federal Government of § 14 para. 2 Reorganization Act.

[128] Marsch-Barner, Kallmeyer, Umwandlungsgesetz, 2nd ed., § 16 annot. 41; Bork, Lutter, Umwandlungsgesetz, 2nd ed., § 16 annot. 19; Bermel, Goutier/Knopf/Tulloch, Kommentar zum Umwandlungsrecht, § 16 annot. 38.

[129] Marsch-Barner, Kallmeyer, Umwandlungsgesetz, 2nd ed., § 16 annot. 43; Bork Lutter, Umwandlungsgesetz, 2nd ed., § 16 annot. 20 et seq.; Bermel, Goutier/Knopf/Tulloch, Kommentar zum Umwandlungsrecht, § 16 annot. 42 et seq.

a) Reorganization Act and Cross-Border Corporate Mergers

The Reorganization Act is applicable only to legal entities having their registered offices in Germany. It does not apply to cross-border transactions. The prevailing opinion is that the German legislature specifically intended to exclude cross-border mergers from the application of the Reorganization Act. Under applicable conflict of law rules, the German Reorganization Act is not applicable to companies with their registered seat abroad.[130] Therefore, a merger of a German company with a foreign company is legally inadmissible, unless the registered seat of the foreign entity is moved to Germany prior to the merger.[131]

b) Principles for Cross-Border Mergers

As a cross-border merger as such is not possible under the Reorganization Act, other solutions are required so that the businesses of different legal entities can be brought together in one cross-border enterprise. Two structures are now described. Such structures must, however, be adjusted in each particular case.

(1) Share exchange

One possibility is a share exchange, by which businesses can be brought together though not directly in one legal entity, at least in one group. The legal entity which absorbs the combined business acts as the dominant company in which all shareholders are brought together. This can be achieved by a capital increase in the future dominant company, and the issue of the new shares to the shareholders in the transferring entity in exchange for their shares. Such exchange offer should be subject to a certain level of acceptance (the majority of shares), so that it is assured that the dominant company does not find itself in a minority position in the transferring company.[132] This deal structure is basically a regular public tender offer of the dominant company if the target is publicly quoted. Should the target have its registered seat in Germany, the German Takeover Act is applicable. If the dominant company is a German corporation then the tender offer rules of the country in which the target has its registered seat apply.

---

[130] Bermel, Goutier/Knopf/Tulloch, Kommentar zum Umwandlungsrecht, § 1 annot. 6, Einführung annot. 46; Lutter, Umwandlungsgesetz, 2nd ed., § 1 annot. 6; Schwarz, Widmann/Mayer, Umwandlungsgesetz, 61st supplementary delivery, § 1 annot. 29; Dehmer, UmwR/UmwStR, § 1 annot. 3.

[131] This legal situation is considered to be in violation of European law (freedom of establishment, Art. 43, 48 EEC), see Lutter, Umwandlungsgesetz, 2nd ed., § 1 annot. 9 et seq.

[132] See Stengel, Weber/Volhard, Arbeitshandbuch für Unternehmensübernahmen, § 17 annot. 357 et seq., noting the example of Hoechst/Rhone Poulenc, 1999.

(2) The participating entities come together in a newly formed stock corporation

It is also possible to combine the businesses of the participating entities in a newly formed stock corporation under German law ("NewCo"). NewCo will make public takeover bids to both participating companies, i.e. under the German Takeover Act, to the shareholders of the German company, and to the shareholders of the foreign company under the tender offer rules applicable in the relevant country. As consideration, NewCo will issue shares to the shareholders of the two companies by means of a capital increase (share exchange plan). A risk of an action to set aside the resolution on this capital increase[133] does not usually exist, because the shares in NewCo are, at the time when the share exchange plan is resolved, held by only one shareholder (for example, a bank as trustee for one of the entities participating in the "merger"). When the share exchange plan is carried out and the shareholders of the two companies become shareholders of NewCo, the deadline for an action to set aside (one month) will usually have expired.

This form of "merger" has the effect that both entities become subsidiaries of the new entity provided that a sufficient exchange threshold is achieved. A weakness of this construction is that minorities possibly remain in each of the future subsidiaries (because not all shareholders accept the public exchange offer).[134] In this respect, it is important if, and in which circumstances, the possibility of a squeeze-out procedure exists in the relevant jurisdiction (for Germany see in detail Ch. 6). In addition, the synergy effects may not be as fully achieved as in the case of a full merger into one legal entity, because the subsidiaries continue to exist.

Case: Fresenius Medical Care AG/Grace & Co.:

A variation of this deal structure was chosen in the cross-border transaction of the dialysis business of Fresenius with the U.S. American Grace & Co. The U.S. American target was merged with a foreign subsidiary of the German Fresenius Medical Care AG (FMC) under U.S. law. The subsidiary was held by a bank as trustee for FMC. The trustee transferred the new shares in the foreign subsidiary created by the merger to FMC as a contribution in kind. In exchange, FMC issued new shares which were converted into American depository shares, and issued by the bank to the former shareholders of the target. This model was later adopted in the Daimler/Chrysler merger 1998.

7. Final Note

A merger under the Reorganization Act offers the possibility of integrating all shareholders in one company as long as only German entities are involved. However, such a merger is not suitable where, as part of a takeover,

---

[133] § 255 para. 2 Stock Corporation Act.
[134] *See* Decher, Festschrift für Lutter, p. 1209, 1215.

it is intended that the portion of minority shareholders be reduced or excluded since the Reorganization Act provides for a cash offer only in certain circumstances. A voluntary cash offer under the Takeover Act would have to be added as a second step. Furthermore, the valuation procedure under the Reorganization Act is more complex than under the Takeover Act. Nevertheless, the Reorganization Act will retain its importance for national mergers and takeovers. But using tender offers under the Takeover Act in combination with the established methods of the Reorganization Act will contribute more effectiveness to mergers under German Law.

Chapter 6. Squeeze-Out

1. Introduction

The legislation regulating public offers also introduced into German corporate law a further significant instrument which shall, according to the legislative history, strengthen Germany's position as a leading industrial and financial location internationally: the so-called squeeze-out procedure,[1] which enables a majority shareholder to exclude minority shareholders from a stock corporation by payment of a cash compensation. The majority shareholder must hold at least 95% of the shares in the targeted corporation or partnership limited by shares.[2] The squeeze-out procedure is applicable irrespective of whether or not the shares of a corporation are listed on the stock exchange and irrespective of the manner in which the majority shareholder acquired its interest; it is not required that the majority shareholding was acquired by way of a takeover offer.

2. Previous Legal Situation

Until the enactment of the squeeze-out procedure as of January 1, 2002, German corporate law did not provide for such a formal procedure to exclude minority shareholders from companies. This led to attempts by major shareholders to exclude minority shareholders by other means. It is true that a majority shareholder controls the shareholders' meeting; however, implementation of shareholders' resolutions was often blocked for years on end by lawsuits instituted by minority shareholders challenging the resolutions, since such lawsuits may have the effect of suspending the relevant resolutions.[3] Often those actions were brought for their tremendous potential for disruption, for the sole purpose of subsequently "selling off" one's right to sue. Also stock corporations in which the minority shareholders hold only a small percentage of the share capital are nevertheless subject to the formal requirements of German stock corporation law, requiring them to call unrea-

---

[1] §§ 327a–327f of the Stock Corporation Act.

[2] The partnership limited by shares is a hybrid form, a combination of a limited partnership and a stock corporation. It has general partners, who are personally responsible for all the liabilities of the partnership limited by shares; in this respect it resembles a limited partnership. These partners are responsible for the management of the company. On the other hand, those of its members who are not liable partners, are shareholders and in this respect this legal form resembles a stock corporation. Despite the personal responsibility of the general partners, the partnership limited by shares is a legal entity with its own legal personality.

[3] E.g., an action to set aside a merger resolution has suspensory effect unless the court issues a preliminary order, § 16 Reorganization Act.

sonably expensive public annual shareholders' meetings and cultivate extensive investor relations.

In order to exclude or minimize as far as possible the potentially disruptive effect of minority shareholders, the measures available under stock corporation law as it was previously in force but, which, however, did not achieve the objective of excluding minority shareholders from the corporation either fully or satisfactorily from the viewpoint of the majority shareholder,[4] were often implemented. These measures were the so-called integration,[5] the "squeeze-out asset deal," delistings, and "control and profit transfer agreements."

a) Integration

In the case of an integration, following registration of a corresponding shareholders' resolution in the commercial register, all shares held by the minority shareholders are automatically transferred to the majority shareholder. This is possible where the majority shareholder holds at least 95% of the shares in the stock corporation to be integrated. The integrated corporation therefore becomes wholly-owned by the majority shareholder and is integrated into its business (the "principal company") to the extent that a particularly close relationship between the companies is created. In particular, the principal company may give binding instructions to the board of the integrated company. Generally, the minority shareholders receive shares in the majority shareholder (share exchange), or – in special cases – cash compensation in exchange for the loss of their shares in the integrated company. Integration, therefore, necessarily results in the minority shareholders' withdrawal from the integrated corporation; however, they may become shareholders in the principal company – and hence would continue to exist as a potential "disruptive factor." Moreover, the principal company is liable for all liabilities of the integrated corporation, i. e. the corporate veil between the principal company and the integrated company is removed. Furthermore, an integration requires the majority shareholder to be a stock corporation with registered office in Germany. Hence, in many cases an integration will not fully correspond to the intentions of the majority shareholder.

b) Squeeze-Out Asset Deal

In the case of a so-called "squeeze-out asset deal," the entire assets of the targeted corporation are transferred to another company, in which the majority shareholder holds all shares, by way of an asset deal; the targeted corporation is subsequently dissolved by liquidation resolution initiated by the majority shareholder.

---

[4] Cancellation of shares in accordance with §§ 237 et seq. German Stock Corporation Act as well as forfeiture of shares in accordance with § 64 of the same Act were not sufficient to achieve this objective. These "instruments" are not capable of directly excluding a shareholder from a corporation.

[5] § 319 et seq. Stock Corporation Act.

The minority shareholders lose their shares upon dissolution of the corporation and receive their portion of the liquidation proceeds.

According to the case law of the German Federal Constitutional Court („Bundesverfassungsgericht"), it is for the courts to ensure that the minority shareholders are fully compensated for the loss of their shares.[6] If the purchase price that is paid for the assets of the company falls short of the true value of the assets (supposedly on a going-concern assumption) then the minority shareholders may file an action to void the shareholders' resolution and block the asset deal.[7] Besides, due to the complexity of the necessary measures and the large tax burden resulting from the sale of hidden reserves, the squeeze-out asset deal has not proved to be a viable alternative in the majority of cases.

c) Delisting

A formal delisting of a publicly traded company places substantial pressure on minority shareholders to dispose of their shares to avoid holding illiquid assets. A formal delisting requires a shareholders' resolution with a 75% voting majority.[8] Extensive reporting duties on the grounds for the decision on the delisting apply.[9] Moreover, the minority shareholders must have the opportunity to dispose of their shares,[10] such as by an adequate takeover offer made by the majority shareholder who initiated the delisting. According to newly enacted regulations of the Frankfurt Stock Exchange, it is likewise sufficient if the delisting is effected after a grace period of no less than six months, so that the minority shareholders have ample time to sell their shares.[11] However, as there is no actual obligation on the minority shareholders to sell their shares, the goal of a complete freeze-out of the minority shareholders is not always achieved.

d) Control and Profit Transfer Agreements

The parent company could enter into a "control and profit transfer agreement." Under such agreement, which requires a 75% approval from the shareholders' meeting of the controlled entity, the management of the latter

---

[6] Federal Constitutional Court BVerfGE 14 p. 263 – „Feldmühle;" BVerfGE 100 p. 289, 303 et seq. – „DAT/Altana."

[7] Federal Constitutional Court, BVerfG DB 2000 p. 1905, 1907 – "Moto Meter AG."

[8] Appeal Court of Munich, OLG München ZIP 2001 p. 700, 703 – "Macrotron."

[9] Analogous application of § 186 para. 4 clause 2 Stock Corporation Act; however, once those reporting duties are duly complied with, a court will not scrutinize the delisting resolution in a substantive way.

[10] *See* § 43 para. 4 Stock Exchange Act which requires that the interests of the minority shareholders are taken into consideration.

[11] § 54a Stock Exchange Regulation („Börsenordnung"); it is questionable, however, whether such grace period really offers an adequate opportunity to dispose of the shares, as active trading might actually cease after the publication of the resolution on the delisting.

is subject to instructions given by the management of the parent company, and all profits and losses are directly transferred to the parent. Therefore, the controlled entity no longer distributes dividends to its shareholders. Thus, the parent company must compensate the minority shareholders of the controlled entity for the loss of future dividends;[12] moreover, the parent company must offer to acquire the shares of the minority shareholders for an adequate consideration, either in shares of the parent company, or in cash.[13] However, the minority shareholders are not obliged to sell their shares.

In the **Vodafone/Mannesmann case,** Vodafone held 98.62% of the shares in Mannesmann AG after the takeover offer. On June 11, 2001, Vodafone announced that Mannesmann AG would become subject to a control and profit transfer agreement with Vodafone.[14] Vodafone offered to buy the shares of the remaining Mannesmann minority shareholders for € 206.53 in cash.[15] This case, by the way, also demonstrates that those of the target's shareholders who reject a public offer may often count on receiving a higher consideration for their shares later on in the context of a control and profit transfer agreement, a delisting or integration. The Mannesmann shareholders who accepted the Vodafone bid in 2000 received for each share 58.9646 Vodafone shares. At the time when Vodafone announced the offer of € 206.53 in June 2001, the Vodafone shares traded around € 2.75, corresponding to € 162 per Mannesmann share based on the conversion ratio of 58.9646 Vodafone shares. Recently, Vodafone has again topped its offer to € 217.91 in cash per Mannesmann share. In the **INA Holding/FAG Kugelfischer case,** following the successful completion of the public bid at € 12 per FAG share, FAG's stock price rose to over €13 (and sometimes reached more than € 16); obviously the market expected that INA Holding would make another offer exceeding € 12 to the remaining minority shareholders in the context of a control and profit transfer agreement.

3. The New Squeeze-Out Provisions

a) Reasons for Introducing the Squeeze-Out

The frequent abuse of marginal minority interests held in stock corporations, with the aim of impeding the management and the implementation of structural measures in order to obtain financial concessions from the majority shareholder, the lack of legal instruments to prevent such conduct satisfactorily, as well as the considerable and costly formal effort even the smallest minority shareholdings entail in many cases, ultimately led the German

---

[12] § 304 Stock Corporation Act.

[13] § 305 para. 1 Stock Corporation Act; the kind of consideration (shares or cash) depends, inter alia, on whether the parent company is an independent or controlled entity, § 305 para. 2 Stock Corporation Act.

[14] Via Vodafone Deutschland GmbH, a German subsidiary of Vodafone Plc.

[15] Vodafone had to offer cash, as Vodafone Deutschland GmbH was a subsidiary of a foreign company, § 305 para. 2 no. 2, 3 Stock Corporation Act.

legislature to introduce the possibility of a squeeze-out into German stock corporation law – also as a reaction to pressure exerted by German industry. Moreover, for reasons of international competitiveness, the objective was to introduce an instrument into German stock corporation law which had long since been employed in numerous other countries.

b) Conditions and Procedure

Under the new regulations, the following stages of procedure and conditions apply to the exclusion of minority shareholders from a stock corporation or a partnership limited by shares:

- The majority shareholder must hold at least 95% of the issued share capital of the relevant company.
- A resolution to effect the squeeze-out must be passed by the shareholders' meeting.
- The squeeze-out resolution must be registered in the commercial register, which results in the automatic transfer of all shares held by the minority shareholders to the majority shareholder.
- Payment of an adequate cash compensation by the majority shareholder to the minority shareholders.

(1) Shareholding of at least 95%

The majority shareholder must hold at least 95% of the issued share capital of the target.[16] A shareholder who satisfies this criterion is referred to in the legislation as the "principal shareholder."[17] Treasury shares held by the target and shares held by another party on behalf of the target (e.g. within the context of a trust) are to be deducted from the issued share capital when calculating the proportion.[18] For example, where a stock corporation has an issued share capital of € 100,000 of which company shares of € 10,000 are held by the corporation, then the majority interest will be calculated on the basis of the issued share capital being € 90,000.

(a) Attribution of indirectly held shares

However, the principal shareholder need not hold the 95% shareholding directly, nor even a small portion thereof. A party will also be deemed a

---

[16] According to the Explanatory Memorandum of the Federal Government on the Takeover Act (BT-Drucks. 14/7034 of October 5, 2001, p. 72), the 95% threshold is based on the fact that, in German stock corporation law, 5% of the capital stock is recognized as being sufficient to establish a minority (cf. e.g. §§ 122 para. 2; 258 para. 2; 260 para. 2; 265, para. 3 Stock Corporation Act). The 95% threshold applicable in case of integration was also taken as an example by the legislature, *see* supra Ch. 6 no. 2. a. (§ 320 para. 1 Stock Corporation Act). From the viewpoint of legal policy, the squeeze-out was to enable a remaining minority to be excluded. The cases discussed during the legislative procedure as requiring regulation in practice involved minority shareholdings of up to 5%.
[17] § 327a Stock Corporation Act.
[18] §§ 327a para. 2, 16 para. 2 clause 2, and para. 3 Stock Corporation Act.

principal shareholder if 95% of the shares can be attributed to it as being *indirectly* held. The following categories of shares, inter alia, will be attributed to the principal shareholder:[19]

(i) shares which belong to an enterprise controlled by the principal shareholder;
(ii) shares which are held by another party on behalf of the principal shareholder, or on behalf of an entity controlled by that shareholder;
(iii) if the principal shareholder is a sole proprietor, the shares constituting assets of his business and the shares constituting the shareholder's private property are added.

(b) Pooling of shares in a partnership

Unless an attribution of indirectly held shares applies, the 95% minimum shareholding must be owned by one single shareholder. A resolution passed with a 95% voting majority by several shareholders is not sufficient. It is not clarified as yet whether several shareholders may "pool" their shareholdings in a partnership in order to reach the 95% threshold.

Imagine a stock corporation the shares of which are distributed among only a few shareholders, say three shareholders with a 33% stake each and one shareholder with a 1% interest. The three large shareholders who together hold 99% are looking for a way to get rid of the awkward 1% shareholder. They decide to join together in a partnership and to transfer all their shares to that partnership so that the latter becomes a majority shareholder owning more than 95% of the share capital and, as the right to invoke a squeeze-out procedure does not depend on the legal form of the majority shareholder, start the squeeze-out procedure.

In general, the exclusion of minority shareholders under the squeeze-out regulations does not need any material justification; it falls within the unfettered discretion of the 95% majority shareholder. Nevertheless, the possibility to exclude shareholders is a narrow exception in German corporate law. As a rule, under German corporate law, a shareholder can only be excluded if good cause exists, since the exclusion of a shareholder is an interference with its constitutional property rights. The German legislature justifies the interference arising from a squeeze-out with the argument that marginal shareholdings in most cases only serve as private wealth[20] and do not have any strategic or economic value, as the owner of a shareholding of less than five percent cannot generally influence the business strategy of a corporation. This may generally be true regarding publicly listed companies, but may be substantially different in a small, non-listed corporation: the ar-

---

[19] §§ 327a para. 2, 16 para. 4 Stock Corporation Act. Through this attribution the legislature sought to avoid the complicated and economically meaningless transfer of shares so as to meet the formal requirements for the squeeze-out; see Explanatory Memorandum of the Federal Government on the Takeover Act, BT-Drucks. 14/7034 of October 5, 2001, p. 72.

[20] Explanatory Memorandum of the Federal Government on the Takeover Act, BT-Drucks. 14/7034 of October 5, 2001, p. 32: Art. 14 of the German Constitution protects the property rights, not the concerns in all private wealth.

guments of a minority shareholder in the case of a small corporation may demand attention and, therefore, even the owner of a one-percent shareholding may be able to influence the business strategy of the company to some extent, in particular if it has certain minority rights in the Articles of Association[21] or under a shareholders' agreement.[22]

Given this situation, the squeeze-out provisions should not be interpreted too broadly. One should think of making a distinction: if the duration of the partnership is intended to be indefinite, the partnership shall have a right to initiate a squeeze-out resolution.[23] The decision to pool shareholdings in a partnership is a business decision to be respected. The need for flexible management decisions justifies the squeeze-out procedure and the exclusion of shareholders.[24]

Such a situation does not, however, exist, if the partnership is formed only as a temporary shareholder for a limited period of time, it being obvious that the *only* purpose of the formation of the new shareholder is the exclusion of other shareholders.[25] In such instance, the squeeze-out regulations would be abused for a purpose not intended by the legislature.

Coming back to our case: if the three major shareholders contribute their shares to a long-term partnership in order to jointly exercise their influence on the corporation, the partnership may very well initiate a squeeze-out of the 1% shareholder. On the other hand, if the three shareholders act in concert only for the one purpose of excluding the 1% minority shareholder then the squeeze-out resolution would be illegal and the minority shareholder could successfully file an action to set the resolution aside.[26]

(2) Determination of the cash compensation and audit

A squeeze-out of minority shareholders is effected against payment of cash compensation which must be paid by the principal shareholder. The amount of cash compensation is determined by the principal shareholder.[27] It must be based on a valuation of the enterprise.

It may appear somewhat disconcerting at first glance that the amount of compensation is determined by the majority shareholder; however, this is in line with the rules on the payment of consideration to minority shareholders under German corporation law in other instances: in the context of control

---

[21] Such as the right to appoint up to one third of the members of the supervisory board, § 101 para. 2 Stock Corporation Act.

[22] If a shareholders' agreement between the minority and majority shareholders exists, the right of the majority shareholder might be excluded anyway; even if not expressly stated such shareholders' agreement may contain an implied waiver of the right to initiate a squeeze-out.

[23] Bolte, DB 2001 p. 2587, 2589.

[24] Explanatory Memorandum of the Federal Government on the Takeover Act, BT-Drucks. 14/7034 of October 5, 2001, p. 32.

[25] Grunewald, ZIP 2002 p. 18, 22.

[26] Baums, WM 2001 p. 1843, 1846; Baums is, however, of the opinion that the resolution is not merely voidable, but null and void in itself.

[27] § 327 b Stock Corporation Act (subject to judicial review, *see* Ch. 6 no. 4. and 5. below).

and profit transfer agreements[28] and integrations (see Ch. 6 no. 2. a. and d. above), the amount of cash compensation is, in the first step, determined unilaterally by the controlling enterprise, while the minority shareholders may file an action to adjust inadequate compensation amounts.

The management board of the corporation must provide the principal shareholder with all the documents and related information required for an appropriate business valuation.

The adequacy of the cash compensation determined and the reasons for such adequacy along with the satisfaction of the other requirements of the proposed squeeze-out must be explained by the principal shareholder in a written report to the shareholders' meeting.[29] This report must be verified by one or more auditors who must provide a written audit report to the shareholders' meeting.[30] The auditors are appointed by the competent court at the request of the principal shareholder. The audit report must state:

- the valuation methods according to which the compensation was determined;
- the reasons why the methods applied are appropriate; and
- the amount of the compensation which would result in each case from the application of different valuation methods, insofar as more than one method was applied. It is also important to state the weighting applied in determining the compensation, according to the different valuation methods.

(3) Passing a resolution on the squeeze-out at the shareholders' meeting

The squeeze-out is effected by a shareholders' resolution on the withdrawal of the minority shareholders (squeeze-out resolution).[31] The resolution must be passed with a simple majority of the issued share capital represented at the meeting. In order to ensure that comprehensive information is provided to the minority shareholders, certain documents are to be displayed in the business premises of the corporation for inspection by the shareholders from the date on which the shareholders' meeting is called. These include, in particular, the report by the principal shareholder,[32] and the auditor's report on the audit of the cash compensation. Each minority shareholder may review these reports and obtain copies thereof free of charge in order to enable it to understand that the essential condition for the squeeze-out regarding the 95% shareholding has been satisfied, and to understand the basis of the calculation of the cash compensation. These documents must also be available at the shareholders' meeting.

During the shareholders' meeting, the management board may allow the principal shareholder to explain the draft squeeze-out resolution and the calculation of the cash compensation.[33]

---

[28] Cf. § 305 para. 1 Stock Corporation Act.
[29] § 327c para. 2 clause 1 Stock Corporation Act.
[30] § 327c para. 2 clause 2 to 5 Stock Corporation Act.
[31] § 327a Stock Corporation Act.
[32] § 327c para. 2 clause 1 Stock Corporation Act, *see* Ch. 4 no. 3. b. (2) above.
[33] § 327d clause 2 Stock Corporation Act.

(4) Registration of the squeeze-out resolution in the commercial register; transfer of the shares

Upon the registration of the squeeze-out resolution in the commercial register all shares held by the minority shareholders are automatically transferred by operation of law to the principal shareholder.[34] Simultaneously with the transfer of the shares, the minority shareholder's right to payment of the cash compensation arises vis-à-vis the principal shareholder. This right is temporarily documented by the share certificates, if such certificates have been issued.[35] As regards the principal shareholder's ability to make the compensation payment, the minority shareholders must be protected by a **guarantee** issued by a German bank. The principal shareholder is responsible for obtaining this guarantee, by which the bank guarantees the prompt performance of the principal shareholder's payment obligations,[36] before the shareholders' meeting is called. The guarantee must cover only the amount that is determined by the majority shareholder. It is not required that the guarantee encompasses any adjustments ordered by a court in the event that a minority shareholder challenges the amount of the compensation.[37] As of the date on which the registration of the resolution in the commercial register is confirmed, the compensation bears interest at a rate of 2% p. a. above the basic interest rate.[38]

A condition for registration of the resolution[39] is the issuance of a so-called **negative declaration** by the management board of the corporation.[40] Such negative declaration must state that no action has been brought in due time[41] challenging the validity of the resolution, or that such an action has been dismissed with final effect or withdrawn. In the absence of a negative declaration, a bar to registration of the resolution exists so that the commercial register is not permitted to register the resolution. The competent court may, however, in a summary proceeding remove the bar to registration if the corporation applies to the court accordingly.[42] The court may remove the bar in this clearance procedure only if the pending action filed by a minority shareholder is frivolous or clearly has no prospects of success, or where the interest of the corporation in the immediate effect of the squeeze-out has precedence over the plaintiff shareholder's interest in obtaining protection. Within the context of the balancing of interests to be undertaken by the court in the latter case, the fact that the principal shareholder is pursuing the squeeze-out within the framework of comprehensive restructuring measures

---

[34] § 327e para. 3 clause 1 Stock Corporation Act.
[35] § 327e para. 3 clause 2 Stock Corporation Act.
[36] § 327b para. 3 Stock Corporation Act.
[37] Geibel/Süßmann/Grzimek, WpÜG, Art. 7 § 327b AktG annot. 42; Meilicke, DB 2001 p. 2387, 2389; Krieger, BB 2002 p. 53, 58; Vetter, AG 2002 p. 176, 189.
[38] § 247 Civil Code.
[39] § 327e para. 1 Stock Corporation Act.
[40] §§ 327e para. 2, 319 para. 5 Stock Corporation Act.
[41] Within one month after the squeeze-out resolution, § 246 para. 1 Stock Corporation Act.
[42] §§ 327e para. 2, 319 para. 6 Stock Corporation Act.

in order to achieve synergies or to ensure the financial survival of the corporation, is of particular relevance.[43]

(5) Holders of options and convertible bonds

The Takeover Act does not clearly specify the legal consequences for holders of options and convertible bonds in the event of a squeeze-out.

Some legal scholars are of the opinion that option and conversion rights survive a squeeze-out, i. e. such right holders might later become shareholders of the company upon exercise of their rights.[44] Should those rights amount to less than 5% after the squeeze-out then another squeeze-out might be initiated. However, a second squeeze-out would not be possible if conversion rights exceeding 5% of the capital are exercised after the first squeeze-out.

We do not follow this opinion. In our view, any option and conversion rights are extinguished by a squeeze-out. As the minority shareholders lose their rights in the event of a squeeze-out, the same must apply to holders of option and conversion rights which are not yet represented by actual shareholdings.[45] This will apply even if the outstanding option and conversion rights would dilute the majority shareholding below the 95% threshold because the Act clearly requires a 95% majority at the time when the squeeze-out resolution is passed.

However, the statutory right to adequate compensation applying to the minority shareholdings of course applies also to the outstanding option and conversion rights, i. e. the rights holders are entitled to the compensation minus the relevant exercise price and discounted to present value if the rights may only be exercised at some point in the future.

4. Calculation of the Cash Compensation

The focal aspect of the squeeze-out procedure is the calculation of the cash compensation by the principal shareholder. As mentioned above, the amount of the cash compensation must be adequate and must take into account the situation of the corporation on the date on which the shareholders' resolution on the squeeze-out is passed.[46] Therefore, the valuation of the enterprise and the choice of objective valuation methods are of crucial im-

---

[43] *See* Appeal Court of Düsseldorf, OLG Düsseldorf, ZIP 1999 p. 793, 798; Lutter/Bork, 2nd ed., § 16 UmwG annot. 21.

[44] Baums, WM 2001 p. 1843, 1848 et seq.

[45] Geibel/Süßmann/Grzimek, WpÜG Art. 7 § 327e annot. 30; Ehricke/Roth, DStR 2001 p. 1120, 1122; regarding the similar problem in cases of integration: Federal Supreme Court, BGH ZIP 1998 p. 560, 561 – „Siemens – Nixdorf."

[46] § 327b para. 1 Stock Corporation Act; the wording corresponds to the statutory provisions regulating the cash compensation within the context of an integration, § 320b Stock Corporation Act, and within the context of control and profit transfer agreements, § 305 of the same Act. Therefore, the case law handed down in those respects may be referred to.

portance. In practice, the valuation method predominantly used is the capitalized earnings method or discounted cashflow method (DCF).

The loss of the shares interferes with the shareholder's status as a (partial) owner of the corporation which is protected under Art. 14 of the Federal Constitution. Within the context of an integration,[47] the German Federal Constitutional Court has held regarding this issue that:

- minority shareholders are to receive full compensation in this respect – hence, adequate cash compensation must reflect the full value of the shares – and
- the amount of the cash compensation must not be lower than the current market value of the shares, hence the compensation in relation to shares quoted on the stock exchange may not be lower than the stock exchange price ("extrinsic value").[48]

Following these principles, the Federal Supreme Court has held – again within the context of an integration – that the average stock exchange price for the last three months prior to the relevant date is decisive, so that unusual, unconsolidated fluctuations and leaps are not taken into account.[49] However, should the stock exchange price remain lower than the value of the enterprise as calculated according to the capitalized income method (constituting the "intrinsic value"), the compensation payment will be determined by this higher intrinsic value.[50] In general, the stock exchange quote (extrinsic value) for shares actively traded in efficient markets should be a powerful factor for the determination of the "true value" of the shares, and reference to a higher intrinsic value should be taken only in exceptional circumstances. However, in the case of a squeeze-out with a majority shareholder owning at least 95% of the shares, active trading may not exist with only a maximum of 5% of free floating shares on the market; therefore, in a squeeze-out context, the intrinsic value based on a normal business valuation is of particular importance,[51] unless the squeeze-out immediately follows a public tender offer in which case the average stock price prior to the takeover might serve as a basis for the extrinsic value.[52]

---

[47] § 320b para. 2 Stock Corporation Act.
[48] Federal Constitutional Court, BVerfGE 100, p. 289, 303 et seq. – „DAT/Altana."
[49] Federal Supreme Court, BGH AG 2001 p. 417, 419 – „DAT/Altana IV."
[50] Federal Supreme Court, BGH AG 2001 p. 417, 418–419 – „DAT/Altana IV."
[51] Vetter, AG 2002 p. 176, 188.
[52] Note that under the current version of the squeeze-out regulations, the price offered in a public bid prior to the squeeze-out is not *necessarily* adequate as compensation in the squeeze-out procedure!

5. Legal Protection for Minority Shareholders

A minority shareholder seeking legal protection against a squeeze-out has recourse to two different procedures:

a) Action to Set Aside

The minority shareholders may challenge the squeeze-out resolution passed by the shareholders' meeting by an action to set it aside on the basis of non-compliance with formal or substantive requirements.

The minority shareholders may claim, for example, that the majority shareholder did not have the required majority of 95% or that rights of the minority shareholders to information were violated (see Ch. 6 no. 3. b. (3) above).

b) Compensation Assessment Proceeding

An action to set aside the squeeze-out resolution cannot be based on the claim that the cash compensation determined by the principal shareholder is inadequate.[53] Rather, the adequacy of the cash compensation may only be reviewed within the context of special proceedings, the so-called Compensation Assessment Proceeding *(Spruchstellenverfahren)*,[54] which may be initiated by any former minority shareholder within two months after notification of the registration of the squeeze-out resolution in the commercial register.[55] The court will determine an adequate cash compensation.

The decisive difference between an action to set aside and the compensation assessment proceeding is that the latter does not have the effect of suspending the squeeze-out resolution. While the management board may not issue the "negative declaration" necessary for the entry in the commercial register in the case of a pending action to set aside (see Ch. 6 no. 3. b. (4) above), a pending compensation assessment procedure does not prevent the entry in the commercial register and the effectiveness of the squeeze-out.

---

[53] According to § 327f para. 1 clause 3 Stock Corporation Act, in the case of a procedurally defective compensation offer or if no offer at all is made, the minority shareholders can either (i) take an action to set aside the squezze-out resolution, or (ii) institute the compensation assement proceeding to have adequate compensation fixed. *See* Hüffer, 5th ed., § 327f AktG annot. 4.

[54] In a court proceeding which is specifically provided for in the Reorganization Act, the shareholders may claim certain compensation. This refers, in particular, to the conversion ratio and certain compensation claims of dissenting shareholders in the case of mergers. This procedure implies a certain interest in excluding disruptive law suits against the validity of the merger by shareholders who are not adequately compensated or who have not been compensated. The compensation assessment proceeding cannot prevent or delay a merger. The shareholder can achieve only an improvement in the conversion ratio or in the level of cash compensation. *See* in detail Ch. 5 no. 5. h.

[55] § 327f para. 2 Stock Corporation Act.

Therefore, it is essential to determine which causes of action fall in the two different categories. According to a variety of court precedents, not only the inadequacy of the compensation as such is the subject matter of the compensation assessment proceedings; the same applies to violations of information and reporting duties in connection with the valuation of the shares.[56] Accordingly, it is not possible to base an action to set aside the squeeze-out resolution on informational deficits as regards the amount of the compensation payment or the valuation of the enterprise.[57] Should a minority shareholder nevertheless file an action to set aside based on such inadmissible causes of action in order to benefit from the suspensory effect of the action and place a bar on the registration of the squeeze-out resolution, then the competent court may nevertheless clear the registration in a summary proceeding for an obvious lack of merit of the action to set aside.[58]

Therefore, an action to set aside may be based on a very limited number of causes of action, in particular on formal grounds only, such as the improper calling of the shareholders' meeting or errors in the voting procedure. Another basis for an action to set aside may be the allegation that the majority shareholder did not own the required 95% shareholding, e. g. because:

- shares indirectly held were wrongfully attributed to the majority shareholder (see Ch. 6 no. 3. b. (1) (a) above);
- the 95% shareholding was based on a wrongful pooling of several shareholders' interests in bad faith (see Ch. 6 no. 3. b. (1) (b) above).

In the vast majority of cases, however, the minority shareholder will be restricted to seeking legal protection within the context of the compensation assessment proceeding. The decisive advantage of this for the principal shareholder is that, contrary to an action challenging a resolution, the proceedings do not have suspensive effect or block the squeeze-out procedure. However, these proceedings may very well take over ten years to complete.

6. Comparison with other Countries

The motivation for drafting legal provisions enabling the squeeze-out in Germany was not least the adjustment to the international situation, since corresponding provisions are anchored in the laws of numerous countries. Hence, as pointed out above, the introduction of the squeeze-out is also viewed as an important contribution towards strengthening Germany's posi-

---

[56] Federal Supreme Court, BGH ZIP 2001 p. 199; ZIP 2001 p. 412.

[57] Vetter, DB 2001 p. 743, 746; Habersack, ZIP 2001 p. 1230, 1237.

[58] The reference to the compensation assessment proceeding in § 327f para. 1 Stock Corporation Act corresponds to the statutory provision for the review of cash compensation within the context of integrations, within the context of control and profit transfer agreements and within the context of methods of reorganization provided for by the Reorganization Act (*„Umwandlungsgesetz"*). The principles developed in case law with respect to these provisions are, therefore, also applicable to the squeeze-out procedure.

tion as an industrial center and financial location. In view of their international orientation, it therefore seems appropriate to compare the provisions with those in force in other countries.

a) Squeeze-out Procedure not Restricted to Corporations Quoted on the Stock Exchange

Apart from the varying majorities of shareholding required to initiate the squeeze-out procedure – 90% in the United Kingdom and Austria, 98% in Italy and Switzerland, and 95% in both France and the Netherlands – it becomes apparent within an international comparison that German law, contrary, for example, to French law, does not restrict the squeeze-out of minority shareholders to corporations which are quoted on the stock exchange; rather, minority shareholders may also be squeezed out of privately held stock corporations.

This fact is of particular significance for the limited liability company:[59] the Act on Limited Liability Companies (*„GmbH-Gesetz"*) does not provide for a squeeze-out. However, it is now possible to implement a "cold" squeeze-out in a limited liability company and thus rid oneself of undesired minority shareholders: by way of a transformation[60] a limited liability company can be transformed into a (privately held) stock corporation, in which a squeeze-out is subsequently conducted.

b) No Prior Takeover Bid Required; No Right of Withdrawal for Minority Shareholders

A further difference to the provisions applicable in other countries – for example in the United Kingdom – is that a squeeze-out is possible without a prior takeover bid or mandatory offer by a majority shareholder being required.

On the other hand, the minority shareholders do not have a "right" of withdrawal corresponding to the majority shareholder's right to exclude them. Such a corresponding right is provided for in numerous countries: in the United Kingdom or in France, for example, the squeeze-out provisions are flanked by a right conferred on the minority vis-à-vis the majority shareholder to sell its shares to the majority shareholder.[61]

7. Facilitated Delisting due to a Squeeze-Out

Apart from its main objective, namely the exclusion of minority shareholders, a squeeze-out may also be relevant with regard to the delisting of a stock corporation, i. e. a withdrawal from the stock exchange. Both the so-

---

[59] This form of corporation is most commonly used for privately held companies.
[60] § 190 et seq. Reorganization Act.
[61] United Kingdom: Section 430 A Companies Act 1985; France: Art. 5–6–1 règlement gènèral CMF, amended by arrêté of Nov. 5, 1998.

called formal delisting[62] and the various forms of the so-called "cold delisting" pursuant to the Reorganization Act, involve a fairly complicated and lengthy procedure which can be obstructed by court proceedings. In contrast, where a squeeze-out is carried out effectively, proper trading on the stock exchange is no longer possible since all shares are held by one single shareholder. The stock exchange will then automatically discontinue trading in the shares. Furthermore, should the stock exchange require, in addition to discontinuing trading, a formal delisting procedure,[63] then this is a mere formality.[64] Therefore, if the conditions for a squeeze-out exist, using the squeeze-out procedure can considerably facilitate a delisting.

8. Conclusion

The squeeze-out provisions introduced into the Stock Corporation Act in connection with the legislation on public bids, offers a majority shareholder the possibility to acquire the remaining shares of the stock corporation and thus to efficiently implement the restructuring measures it considers economically rational, without any delay being caused by minority shareholders. The problem of "rogue shareholders" is effectively prevented by a squeeze-out, the entrepreneurial flexibility available to the majority shareholder is strengthened, and a better control of the capital employed is facilitated. Expensive public shareholders' meetings for the benefit of a small number of minority shareholders can be avoided in future in this way. However, it is important to note that the squeeze-out provisions interfere considerably with the rights of the minority shareholders. The scope of the German provisions exceed the provisions applicable in the majority of other countries; there are similarly far-reaching provisions only in the Netherlands. One must assume that the strong position occupied by the majority shareholder, when compared internationally, will, in accordance with the intentions of the legislature, ultimately increase the attractiveness of Germany as an industrial centre for (overseas) investors and also enhance Germany's international competitiveness as an industrial and financial location.

---

[62] § 43 para. 4 Stock Exchange Act.
[63] § 43 para. 4 Stock Exchange Act.
[64] Vetter DB 2001, p. 743, 745, proceeds on the assumption that the stock exchange listing will be lost automatically.

Chapter 7. Comparison with UK City Code on Takeovers and Mergers

The UK system is self-regulatory[1] rather than statutory as in Germany and the U. S., comparable with the previous German Takeover Code. This chapter provides a brief overview of the UK takeover regulatory system and highlights the differences between this and the law relating to takeovers in Germany.

1. Self-Regulation

At the heart of the takeover regulatory system in the UK is The City Code on Takeovers and Mergers ("City Code") which is issued and administered by the Panel on Takeovers and Mergers ("Panel").[2] The City Code does not and does not seek to have the force of law but rather is a non-statutory, self-regulatory code of behavior developed and largely observed by the UK securities markets. It is designed principally to ensure fair and equal treatment of all the target's shareholders and it regulates the conduct, structure and timetable of UK takeovers. Only a few provisions relating to takeovers are regulated by statute.[3] The Panel, too, is a non-statutory, self-regulatory body comprised of a number of people appointed by the Governor of the Bank of England and representatives of professional organisations and financial institutions involved in the UK securities markets.[4] The Panel meets rarely, the day-to-day administration of the City Code being undertaken by the Panel Executive of which the Director General is in charge and the members

---

[1] The EU directive on takeovers (Thirteenth Company Law Directive), which was originally modelled on the UK system, has been under consideration since 1989. If changes are made to the directive in order to take into account reservations and compromises which are being sought by some member states, the directive will need to be considered for a second time by the European Parliament, before being considered again by the Council in light of any amendments of the European Parliament. If the directive is adopted and provides, as in the current draft, for a supervisory authority to "have all the powers necessary for the exercise of [its] functions," then self-regulation will give way to statutory control. *See* in more detail Ch. 2 no. 3.

[2] The City Code, together with The Rules Governing Substantial Issues of Shares ("SARs") forms the so-called "Blue Book." The Listing Rules, which are issued by the London Stock Exchange and also referred to as the "Yellow Book" contain further self-regulatory provisions relating to takeover offers.

[3] For example, provisions relating to disclosure obligations and mandatory offers are contained in the Companies Act 1985, as amended by the Financial Services Act 1986. Insider dealing legislation is contained in the Criminal Justice Act 1993. Antitrust legislation may also apply.

[4] The membership of the Panel is therefore similar to that of the German Takeover Committee.

of which are City practitioners. The Panel has many years of experience with takeovers in the UK.[5]

The City Code is comprised of first, some general principles and secondly, a series of rules. It is not written in technical language and the introduction to the City Code specifies that the underlying purpose and spirit, and not just the letter, of the general principles and the rules must be observed. This is surprising for those from a common law jurisdiction such as Germany, where the letter of the law is usually paramount. The City Code's strength lies in the freedom given to the Panel to interpret it flexibly to achieve a speedy and sensible outcome. As the spirit of the City Code must be observed, it will apply in areas or circumstances not expressly covered by any rule. The Panel can (and should) be consulted quickly on matters of interpretation of the City Code without the formality, cost and delay of a court hearing.[6] Where appropriate, the Panel will be prepared to modify or relax the effect of a rule. Finally, the City Code can be amended quickly in order to take into account new business practices or takeover situations. This ability to react quickly to fast-moving events and, by applying the spirit of the City Code, to treat each (often complex) case on its own merits with little fear that decisions taken by it in the heat of the bid will be overturned on appeal to the courts[7] is the great advantage of the self-regulatory system.

Although the City Code does not have the force of law, and indeed may be assumed at first glance to be for the purposes of guidance only, it is in practice mandatory to comply with its provisions. The Panel is able to impose stringent sanctions on those who do not do so.[8] Which sanctions are imposed depends on the seriousness and nature of the breach and include public or private censure, a reference to another regulatory authority which in its turn might hold disciplinary proceedings and withdraw a financial adviser's authority to carry on investment business (so-called "cold-shoulder" treatment) and a direction that remedial action be taken. Remedial action may take the form of fines. For example, in one extreme case in 1989 Guinness plc was required by the Panel to pay approximately GBP 85 million to former Distillers shareholders following a breach of one of the rules of the City Code during the battle for control of Distillers.

---

[5] The Panel was set up in 1968. The City Code was first published in March 1968.

[6] The Panel decides on the interpretation and application of the City Code for the particular circumstances and legal advice is therefore no substitute for consultation with the Panel.

[7] Appeals can be made to an Appeal Committee within the Panel. Decisions of the Panel are subject to judicial review by the courts. However, the principle that the court's role is not to reverse Panel decisions made during a takeover bid in order that judicial review proceedings are not used as a tactic (so-called "tactical litigation") to disrupt the bid was well-established by the Court of Appeal in *R v Panel on Takeovers and Mergers, ex parte Datafin plc [1987] 1 All ER 564*. To date the courts have not intervened in any Panel ruling.

[8] Further, the courts may refer to the standards outlined in the City Code to determine whether a financial adviser or director of a company is legally liable for acting in breach of its fiduciary duty of care.

2. Application of the City Code

The City Code is concerned with "takeover and merger transactions, however effected, of all relevant companies." These include offers for the whole of the share capital of a company, partial offers,[9] offers by a parent company for shares in its subsidiary and certain other transactions where control of a company is to be obtained or consolidated. As is the case under the German Takeover Act, the threshold at which control is obtained is when 30% of the voting rights are held.[10]

In determining whether or not the City Code applies, the nature of the company in respect of which an offer is made or control sought is decisive. **Relevant companies** are all listed and unlisted public companies considered by the Panel to be resident in the UK, the Channel Islands and the Isle of Man (but not open-ended investment companies). The Code also applies to certain private companies considered to be so resident which have at any time during the previous ten years had certain public features (e.g. their share capital has been listed on the London Stock Exchange or they have filed a prospectus for the issue of share capital with the registrar of companies). The Panel will usually consider a company to be resident in the UK, the Channel Islands or the Isle of Man only if it is incorporated and has its place of central management in these jurisdictions.

All those participating in a transaction to which the City Code applies must comply with it. This includes the directors of the offeror and the target and all professional advisers acting in connection with the transaction. Financial advisers, in particular, must not only observe the City Code themselves but also ensure "so far as they are reasonably able" that the offeror, the target and their respective directors do so as well.

As has already been discussed in relation to Germany, an offer may be subject to the regulations of an overseas jurisdiction in addition to the City Code, for example if the target has shareholders or is listed in an overseas jurisdiction or if the offeror wishes to offer its own shares in consideration for shares in the target. This problem arises frequently in the UK in relation to the U.S. where certain rules of the U.S. Securities Exchange Act 1934 conflict with those of the City Code, for example, the rules relating to the timetable of an offer. In such cases, a waiver of the requirements must be obtained from both regulatory authorities or the offer must be structured so as to circumvent the requirements. Standard City practice in these cases is

---

[9] Panel consent to any partial offer is required (Rule 36) and the Panel may impose stringent conditions. Partial offers occur rarely in the UK; generally a maximum of ten partial offers are made each year. This rule aims to avoid the undesirable effect of all shareholders not being treated equally. In Germany, partial offers are only admissible if the offeror will not reach the 30% control threshold, § 32 German Takeover Act.

[10] Control is defined as "a holding, or aggregate holding, of shares carrying 30% or more of the voting rights of a company, irrespective of whether the holding or holdings gives de facto control." Voting rights are those which are "currently exercisable at a general meeting." Note that the SARs (*see* footnote 2) apply where a person acquires an aggregate of between 15% and 30% of the voting rights of a company.

not to communicate a takeover offer to shareholders in the "forbidden territories" and, upon receiving acceptances of at least 90%, compulsorily acquiring the shares of the minority shareholders in the "forbidden territories" pursuant to Sec. 429 of the Companies Act 1985 (comparable to a "squeeze-out" under German law; see in detail Ch. 6).[11]

3. General Principles

The general principles of the City Code are very similar to those in the German Takeover Act. In addition to the following general principles contained in the German Takeover Act, namely:

(i) Shareholders must be treated equally;
(ii) Shareholders must be given sufficient information and time to allow them to reach a properly informed decision;
(iii) The target's board must act in the interests of the target;
(iv) Expeditious completion of the process (this is dealt with in the rules of the City Code rather than in the general principles); and
(v) Prohibition on market manipulation or the creation of a false market;

the City Code includes additional general principles relating to the following:

(vi) An offeror should announce an offer only if it has every reason to believe that it will be able to implement the offer; in particular, since it is mandatory for a person or persons acting in concert who acquire or consolidate control over a company to make an offer to all shareholders, the person or persons concerned must ensure that they are is able to implement such an offer;
(vii) The directors of the target must not, without the shareholders' approval, take any frustrating action, i.e. do anything that may frustrate a bona fide offer or deny the shareholders the opportunity to decide on the merits of an offer (comparable with the **duty of neutrality** under German law); and
(viii) There is an obligation on a person having control over a company to exercise its rights of control in good faith and not to oppress the minority. Under German law, this duty of good faith is part of general corporate law.[12]

In particular the general principle concerning the ability of the offeror to implement the offer has considerable importance in practice. Responsibility

---

[11] In *In re Joseph Holt plc, Winpar Holdings Ltd v Joseph Holt Group plc, The Times, 24 May 2001* the Court of Appeal held that it was clear that the terms of an offer – which had not been made to shareholders in "forbidden territories" because of expensive and complicated local securities procedures – did extend to all shares, including those in the "forbidden territories" and that the offeror was able to compulsorily acquire the remaining shares. However, shareholders might apply to the court for a declaration that their shares are exempt from the compulsory acquisition or that the acquisition of those shares is made on terms more favourable to the relevant shareholders.

[12] If the minority shareholders are oppressed, e.g. by way of a control and profit transfer agreement, they are entitled to receive adequate compensation.

in this connection rests also on the offeror's financial advisor.[13] For example, the offeror should obtain an irrevocable commitment of financing from a lender before making an offer, although it may in certain circumstances be sufficient if the offeror's financial adviser is satisfied that the offeror will be able to satisfy the offer consideration.[14] Further, if anti-trust clearance for the transaction is not likely to be obtained by Day 81 of the offer timetable (when all conditions to which the offer is subject must be satisfied or waived), the offeror should make a pre-conditional offer instead in order not to breach this general principle. Alternatively, the Panel may be prepared to extend Day 81, although it will only do this if the offer timetable has already begun.

One example of a pre-conditional offer was the Guiness/Grand Met merger, which was subject to the pre-condition that working capital would be put into place for the whole group.

4. Mandatory Offers

a) Obligation to Make a Mandatory Offer

A mandatory offer for all shares must be made on acquisition of more than 30% of the voting rights or if more than 1% of voting rights is acquired within 12 months of an already existing holding of between 30% and 50% of voting rights. The method of acquisition of the relevant proportion of the voting rights is irrelevant. A mandatory offer is binding only if the offeror receives a level of acceptances which brings its holding of voting rights to over 50%. If insufficient acceptances are received, the offeror must return shares which it has acquired pursuant to the acceptances and must reduce its share of the voting rights to less than 30%. This means that it is not possible to acquire a holding of between 30% and 50% by way of a mandatory offer. In the case of voluntary offers, the Panel may, however, waive the 50% condition.[15] The acquisition of shares in a target is restricted if such acquisition (which excludes gifts, the issue of new shares and convertible shares) would result in a holding of more than 30% or if more than 1% of voting rights are acquired within 12 months of an already existing holding of between 30% and 50%, unless:

(i) the acquisitions take place within 7 days and the purchaser states its intention to make a bid;
(ii) the acquisition is effected immediately prior to a statement of intention to make a bid and the management of the target consents to the acquisition; or

---

[13] In relation to the recommended offer in 1989 by WM Low and Co plc for Budgens plc, which was conditional upon the approval of WM Low's shareholders and later withdrawn when the directors of WM Low received additional information about the financing of Budgens and no longer felt able to recommend the offer to their shareholders, the Panel decided that the financial advisers of WM Low should have pressed harder for the crucial information before any announcement of an offer.
[14] This is comparable with § 13 German Takeover Act.
[15] Note 1 to Rule 10: "in certain exceptional cases."

(iii) the acquisition is immediately followed by a statement of intention to make a bid and the management of the target consents to the acquisition.

This latter exception to the restriction applies also where a rival offer has been publicly welcomed by the target's management or where the offer has already expired and the Secretary of State has stated that there would be no referral of the transaction to the UK merger control entity, the Monopolies and Mergers Commission.

b) Exemptions

The Panel may declare **exemptions** from the obligation to make a bid and usually does this where there is no risk that the interests of the minority shareholders will be disadvantaged. In particular, it will usually declare an exemption from the obligation to make a bid in the following cases:

(i) **Whitewash Procedure:**

Cases where the so-called "whitewash procedure" is used: the shareholders in general meeting consent to a transaction which would result in a change of control of the company, for example following the issue of new shares or the transfer of shares. A voting majority of those not involved in the transaction is required. Details of the transaction must be provided to the shareholders in writing in advance, and such letter must be approved by Panel beforehand. The procedure allows shareholders to object to transactions involving a change of control of the company. However, if they approve the transaction, the Panel will usually declare an exemption from the duty to make a bid, on the assumption that the minority shareholders do not need protection, given that they have approved the transaction.

(ii) **Restructurings:**

Restructurings, including those carried out by way of the issue of new shares or by way of an agreement with creditors concerning cancellation of debt in return for shares, provided that it is convinced of the extremely desolate financial position of the company and the urgency of the action to be taken.

(iii) **Accidental exceeding of the 30% threshold:**

Cases whether the 30% threshold is accidentally exceeded, provided that it is convinced that it was indeed accidental and the purchaser reduces its shareholding to below the threshold.

(iv) **Anticipated lack of success chances:**

Cases where the Panel receives prior written notice that acceptances bringing the total to 50% of the voting rights will not be reached, since an offer without a sufficient level of acceptances is not binding anyway.

(v) **Immediate resale of the shares:**

Cases where the shares are sold on immediately, provided that it has been informed of the relevant agreements in advance.

As under the German legislation, the mandatory offer obligation is triggered upon reaching a certain threshold. Thus there is certainty as regards the obligation to make a bid. In unusual circumstances and where there is no risk that the interests of minority shareholders will be prejudiced, however, the Panel is entitled to declare an exemption.

5. Conclusion

There are many differences between the German and the UK regulatory systems, of which this chapter has mentioned only a few. One difference which illustrates the differences in general approach between the two systems, and the importance placed on consultation with the Panel at every step of the way before, during and after an offer has been made and the transaction has been implemented, is in relation to statements made by the target's board to the target's shareholders (which can have huge influence on the outcome of an offer). In Germany, the board must not make use of its obligation to inform the shareholders and its duty to take a view of the offer to such extent that shareholders are misled in such a way as to affect their decision. In the UK, all communications to shareholders are subject to a stringent duty of care and accuracy and must be agreed with Panel prior to their release.

Case: Carnival/P&O Princess:

The great advantage of the UK system is its flexibility, which is perhaps best illustrated by a recent case. In February 2002 the Panel took unusual action in the hostile bid by U.S. cruise company Carnival for UK rival P&O Princess ("P&O") by deciding halfway through the process to extend the deadline for the process. The Panel has allowed Carnival a long delay in posting its offer document after antitrust regulators rule on its offer.

The reason for this is that P&O already has a rival plan to merge with Royal Caribbean Cruises ("Royal") which is not subject to the City Code because the merged entity would be a dual-listed company, i.e. the merger would create a single economic unit without any shares changing hands and with the shares of P&O and Royal remaining independently listed. As Royal's merger deal is not a "takeover offer" for P&O, the P&O-Royal merger deal is outside the remit of the Panel. Further, the merger deal includes two "poison pills" (which the Panel frowns on and which are generally not permitted under the City Code), one in the form of a joint venture between P&O and Royal which can be unwound in January 2003, and the other in the form of large break fees payable if one side terminated the deal.

One of the Panel's basic principles is a level playing field in bids, allowing shareholders to decide between the rival offers. Extending the timetable of the Carnival bid to allow Carnival to time the end of its bid with the date of termination of the P&O-Royal joint venture allows the P&O shareholders a clearer choice between the Carnival offer and the Royal merger plan. The "state of siege" argument[16] for adhering to the usual timetable is not very strong in these

---

[16] The City Code subjects offerors to a strict timetable. An offeror must promptly post an offer document to shareholders and then has a maximum of 60 days to clinch

circumstances as the P&O-Royal merger deal is also subject to regulatory investigations. The spirit of the City Code is therefore adhered to in this case.[17]

In order to close this loophole in relation to future transactions and as a result of representations being made to the Panel by institutional shareholder bodies on the issue of dual-listed companies, the Panel is now considering and has published proposals to bring the establishment of such structures within the City Code.[18] According to these proposals, the Code will apply either to dual-listed company transactions from the start or only if one of the companies involved in a dual-listed company structure is the subject of a hostile bid. The Panel sensibly recommends the former option. The Panel also proposes to amend the existing rule of the Code which does not permit large poison pills in the form of break fees[19] to make clear that the City Code imposes strict financial limits on all provisions which may be used by an offeror as bid repellents, including dual-listed company structures. Until these amendments to the City Code are effected, the Panel advises parties or their advisers proposing to implement a dual-listed company structure in relation to a company to which the City Code applies to consult the Panel. Thus, even though the proposed amendments have not yet been made, the sanctions resulting from non-compliance with the spirit of the City Code mean that the loophole has effectively already been closed.

The disadvantages of a self-regulatory system relate to the areas of investigation and enforcement by the Panel. While the Panel is usually successful in ensuring compliance with the City Code (and in this respect in particular the "cold shoulder" approach appears to be an effective deterrent), it has no statutory powers to investigate breaches of the City Code and therefore relies heavily on receiving information from those involved in the takeover market. Nevertheless, the Panel does have access to certain documents which the Secretary of State of the Department of Trade and Industry has power to require to be produced. It also has access to the computerized records of the London Stock Exchange and is therefore able to monitor dealings. Finally, the rules of other City regulatory organisations require their members to cooperate with the Panel in its investigations. There are those who believe that the Panel requires more vigorous statutory powers. The author is not one of these and believes that the Panel's advantage of flexibility, which derives largely from fine-tuning the provisions of the City Code over the course of many years of the Panel's experience, should not be put at risk by attempting to implement the provisions of the City Code into statute, however thoughtfully this may be carried out.

---

victory. This is to prevent defending executives being subject to an endless state of siege that eventually undermines effective management of the company.

[17] The European Commission controversially approved Carnival's bid for P&O on July 7, 2002.

[18] Statements 2002/5 and 2002/10, Consultation Paper PCP 11.

[19] Rule 21.2, which restricts the amount of inducement fees to 1% of the offer value.

Gesetzestexte

Appendix 1
The Act on the Purchase of Securities and on Takeovers 2002 (German Takeover Act)

(Unofficial Translation of the German „Wertpapiererwerbs- und Übernahmegesetz" (2002) by NÖRR STIEFENHOFER LUTZ)

Table of Contents

Part 1. General Provisions

§ 1 Scope of Application	144
§ 2 Definitions	144
§ 3 General Principles	146

Part 2. Jurisdiction of the Federal Supervisory Office for Financial Services

§ 4 Duties and Rights	146
§ 5 Commission	146
§ 6 Objections Committee	148
§ 7 Co-operation with Supervisory Authorities in Germany	150
§ 8 Co-operation with the Competent Bodies in other Countries	150
§ 9 Duty of Confidentiality	152

Part 3. Bid to Purchase Securities

§ 10 Publication of the Decision to make a Bid	154
§ 11 Offer Document	156
§ 12 Liability for the Offer Document	158
§ 13 Financing of the Bid	160
§ 14 Sending and Publishing the Offer Document	160
§ 15 Prohibition of a Bid	162
§ 16 Periods for Acceptance, Calling of General Meeting	162
§ 17 Inadmissibility of Public Demand to Make Bids	164
§ 18 Conditions; Inadmissibility of the Reservation of the Right to Withdraw and Revoke	164
§ 19 Acceptance in the case of a Partial Bid	166
§ 20 Trading Portfolio	166
§ 21 Change to the Bid	166
§ 22 Competing Bids	168
§ 23 Publication Obligations of the Offeror after Making a Bid	168
§ 24 Cross-Border Bids	170
§ 25 Resolution of the Shareholders' Meeting of the Offeror	170
§ 26 Waiting Period	170
§ 27 The Opinion of the Board of Management and of the Supervisory Board of the Target Company	172
§ 28 Advertising	172

Anhang 1
Wertpapiererwerbs- und Übernahmegesetz (WpÜG)

Vom 20. Dezember 2001 (BGBl. I S. 3822),
zuletzt geändert durch Gesetz vom 23. 7. 2002 (BGBl. I S. 2850)

Inhaltsübersicht

Abschnitt 1. Allgemeine Vorschriften

§ 1 Anwendungsbereich	145
§ 2 Begriffsbestimmungen	145
§ 3 Allgemeine Grundsätze	147

Abschnitt 2. Zuständigkeit der Bundesanstalt für Finanzdienstleistungsaufsicht

§ 4 Aufgaben und Befugnisse	147
§ 5 Beirat	147
§ 6 Widerspruchsausschuss	149
§ 7 Zusammenarbeit mit Aufsichtsbehörden im Inland	151
§ 8 Zusammenarbeit mit zuständigen Stellen im Ausland	151
§ 9 Verschwiegenheitspflicht	153

Abschnitt 3. Angebote zum Erwerb von Wertpapieren

§ 10 Veröffentlichung der Entscheidung zur Abgabe eines Angebots	155
§ 11 Angebotsunterlage	157
§ 12 Haftung für die Angebotsunterlage	159
§ 13 Finanzierung des Angebots	161
§ 14 Übermittlung und Veröffentlichung der Angebotsunterlage	161
§ 15 Untersagung des Angebots	163
§ 16 Annahmefristen; Einberufung der Hauptversammlung	163
§ 17 Unzulässigkeit der öffentlichen Aufforderung zur Abgabe von Angeboten	165
§ 18 Bedingungen; Unzulässigkeit des Vorbehalts des Rücktritts und des Widerrufs	165
§ 19 Zuteilung bei einem Teilangebot	167
§ 20 Handelsbestand	167
§ 21 Änderung des Angebots	167
§ 22 Konkurrierende Angebote	169
§ 23 Veröffentlichungspflichten des Bieters nach Abgabe des Angebots	169
§ 24 Grenzüberschreitende Angebote	171
§ 25 Beschluss der Gesellschafterversammlung des Bieters	171
§ 26 Sperrfrist	171
§ 27 Stellungnahme des Vorstands und Aufsichtsrats der Zielgesellschaft	173
§ 28 Werbung	173

Part 4. Takeover Bids

§ 29 Definitions	172
§ 30 Attribution of Voting Rights	174
§ 31 Consideration	174
§ 32 Inadmissibility of Partial Bids	176
§ 33 Acts of the Board of Management of the Target Company	176
§ 34 Application of the Provisions of Part 3	178

Part 5. Mandatory Offers

§ 35 Obligation to Publish and Make an Offer	178
§ 36 Voting Rights not taken into Account	180
§ 37 Exemption from the Publication Obligation and from the Making of an Offer	180
§ 38 Right to Interest	180
§ 39 Application of the Provisions of Parts 3 and 4	180

Part 6. Procedure

§ 40 The Authority of the Federal Supervisory Office to Investigate	182
§ 41 Objections Procedure	182
§ 42 Immediate Enforceability	184
§ 43 Notification and Service	184
§ 44 The Federal Supervisory Office's Right of Publication	184
§ 45 Communications to the Federal Supervisory Office	186
§ 46 Penalties	186
§ 47 Costs	186

Part 7. Legal Remedies

§ 48 Admissibility, Jurisdiction	186
§ 49 Suspensory Effect	188
§ 50 Order of Immediate Enforcement	188
§ 51 Time-Limits and Form	188
§ 52 Participants in the Appeal	190
§ 53 Compulsory Legal Representation	190
§ 54 Oral Hearing	190
§ 55 Principle of Investigation	190
§ 56 Appeal Decision; Obligation to Present Documents	190
§ 57 Inspection of Files	192
§ 58 Application of the Court Constitution Act and the Code of Civil Procedure	194

Part 8. Penalties

§ 59 Forfeiture of Rights	194
§ 60 Fines	194
§ 61 The Competent Administrative Authority	196
§ 62 Jurisdiction of the Oberlandesgericht[1] in Court Proceedings	198
§ 63 Appeal on a Point of Law to the Bundesgerichtshof[2]	198
§ 64 Reinstatement with Fine	198
§ 65 Court Decision on Enforcement	198

---

[1] Court of Appeal.
[2] Federal Supreme Court.

Wertpapiererwerbs- und Übernahmegesetz 143

Abschnitt 4. Übernahmeangebote

§ 29 Begriffsbestimmungen 173
§ 30 Zurechnung von Stimmrechten 175
§ 31 Gegenleistung 175
§ 32 Unzulässigkeit von Teilangeboten 177
§ 33 Handlungen des Vorstands der Zielgesellschaft 177
§ 34 Anwendung der Vorschriften des Abschnitts 3 179

Abschnitt 5. Pflichtangebote

§ 35 Verpflichtung zur Veröffentlichung und zur Abgabe eines Angebots 179
§ 36 Nichtberücksichtigung von Stimmrechten 181
§ 37 Befreiung von der Verpflichtung zur Veröffentlichung und zur Abgabe eines Angebots 181
§ 38 Anspruch auf Zinsen 181
§ 39 Anwendung der Vorschriften des Abschnitts 3 und 4 181

Abschnitt 6. Verfahren

§ 40 Ermittlungsbefugnisse der Bundesanstalt 183
§ 41 Widerspruchsverfahren 183
§ 42 Sofortige Vollziehbarkeit 185
§ 43 Bekanntgabe und Zustellung 185
§ 44 Veröffentlichungsrecht der Bundesanstalt 185
§ 45 Mitteilungen an die Bundesanstalt 187
§ 46 Zwangsmittel 187
§ 47 Kosten 187

Abschnitt 7. Rechtsmittel

§ 48 Statthaftigkeit, Zuständigkeit 187
§ 49 Aufschiebende Wirkung 189
§ 50 Anordnung der sofortigen Vollziehung 189
§ 51 Frist und Form 189
§ 52 Beteiligte am Beschwerdeverfahren 191
§ 53 Anwaltszwang 191
§ 54 Mündliche Verhandlung 191
§ 55 Untersuchungsgrundsatz 191
§ 56 Beschwerdeentscheidung; Vorlagepflicht 191
§ 57 Akteneinsicht 193
§ 58 Geltung von Vorschriften des Gerichtsverfassungsgesetzes und der Zivilprozessordnung 195

Abschnitt 8. Sanktionen

§ 59 Rechtsverlust 195
§ 60 Bußgeldvorschriften 195
§ 61 Zuständige Verwaltungsbehörde 197
§ 62 Zuständigkeit des Oberlandesgerichts im gerichtlichen Verfahren 199
§ 63 Rechtsbeschwerde zum Bundesgerichtshof 199
§ 64 Wiederaufnahme gegen Bußgeldbescheid 199
§ 65 Gerichtliche Entscheidung bei der Vollstreckung 199

Part 9. Court Jurisdiction; Transitional Arrangements

§ 66 The Court in Matters of the Purchase of Securities and of Takeovers 198
§ 67 The Oberlandesgericht[3] Panel for Matters Concerning the Acquisition of Securities and Takeovers 200
§ 68 Transitional Provisions 200

Part 1. General Provisions

§ 1. Scope of Application

This Act is to be applied to offers for the purchase of securities which are issued by a company and admitted to trading on an organised market.

§ 2. Definitions

(1) Bids are public offers of purchase or exchange made freely or on the basis of an obligation under this Act for acquiring securities of a company.

(2) Securities are
1. shares, similar securities and certificates which represent shares,

2. other securities which have as their subject matter the acquisition of shares, similar securities or certificates which represent shares, even if certificates have not been issued.

(3) Companies are companies limited by shares or partnerships limited by shares having their registered offices in Germany.

(4) Offerors are natural persons or legal entities or partnerships which, alone or together with other persons, make a bid, intend to do so or are obliged to do so.

(5) Persons acting in common are natural persons or legal entities which co-ordinate their conduct in relation to their acquisition of securities of the target company or their exercise of voting rights of shares of the target company with the offeror on the basis of an agreement or in any other manner. Subsidiaries of the offeror shall be deemed to be persons acting in common with the offeror.

(6) Subsidiaries are enterprises which are deemed to be subsidiaries within the meaning of § 290 of the Commercial Code or on which a dominant influence can be exercised, without this depending on the legal form or the location of the registered office.

(7) Organised market is the official trading or regulated market on a stock exchange in Germany and the regulated market within the meaning of Art. 1 no. 13 of the *Council Directive 93/22/EEC of 10 May 1993 on investment services in the securities field (OJ EC L 141 p. 27)* in another State of the European Economic Area.

---

[3] Court of Appeal.

Abschnitt 9. Gerichtliche Zuständigkeit; Übergangsregelungen

§ 66 Gerichte für Wertpapiererwerbs- und Übernahmesachen 199
§ 67 Senat für Wertpapiererwerbs- und Übernahmesachen beim Oberlandesgericht 201
§ 68 Übergangsregelungen 201

Abschnitt 1. Allgemeine Vorschriften

§ 1. Anwendungsbereich

Dieses Gesetz ist anzuwenden auf Angebote zum Erwerb von Wertpapieren, die von einer Zielgesellschaft ausgegeben wurden und zum Handel an einem organisierten Markt zugelassen sind.

§ 2. Begriffsbestimmungen

(1) Angebote sind freiwillige oder auf Grund einer Verpflichtung nach diesem Gesetz erfolgende öffentliche Kauf- oder Tauschangebote zum Erwerb von Wertpapieren einer Zielgesellschaft.

(2) Wertpapiere sind, auch wenn für sie keine Urkunden ausgestellt sind,
1. Aktien, mit diesen vergleichbare Wertpapiere und Zertifikate, die Aktien vertreten,
2. andere Wertpapiere, die den Erwerb von Aktien, mit diesen vergleichbaren Wertpapieren oder Zertifikaten, die Aktien vertreten, zum Gegenstand haben.

(3) Zielgesellschaften sind Aktiengesellschaften oder Kommanditgesellschaften auf Aktien mit Sitz im Inland.

(4) Bieter sind natürliche oder juristische Personen oder Personengesellschaften, die allein oder gemeinsam mit anderen Personen ein Angebot abgeben, ein solches beabsichtigen oder zur Abgabe verpflichtet sind.

(5) Gemeinsam handelnde Personen sind natürliche oder juristische Personen, die ihr Verhalten im Hinblick auf ihren Erwerb von Wertpapieren der Zielgesellschaft oder ihre Ausübung von Stimmrechten aus Aktien der Zielgesellschaft mit dem Bieter auf Grund einer Vereinbarung oder in sonstiger Weise abstimmen. Tochterunternehmen des Bieters gelten als mit diesem gemeinsam handelnde Personen.

(6) Tochterunternehmen sind Unternehmen, die als Tochterunternehmen im Sinne des § 290 des Handelsgesetzbuchs gelten oder auf die ein beherrschender Einfluss ausgeübt werden kann, ohne dass es auf die Rechtsform oder den Sitz ankommt.

(7) Organisierter Markt sind der amtliche Handel oder geregelte Markt an einer Börse im Inland und der geregelte Markt im Sinne des Artikels 1 Nr. 13 der Richtlinie 93/22/EWG des Rates vom 10. Mai 1993 über Wertpapierdienstleistungen (ABl. EG Nr. L 141 S. 27) in einem anderen Staat des Europäischen Wirtschaftsraums.

(8) The European Economic Area includes the States of the European Communities together with the States of the Treaty on the European Economic Area.

§ 3. General Principles

(1) The holders of securities of the same class in the target company are to be treated equally.

(2) The holders of securities in the target company must be provided with sufficient time and adequate information to enable them to reach a properly informed decision on the bid.

(3) The management board and supervisory board of the target company must act in the interests of the company.

(4) The offeror and the target company shall carry through the procedure expeditiously. The target company may not be hindered in the conduct of its affairs for longer than is reasonable.

(5) While trading in the securities of the target company, of the offeror company or of any other company affected by the bid, market distortions shall not be created.

Part 2. Jurisdiction of the Federal Supervisory Office for Financial Services

§ 4. Duties and Rights

(1) The Federal Supervisory Office for for Financial Services (the Supervisory Office) shall supervise bids in accordance with the provisions of this Act. It shall, in the framework of the duties ascribed to it, take measures to counter abuses which affect the proper conduct of the procedure or which could result in significant disadvantages for the securities market. The Supervisory Office may issue such orders as are effective and necessary for the removal or prevention of abuses.

(2) The Supervisory Office shall undertake the tasks and entitlements ascribed to it in this Act only in the public interest.

§ 5. Commission

(1) A commission shall be formed at the Supervisory Office. The commission shall consist of
1. four representatives of the issuers,
2. two representatives each of the institutional and private investors,
3. three representatives of investment services enterprises within the meaning of § 2 para. 4 of the Securities Trading Act.
4. two employees' representatives,
5. two representatives from the academic world.

(8) Der Europäische Wirtschaftsraum umfasst die Staaten der Europäischen Gemeinschaften sowie die Staaten des Abkommens über den Europäischen Wirtschaftsraum.

§ 3. Allgemeine Grundsätze

(1) Inhaber von Wertpapieren der Zielgesellschaft, die derselben Gattung angehören, sind gleich zu behandeln.

(2) Inhaber von Wertpapieren der Zielgesellschaft müssen über genügend Zeit und ausreichende Informationen verfügen, um in Kenntnis der Sachlage über das Angebot entscheiden zu können.

(3) Vorstand und Aufsichtsrat der Zielgesellschaft müssen im Interesse der Zielgesellschaft handeln.

(4) Der Bieter und die Zielgesellschaft haben das Verfahren rasch durchzuführen. Die Zielgesellschaft darf nicht über einen angemessenen Zeitraum hinaus in ihrer Geschäftstätigkeit behindert werden.

(5) Beim Handel mit Wertpapieren der Zielgesellschaft, der Bietergesellschaft oder anderer durch das Angebot betroffener Gesellschaften dürfen keine Marktverzerrungen geschaffen werden.

Abschnitt 2. Zuständigkeit der Bundesanstalt für Finanzdienstleistungsaufsicht

§ 4. Aufgaben und Befugnisse

(1) Die Bundesanstalt für Finanzdienstleistungsaufsicht (Bundesanstalt) übt die Aufsicht bei Angeboten nach den Vorschriften dieses Gesetzes aus. Sie hat im Rahmen der ihr zugewiesenen Aufgaben Missständen entgegenzuwirken, welche die ordnungsmäßige Durchführung des Verfahrens beeinträchtigen oder erhebliche Nachteile für den Wertpapiermarkt bewirken können. Die Bundesanstalt kann Anordnungen treffen, die geeignet und erforderlich sind, diese Missstände zu beseitigen oder zu verhindern.

(2) Die Bundesanstalt nimmt die ihm nach diesem Gesetz zugewiesenen Aufgaben und Befugnisse nur im öffentlichen Interesse wahr.

§ 5. Beirat

(1) Bei der Bundesanstalt wird ein Beirat gebildet. Der Beirat besteht aus
1. vier Vertretern der Emittenten,
2. je zwei Vertretern der institutionellen und der privaten Anleger,
3. drei Vertretern der Wertpapierdienstleistungsunternehmen im Sinne des § 2 Abs. 4 des Wertpapierhandelsgesetzes,
4. zwei Vertretern der Arbeitnehmer,
5. zwei Vertretern der Wissenschaft.

The members of the commission will be appointed by the Federal Ministry of Finance for five years in each case. The appointment of the members described at sentence 2 nos. 1 to 4 shall be made after the affected group of persons has been heard. The members of the commission must be particularly suitable in their knowledge of the subject; in particular, they must have knowledge of the functioning of the capital markets and knowledge in the area of corporate law, accountancy or labour law. The members of the commission shall exercise their office as an honorary office without remuneration. They shall receive per diem and the reimbursement of their travelling costs for participation in meetings according to the fixed amounts determined by the Federal Ministry of Finance. Representatives of the Federal Ministries of Finance, of Justice and of Economic Affairs and Technology may take part in the meetings.

(2) The Federal Ministry of Finance, by legal regulation, which shall not require the approval of the Bundesrat,[4] may issue more detailed provisions for the composition of the commission, the details of appointment of its members, the premature ending of membership, the procedure and the costs. The Federal Ministry of Finance may delegate this authority to the Supervisory Office.

(3) The commission shall participate in the supervision. It shall advise the Supervisory Office on the supervision, in particular, concerning the issuing of legal regulations for the supervisory activity of the Supervisory Office. It shall, with the agreement of two thirds of its members, propose honorary advisory members and their deputies for the objections committee.

(4) The President of the Supervisory Office shall call the meetings of the commission. The meetings will be chaired by the President of the Supervisory Office or an official delegated by him.

(5) The commission shall provide its own rules of procedure.

§ 6. Objections Committee

(1) An objections committee shall be formed at the Supervisory Office. This will decide on objections to rulings of the Supervisory Office under § 4 para. 1 clause 3, §§ 10 para. 1 sentence 3, para. 2 sentence 3, § 15 para. 1 and 2, § 20 para. 1, § 24, § 28 para. 1, § 36 and § 37.

(2) The objections committee shall consist of
1. the President of the Supervisory Office or an official delegated by him, who is qualified to hold judicial office, as chairman,

2. two officials delegated by the President of the Supervisory Office as advisory members,
3. three honorary advisory members appointed by the President of the Supervisory Office.
In the case of a tie, the chairman shall decide.

---

[4] Chamber of State Governments.

Die Mitglieder des Beirates werden vom Bundesministerium der Finanzen für jeweils fünf Jahre bestellt; die Bestellung der in Satz 2 Nr. 1 bis 4 genannten Mitglieder erfolgt nach Anhörung der betroffenen Kreise. Die Mitglieder des Beirates müssen fachlich besonders geeignet sein; insbesondere müssen sie über Kenntnisse über die Funktionsweise der Kapitalmärkte sowie über Kenntnisse auf dem Gebiet des Gesellschaftsrechts, des Bilanzwesens oder des Arbeitsrechts verfügen. Die Mitglieder des Beirates verwalten ihr Amt als unentgeltliches Ehrenamt. Für ihre Teilnahme an Sitzungen erhalten sie Tagegelder und Vergütung der Reisekosten nach festen Sätzen, die das Bundesministerium der Finanzen bestimmt. An den Sitzungen können Vertreter der Bundesministerien der Finanzen, der Justiz sowie für Wirtschaft und Technologie teilnehmen.

(2) Das Bundesministerium der Finanzen kann durch Rechtsverordnung, die nicht der Zustimmung des Bundesrates bedarf, nähere Bestimmungen über die Zusammensetzung des Beirates, die Einzelheiten der Bestellung seiner Mitglieder, die vorzeitige Beendigung der Mitgliedschaft, das Verfahren und die Kosten erlassen. Das Bundesministerium der Finanzen kann die Ermächtigung durch Rechtsverordnung auf die Bundesanstalt übertragen.

(3) Der Beirat wirkt bei der Aufsicht mit. Er berät die Bundesanstalt, insbesondere bei dem Erlass von Rechtsverordnungen für die Aufsichtstätigkeit der Bundesanstalt. Er unterbreitet mit Zustimmung von zwei Dritteln seiner Mitglieder Vorschläge für die ehrenamtlichen Beisitzer des Widerspruchsausschusses und deren Vertreter.

(4) Der Präsident der Bundesanstalt lädt zu den Sitzungen des Beirates ein. Die Sitzungen werden vom Präsidenten der Bundesanstalt oder einem von ihm beauftragten Beamten geleitet.

(5) Der Beirat gibt sich eine Geschäftsordnung.

§ 6. Widerspruchsausschuss

(1) Bei der Bundesanstalt wird ein Widerspruchsausschuss gebildet. Dieser entscheidet über Widersprüche gegen Verfügungen der Bundesanstalt nach § 4 Abs. 1 Satz 3, § 10 Abs. 1 Satz 3, Abs. 2 Satz 3, § 15 Abs. 1 und 2, § 20 Abs. 1, §§ 24, 28 Abs. 1, §§ 36 und 37.

(2) Der Widerspruchsausschuss besteht aus
1. dem Präsidenten der Bundesanstalt oder einem von ihm beauftragten Beamten, der die Befähigung zum Richteramt hat, als Vorsitzendem,
2. zwei vom Präsidenten der Bundesanstalt beauftragten Beamten als Beisitzern,
3. drei vom Präsidenten der Bundesanstalt bestellten ehrenamtlichen Beisitzern.

Bei Stimmengleichheit entscheidet der Vorsitzende.

(3) The honorary advisory members will be appointed members of the objections committee by the President of the Supervisory Office for five years.

(4) The Federal Ministry of Finance can, by legal regulation, which does not require the approval of the Bundesrat, issue more particular provisions as to the procedure, the details of appointment of the honorary advisory members, the premature ending and the representation. The Federal Ministry of Finance can delegate this authority to the Supervisory Office.

§ 7. Co-operation with Supervisory Authorities in Germany

(1) The Federal Cartel Office and the Federal Supervisory Office for Securities Trading shall provide each other with information necessary for the fulfilment of their duties. In the case of the communication of personal data, § 15 of the Federal Data Protection Act applies.

(2) The Supervisory Office can engage the services of private persons and institutions for the carrying out of its functions under this law.

§ 8. Co-operation with the Competent Bodies in other Countries

(1) The Supervisory Office shall handle co-operation with the authorities of other countries competent for the supervision of bids for the purchase of securities, stock exchanges or other securities' or derivatives' markets and trading in securities and derivatives.

(2) In the context of the co-operation under para. 1, the Supervisory Office may communicate facts necessary for the supervision of bids for the purchase of securities or the administrative or court proceedings connected therewith: in this respect, it may avail of its authority under § 40 para. 1 to 4. In the case of the communication of personal data, the Supervisory Office shall specify the purpose for which such data may be used. The recipient shall be instructed that the data may be processed or used only for the purpose for which they have been communicated. Data shall not be communicated insofar as there are reasons to suspect that a breach of the purpose of a German law will take place thereby. Communication is also forbidden if interests of the party affected which are worthy of protection would be affected thereby, in particular if an adequate standard of data protection is not guaranteed in the receiving country.

(3) If personal data is communicated to the Supervisory Office by the competent authority of another country, such data may be processed or used only in accordance with the purpose specified by the said competent authority. The Supervisory Office may communicate such data, observing the specified purpose, to the stock exchange supervisory authorities and the trading supervisory offices of the stock exchanges.

(3) Die ehrenamtlichen Beisitzer werden vom Präsidenten des Bundesaufsichtsamtes für fünf Jahre als Mitglieder des Widerspruchsausschusses bestellt.

(4) Das Bundesministerium der Finanzen kann durch Rechtsverordnung, die nicht der Zustimmung des Bundesrates bedarf, nähere Bestimmungen über das Verfahren, die Einzelheiten der Bestellung der ehrenamtlichen Beisitzer, die vorzeitige Beendigung und die Vertretung erlassen. Das Bundesministerium der Finanzen kann die Ermächtigung durch Rechtsverordnung auf die Bundesanstalt übertragen.

§ 7. Zusammenarbeit mit Aufsichtsbehörden im Inland

(1) Das Bundeskartellamt und die Bundesanstalt haben einander die für die Erfüllung ihrer Aufgaben erforderlichen Informationen mitzuteilen. Bei der Übermittlung personenbezogener Daten ist § 15 des Bundesdatenschutzgesetzes anzuwenden.

(2) Die Bundesanstalt kann sich bei der Durchführung ihrer Aufgaben nach diesem Gesetz privater Personen und Einrichtungen bedienen.

§ 8. Zusammenarbeit mit zuständigen Stellen im Ausland

(1) Die Bundesanstalt obliegt die Zusammenarbeit mit den für die Überwachung von Angeboten zum Erwerb von Wertpapieren, Börsen oder anderen Wertpapier- oder Derivatemärkten sowie den Handel in Wertpapieren und Derivaten zuständigen Stellen anderer Staaten.

(2) Im Rahmen der Zusammenarbeit nach Absatz 1 darf die Bundesanstalt Tatsachen übermitteln, die für die Überwachung von Angeboten zum Erwerb von Wertpapieren oder damit zusammenhängender Verwaltungs- oder Gerichtsverfahren erforderlich sind; hierbei kann sie von ihren Befugnissen nach § 40 Abs. 1 bis 4 Gebrauch machen. Bei der Übermittlung personenbezogener Daten hat die Bundesanstalt den Zweck zu bestimmen, für den diese verwendet werden dürfen. Der Empfänger ist darauf hinzuweisen, dass die Daten nur zu dem Zweck verarbeitet oder genutzt werden dürfen, zu dessen Erfüllung sie übermittelt wurden. Eine Übermittlung unterbleibt, soweit Grund zu der Annahme besteht, dass durch sie gegen den Zweck eines deutschen Gesetzes verstoßen wird. Die Übermittlung unterbleibt außerdem, wenn durch sie schutzwürdige Interessen des Betroffenen beeinträchtigt würden, insbesondere wenn im Empfängerland ein angemessener Datenschutzstandard nicht gewährleistet wäre.

(3) Werden der Bundesanstalt von einer Stelle eines anderen Staates personenbezogene Daten mitgeteilt, so dürfen diese nur unter Beachtung der Zweckbestimmung durch diese Stelle verarbeitet oder genutzt werden. Die Bundesanstalt darf die Daten unter Beachtung der Zweckbestimmung den Börsenaufsichtsbehörden und den Handelsüberwachungsstellen der Börsen mitteilen.

(4) The provisions on international judicial assistance in criminal matters remain unaffected.

§ 9. Duty of Confidentiality

(1) The personnel of the Supervisory Office and of institutions referred to in § 7 para. 2, persons whose services are availed of by the Supervisory Office in accordance with § 7 para. 2, and the members of the commission and advisory members of the objections committee may not, without authority, disclose or use information obtained in the course of their activity, the confidentiality of which is in the interest of one of the parties subject to obligations under this law or of a third party, in particular business and operation secrets, and personal data, including after the ending of the employment or service of such persons. This applies also to other persons who acquire information of matters referred to in sentence 1 through the preparation of official reports in the course of their duties. Unauthorised disclosure or use in the meaning of sentence 1 does not arise, in particular, if facts are passed to
1. criminal prosecution authorities or courts with jurisdiction in criminal matters and matters involving administrative fines,
2. offices, which by law or public appointment are entrusted with combating restrictions on competition, with the supervision of bids for the purchase of securities or the supervision of stock exchanges or other securities' or derivatives' markets, trading in securities or derivatives, financial institutions, financial services institutions, investment companies, finance companies or insurance companies, and persons engaged by such offices,

insofar as the facts are necessary to the fulfilment by these offices or persons of their functions. Persons who are employed at the offices mentioned in sentence 3 or persons engaged by them, are subject to the duty of confidentiality in accordance with sentences 1 to 3, mutatis mutandis. Facts may be communicated to offices located abroad only if these offices and persons engaged by them are subject to a duty of confidentiality corresponding to sentences 1 and 3.

(2) §§ 93, 97, 105 para. 1, § 111 para. 5 in conjunction with § 105 para. 1 and § 116 para. 1 of the Tax Code [Abgabenordnung] shall not apply to the persons described in para. 1 sentences 1 and 2 insofar as they are engaged in the implementation of this law. They will apply insofar as the tax authorities require the knowledge for the carrying through of a proceeding concerning a tax offence and a tax proceeding connected therewith, the pursuit of which is a matter of mandatory public interest and not concerning facts of which the persons described in para. 1 sentence 1 or 2 have been informed by an office of another country within the meaning of para. 1 sentence 3 no. 2 or by a person instructed by such office.

(3) The members of the commission and the honorary advisory members to the objections committee shall be bound by the Supervisory Office to the conscientious performance of their obligations in accordance with the Act on Formal Confidentiality Obligations of 2 March 1974 (Federal Law Ga-

(4) Die Regelungen über die internationale Rechtshilfe in Strafsachen bleiben unberührt.

§ 9. Verschwiegenheitspflicht

(1) Die bei der Bundesanstalt und bei Einrichtungen nach § 7 Abs. 2 Beschäftigten, die Personen, derer sich die Bundesanstalt nach § 7 Abs. 2 bedient, sowie die Mitglieder des Beirates und Beisitzer des Widerspruchsausschusses dürfen ihnen bei ihrer Tätigkeit bekannt gewordene Tatsachen, deren Geheimhaltung im Interesse eines nach diesem Gesetz Verpflichteten oder eines Dritten liegt, insbesondere Geschäfts- und Betriebsgeheimnisse, sowie personenbezogene Daten auch nach Beendigung ihres Dienstverhältnisses oder ihrer Tätigkeit nicht unbefugt offenbaren oder verwerten. Dies gilt auch für andere Personen, die durch dienstliche Berichterstattung Kenntnis von den in Satz 1 bezeichneten Tatsachen erhalten. Ein unbefugtes Offenbaren oder Verwerten im Sinne des Satzes 1 liegt insbesondere nicht vor, wenn Tatsachen weitergegeben werden an
1. Strafverfolgungsbehörden oder für Straf- und Bußgeldsachen zuständige Gerichte,
2. Stellen, die kraft Gesetzes oder im öffentlichen Auftrag mit der Bekämpfung von Wettbewerbsbeschränkungen, der Überwachung von Angeboten zum Erwerb von Wertpapieren oder der Überwachung von Börsen oder anderen Wertpapier- oder Derivatemärkten, des Wertpapier- oder Derivatehandels, von Kreditinstituten, Finanzdienstleistungsinstituten, Investmentgesellschaften, Finanzunternehmen oder Versicherungsunternehmen betraut sind, sowie von solchen Stellen beauftragte Personen, soweit die Tatsachen für die Erfüllung der Aufgaben dieser Stellen oder Personen erforderlich sind. Für die bei den in Satz 3 genannten Stellen beschäftigten oder von ihnen beauftragten Personen gilt die Verschwiegenheitspflicht nach den Sätzen 1 bis 3 entsprechend. An eine ausländische Stelle dürfen die Tatsachen nur weitergegeben werden, wenn diese Stelle und die von ihr beauftragten Personen einer den Sätzen 1 bis 3 entsprechenden Verschwiegenheitspflicht unterliegen.

(2) Die §§ 93, 97, 105 Abs. 1, § 111 Abs. 5 in Verbindung mit § 105 Abs. 1 sowie § 116 Abs. 1 der Abgabenordnung gelten nicht für die in Absatz 1 Satz 1 und 2 bezeichneten Personen, soweit sie zur Durchführung dieses Gesetzes tätig werden. Sie finden Anwendung, soweit die Finanzbehörden die Kenntnisse für die Durchführung eines Verfahrens wegen einer Steuerstraftat sowie eines damit zusammenhängenden Besteuerungsverfahrens benötigen, an deren Verfolgung ein zwingendes öffentliches Interesse besteht, und nicht Tatsachen betroffen sind, die den in Absatz 1 Satz 1 oder 2 bezeichneten Personen durch eine Stelle eines anderen Staates im Sinne von Absatz 1 Satz 3 Nr. 2 oder durch von dieser Stelle beauftragte Personen mitgeteilt worden sind.

(3) Die Mitglieder des Beirates und die ehrenamtlichen Beisitzer des Widerspruchsausschusses sind nach dem Verpflichtungsgesetz vom 2. März 1974 (BGBl. I S. 469, 547), geändert durch § 1 Nr. 4 des Gesetzes vom 15. August 1974 (BGBl. I S. 1942), in der jeweils geltenden Fassung von

zette I p. 469, 547), as amended by § 1 no. 4 of the law of 15 August 1974 (Federal Law Gazette I p. 1942).

Part 3. Bid to Purchase Securities

§ 10. Publication of the Decision to make a Bid

(1) The offeror shall publish its decision to make a bid without delay in accordance with para. 3 sentence 1. The obligation in accordance with sentence 1 exists also if a resolution of the shareholders' meeting of the offeror is necessary for the decision in accordance with sentence 1 and such a resolution has not yet been passed. The Supervisory Office may permit the offeror on application, in deviation from sentence 2, to publish only after the resolution of the shareholders' meeting if the offeror ensures by means of adequate precautions that this will not give rise to a risk of market distortion.

(2) The offeror shall notify the decision in accordance with para. 1 sentence 1 prior to publication to
1. the management of the stock exchanges on which securities of the offeror, the company and other companies directly affected by the bid are admitted to trading,
2. the management of the stock exchanges on which derivatives within the meaning of § 2 para. 2 of the Securities Trading Act are traded, insofar as the securities are objects of the derivatives, and
3. the Supervisory Office.

The managements may use the decisions notified in accordance with sentence 1 to them prior to its publication only for the purposes of deciding whether the stock exchange quotation should be suspended or discontinued. The Supervisory Office may permit that an offeror with residence or registered office abroad makes a notification in accordance with sentence 1 simultaneously with the publication, if the decisions of the managements as to the suspension or discontinuance of the stock exchange quotation are not thereby affected.

(3) The publication of the decision in accordance with para. 1 sentence 1 is to be made, in German,
1. in at least one supra-regional official stock exchange gazette or
2. by means of an electronically operated information distribution system which is widely used by credit institutions, financial services institutions, companies operating in accordance with § 53 para. 1 of the Banking Act,[5] other companies having their registered offices in Germany and admitted to trading on a German stock exchange, and insurance companies.

The offeror shall state the address under which the publication of the offer document will take place on the Internet in accordance with § 14 para 3 sentence 1 no. 1. A publication in any other manner may not take place prior to the publication in accordance with sentence 1.

---

[5] Gesetz über das Kreditwesen.

der Bundesanstalt auf eine gewissenhafte Erfüllung ihrer Obliegenheiten zu verpflichten.

Abschnitt 3. Angebote zum Erwerb von Wertpapieren

§ 10 Veröffentlichung der Entscheidung zur Abgabe eines Angebots

(1) Der Bieter hat seine Entscheidung zur Abgabe eines Angebots unverzüglich gemäß Absatz 3 Satz 1 zu veröffentlichen. Die Verpflichtung nach Satz 1 besteht auch, wenn für die Entscheidung nach Satz 1 der Beschluss der Gesellschafterversammlung des Bieters erforderlich ist und ein solcher Beschluss noch nicht erfolgt ist. Die Bundesanstalt kann dem Bieter auf Antrag abweichend von Satz 2 gestatten, eine Veröffentlichung erst nach dem Beschluss der Gesellschafterversammlung vorzunehmen, wenn der Bieter durch geeignete Vorkehrungen sicherstellt, dass dadurch Marktverzerrungen nicht zu befürchten sind.

(2) Der Bieter hat die Entscheidung nach Absatz 1 Satz 1 vor der Veröffentlichung
1. den Geschäftsführungen der Börsen, an denen Wertpapiere des Bieters, der Zielgesellschaft und anderer durch das Angebot unmittelbar betroffener Gesellschaften zum Handel zugelassen sind,
2. den Geschäftsführungen der Börsen, an denen Derivate im Sinne des § 2 Abs. 2 des Wertpapierhandelsgesetzes gehandelt werden, sofern die Wertpapiere Gegenstand der Derivate sind, und
3. der Bundesanstalt
mitzuteilen. Die Geschäftsführungen dürfen die ihnen nach Satz 1 mitgeteilten Entscheidungen vor der Veröffentlichung nur zum Zwecke der Entscheidung verwenden, ob die Feststellung des Börsenpreises auszusetzen oder einzustellen ist. Die Bundesanstalt kann gestatten, dass Bieter mit Wohnort oder Sitz im Ausland die Mitteilung nach Satz 1 gleichzeitig mit der Veröffentlichung vornehmen, wenn dadurch die Entscheidungen der Geschäftsführungen über die Aussetzung oder Einstellung der Feststellung des Börsenpreises nicht beeinträchtigt werden.

(3) Die Veröffentlichung der Entscheidung nach Absatz 1 Satz 1 ist

1. in mindestens einem überregionalen Börsenpflichtblatt oder
2. über ein elektronisch betriebenes Informationsverbreitungssystem, das bei Kreditinstituten, Finanzdienstleistungsinstituten, nach § 53 Abs. 1 des Gesetzes über das Kreditwesen tätigen Unternehmen, anderen Unternehmen, die ihren Sitz im Inland haben und an einer inländischen Börse zur Teilnahme am Handel zugelassen sind, und Versicherungsunternehmen weit verbreitet ist,

in deutscher Sprache vorzunehmen. Dabei hat der Bieter auch die Adresse anzugeben, unter der die Veröffentlichung der Angebotsunterlage im Internet nach § 14 Abs. 3 Satz 1 Nr. 1 erfolgen wird. Eine Veröffentlichung in anderer Weise darf nicht vor der Veröffentlichung nach Satz 1 vorgenommen werden.

(4) The offeror shall send the publication under para. 3 sentence 1 without delay to the management of the stock exchanges mentioned in para. 2 sentence 1 nos. 1 and 2 and to the Supervisory Office. This shall not apply insofar as the Supervisory Office has permitted under para. 2 sentence 3 that the notice under para. 2 sentence 1 be made simultaneously with the publication.

(5) The offeror shall notify the management board of the target company in writing of the decision to make a bid without delay after the publication in accordance with para. 3 sentence 1. The management board of the target company shall inform the relevant works council or, insofar as there is none such, the employees directly without delay of the notice under sentence 1.

(6) § 15 of the Securities Trading Act shall not apply to decisions on the making of a bid.

§ 11. Offer Document

(1) The offeror shall prepare and publish a document on the bid (the offer document). The offer document shall contain the information necessary to enable a properly informed decision on the bid to be reached. The information must be correct and complete. The offer document is to be written in German and in a form which facilitates its understanding and evaluation. It shall be signed by the offeror.

(2) The offer document shall contain the content of the bid and additional information.
Information on the content of the bid shall be
1. the name or business name and address or registered office and, if a company is involved, the legal form of the offeror,
2. the business name, the registered office and legal form of the target company,
3. the securities which are the subject matter of the bid,
4. the nature and the amount of the consideration offered for the securities of the target company,
5. the conditions to which the effectiveness of the bid is subject,
6. the commencement and ending of the acceptance period.
Additional information shall be
1. information on the measures necessary to ensure that the offeror has the necessary funds available for the complete performance of the bid and as to the anticipated effects of a successful bid on the assets, finance and profitability of the offeror,
2. details as to the intentions of the offeror in relation to the future business of the target company, in particular in relation to the registered office and the locations of important facilities of the business, the application of its assets, its future obligations, the employees and their representation, the members of the management organs and significant changes of the employment conditions including the measures intended in relation thereto,

(4) Der Bieter hat die Veröffentlichung nach Absatz 3 Satz 1 unverzüglich den Geschäftsführungen der in Absatz 2 Satz 1 Nr. 1 und 2 erfassten Börsen und der Bundeanstalt zu übersenden. Dies gilt nicht, soweit die Bundesanstalt nach Absatz 2 Satz 3 gestattet hat, die Mitteilung nach Absatz 2 Satz 1 gleichzeitig mit der Veröffentlichung vorzunehmen.

(5) Der Bieter hat dem Vorstand der Zielgesellschaft unverzüglich nach der Veröffentlichung nach Absatz 3 Satz 1 die Entscheidung zur Abgabe eines Angebots schriftlich mitzuteilen. Der Vorstand der Zielgesellschaft unterrichtet den zuständigen Betriebsrat oder, sofern ein solcher nicht besteht, unmittelbar die Arbeitnehmer, unverzüglich über die Mitteilung nach Satz 1.

(6) § 15 des Wertpapierhandelsgesetzes gilt nicht für Entscheidungen zur Abgabe eines Angebots.

§ 11. Angebotsunterlage

(1) Der Bieter hat eine Unterlage über das Angebot (Angebotsunterlage) zu erstellen und zu veröffentlichen. Die Angebotsunterlage muss die Angaben enthalten, die notwendig sind, um in Kenntnis der Sachlage über das Angebot entscheiden zu können. Die Angaben müssen richtig und vollständig sein. Die Angebotsunterlage ist in deutscher Sprache und in einer Form abzufassen, die ihr Verständnis und ihre Auswertung erleichtert. Sie ist von dem Bieter zu unterzeichnen.

(2) Die Angebotsunterlage hat den Inhalt des Angebots und ergänzende Angaben zu enthalten.
Angaben über den Inhalt des Angebots sind
1. Name oder Firma und Anschrift oder Sitz sowie, wenn es sich um eine Gesellschaft handelt, die Rechtsform des Bieters,
2. Firma, Sitz und Rechtsform der Zielgesellschaft,
3. die Wertpapiere, die Gegenstand des Angebots sind,
4. Art und Höhe der für die Wertpapiere der Zielgesellschaft gebotenen Gegenleistung,
5. die Bedingungen, von denen die Wirksamkeit des Angebots abhängt,
6. der Beginn und das Ende der Annahmefrist.

Ergänzende Angaben sind
1. Angaben zu den notwendigen Maßnahmen, die sicherstellen, dass dem Bieter die zur vollständigen Erfüllung des Angebots notwendigen Mittel zur Verfügung stehen, und zu den erwarteten Auswirkungen eines erfolgreichen Angebots auf die Vermögens-, Finanz- und Ertragslage des Bieters,
2. Angaben über die Absichten des Bieters im Hinblick auf die künftige Geschäftstätigkeit der Zielgesellschaft, insbesondere den Sitz und den Standort wesentlicher Unternehmensteile, die Verwendung ihres Vermögens, ihre künftigen Verpflichtungen, die Arbeitnehmer und deren Vertretungen, die Mitglieder ihrer Geschäftsführungsorgane und wesentliche Änderungen der Beschäftigungsbedingungen einschließlich der insoweit vorgesehenen Maßnahmen,

3. details of payments or other benefits in money's worth made or promised to members of the management board or the supervisory board of the target company,
4. the confirmation in accordance with § 13 para. 1 sentence 2 stating the name, registered office and legal form of the investment services enterprise.

(3) The offer document must state the name and address, in the case of legal persons or companies, the business name, registered office and legal form, of the persons or companies responsible for the contents of the offer document; it must contain a declaration by these persons or companies that the data are correct to the best of their knowledge and that no significant information has been omitted.

(4) The Federal Ministry of Finance may, by legal regulation, which does not require the agreement of the Bundesrat,
1. issue more detailed provisions as to the form and data to be included in the offer document and
2. prescribe other additional data insofar as such may be necessary for the recipient of the bid to make an accurate and complete assessment of the offeror, the persons acting in common with the offeror and the bid.

(5) The Federal Ministry of Finance may delegate the authority under para. 4 by legal regulation to the Supervisory Office.

§ 12. Liability for the Offer Document

(1) If data in the offer document significant for the assessment of the bid are inaccurate or incomplete, an acceptor of the bid can demand compensation for the damage caused to him by acceptance of the bid from
1. the party which takes responsibility for the offer document, and

2. the party from which the issue of the offer document originates,
   as jointly and severally liable parties.

(2) A party who proves that he was not aware of the inaccuracy or incompleteness of the data contained in the offer document and that this lack of knowledge was not due to gross negligence, cannot be made liable in accordance with para. 1.

(3) The claim under para. 1 does not arise insofar as
1. the acceptance of the bid did not take place on the basis of the offer document,
2. the acceptor of the bid was aware of the inaccuracy or incompleteness of the data contained in the offer document when making the declaration of acceptance, or
3. prior to the acceptance of the bid, a clearly worded correction of the inaccurate or incomplete data was published in Germany in a publication under § 15 para. 1 of the Securities Trading Act or a similar notification was made.

3. Angaben über Geldleistungen oder andere geldwerte Vorteile, die Vorstands- oder Aufsichtsratsmitgliedern der Zielgesellschaft gewährt oder in Aussicht gestellt werden,
4. die Bestätigung nach § 13 Abs. 1 Satz 2 unter Angabe von Firma, Sitz und Rechtsform des Wertpapierdienstleistungsunternehmens.

(3) Die Angebotsunterlage muss Namen und Anschrift, bei juristischen Personen oder Gesellschaften Firma, Sitz und Rechtsform, der Personen oder Gesellschaften aufführen, die für den Inhalt der Angebotsunterlage die Verantwortung übernehmen; sie muss eine Erklärung dieser Personen oder Gesellschaften enthalten, dass ihres Wissens die Angaben richtig und keine wesentlichen Umstände ausgelassen sind.

(4) Das Bundesministerium der Finanzen kann durch Rechtsverordnung, die nicht der Zustimmung des Bundesrates bedarf,
1. nähere Bestimmungen über die Gestaltung und die in die Angebotsunterlage aufzunehmenden Angaben erlassen und
2. weitere ergänzende Angaben vorschreiben, soweit dies notwendig ist, um den Empfängern des Angebots ein zutreffendes und vollständiges Urteil über den Bieter, die mit ihm gemeinsam handelnden Personen und das Angebot zu ermöglichen.

(5) Das Bundesministerium der Finanzen kann die Ermächtigung nach Absatz 4 durch Rechtsverordnung auf die Bundesanstalt übertragen.

§ 12 Haftung für die Angebotsunterlage

(1) Sind für die Beurteilung des Angebots wesentliche Angaben der Angebotsunterlage unrichtig oder unvollständig, so kann derjenige, der das Angebot angenommen hat,
1. von denjenigen, die für die Angebotsunterlage die Verantwortung übernommen haben, und
2. von denjenigen, von denen der Erlass der Angebotsunterlage ausgeht,
als Gesamtschuldner den Ersatz des ihm aus der Annahme des Angebots entstandenen Schadens verlangen.

(2) Nach Absatz 1 kann nicht in Anspruch genommen werden, wer nachweist, dass er die Unrichtigkeit oder Unvollständigkeit der Angaben der Angebotsunterlage nicht gekannt hat und die Unkenntnis nicht auf grober Fahrlässigkeit beruht.

(3) Der Anspruch nach Absatz 1 besteht nicht, sofern
1. die Annahme des Angebots nicht auf Grund der Angebotsunterlage erfolgt ist,
2. derjenige, der das Angebot angenommen hat, die Unrichtigkeit oder Unvollständigkeit der Angaben der Angebotsunterlage bei der Abgabe der Annahmeerklärung kannte oder
3. vor der Annahme des Angebots in einer Veröffentlichung nach § 15 Abs. 3 des Wertpapierhandelsgesetzes oder einer vergleichbaren Bekanntmachung eine deutlich gestaltete Berichtigung der unrichtigen oder unvollständigen Angaben im Inland veröffentlicht wurde.

(4) The claim under para. 1 shall be statute barred one year after the date on which the acceptor of the bid obtains knowledge of the inaccuracy or incompleteness of the data contained in the offer document, at the latest, however, three years after the publication of the offer document.

(5) An agreement reducing or dispensing with the claim under para. 1 in advance, shall be invalid.

(6) Additional claims which can be made under the provisions of civil law on the basis of contracts or intentional tortious acts remain unaffected.

§ 13. Financing of the Bid

(1) The offeror shall, prior to the publication of the offer document, take the necessary measures to ensure that the funds necessary for the complete performance of the bid are available to it at the point in time when the right to payment of the consideration accrues. If payment of money is intended to be the consideration for the bid, an investment services enterprise, independent of the offeror, shall confirm in writing that the offeror has taken the necessary measures to ensure that the necessary funds are available for complete performance of the bid at the point in time when the right to payment of the consideration accrues.

(2) If an offeror has not taken the necessary measures in accordance with para. 1 sentence 2 and if, at the time when the right to payment of the consideration accrues, the necessary funds are not available for this reason, the acceptor of the bid may demand compensation from the investment services enterprise which has issued the written confirmation for the damage caused to him due to the incomplete performance.

(3) § 12 para. 2 to 6 shall apply mutatis mutandis.

§ 14. Sending and Publishing the Offer Document

(1) The offeror shall communicate the offer document to the Supervisory Office within four weeks after publication of the decision to make a bid. The Supervisory Office shall confirm to the offeror the day of receipt of the offer document. The Supervisory Office can, on application, extend the period in accordance with sentence 1 by up to four weeks, if the offeror is unable to comply with the period in accordance with sentence 1 due to a cross-border bid or necessary capital measures.

(2) The offer document is to be published in accordance with para. 3 sentence 1 without delay, if the Supervisory Office has permitted the publication or if ten working days have passed from the receipt of the offer document without the Supervisory Office having prohibited the bid. Prior to the publication in accordance with sentence 1, the offer document may not be made known. The Supervisory Office may, prior to prohibiting the bid, ex-

(4) Der Anspruch nach Absatz 1 verjährt in einem Jahr seit dem Zeitpunkt, zu dem derjenige, der das Angebot angenommen hat, von der Unrichtigkeit oder Unvollständigkeit der Angaben der Angebotsunterlage Kenntnis erlangt hat, spätestens jedoch in drei Jahren seit der Veröffentlichung der Angebotsunterlage.

(5) Eine Vereinbarung, durch die der Anspruch nach Absatz 1 im Voraus ermäßigt oder erlassen wird, ist unwirksam.

(6) Weitergehende Ansprüche, die nach den Vorschriften des bürgerlichen Rechts auf Grund von Verträgen oder vorsätzlichen unerlaubten Handlungen erhoben werden können, bleiben unberührt.

§ 13. Finanzierung des Angebots

(1) Der Bieter hat vor der Veröffentlichung der Angebotsunterlage die notwendigen Maßnahmen zu treffen, um sicherzustellen, dass ihm die zur vollständigen Erfüllung des Angebots notwendigen Mittel zum Zeitpunkt der Fälligkeit des Anspruchs auf die Gegenleistung zur Verfügung stehen. Für den Fall, dass das Angebot als Gegenleistung die Zahlung einer Geldleistung vorsieht, ist durch ein vom Bieter unabhängiges Wertpapierdienstleistungsunternehmen schriftlich zu bestätigen, dass der Bieter die notwendigen Maßnahmen getroffen hat, um sicherzustellen, dass die zur vollständigen Erfüllung des Angebots notwendigen Mittel zum Zeitpunkt der Fälligkeit des Anspruchs auf die Geldleistung zur Verfügung stehen.

(2) Hat der Bieter die nach Absatz 1 Satz 2 notwendigen Maßnahmen nicht getroffen und stehen ihm zum Zeitpunkt der Fälligkeit des Anspruchs auf die Geldleistung aus diesem Grunde die notwendigen Mittel nicht zur Verfügung, so kann derjenige, der das Angebot angenommen hat, von dem Wertpapierdienstleistungsunternehmen, das die schriftliche Bestätigung erteilt hat, den Ersatz des ihm aus der nicht vollständigen Erfüllung entstandenen Schadens verlangen.

(3) § 12 Abs. 2 bis 6 gilt entsprechend.

§ 14. Übermittlung und Veröffentlichung der Angebotsunterlage

(1) Der Bieter hat die Angebotsunterlage innerhalb von vier Wochen nach der Veröffentlichung der Entscheidung zur Abgabe eines Angebots der Bundesanstalt zu übermitteln. Die Bundesanstalt bestätigt dem Bieter den Tag des Eingangs der Angebotsunterlage. Die Bundesanstalt kann die Frist nach Satz 1 auf Antrag um bis zu vier Wochen verlängern, wenn dem Bieter die Einhaltung der Frist nach Satz 1 auf Grund eines grenzüberschreitenden Angebots oder erforderlicher Kapitalmaßnahmen nicht möglich ist.

(2) Die Angebotsunterlage ist gemäß Absatz 3 Satz 1 unverzüglich zu veröffentlichen, wenn die Bundesanstalt die Veröffentlichung gestattet hat oder wenn seit dem Eingang der Angebotsunterlage zehn Werktage verstrichen sind, ohne dass das Bundesaufsichtsamt das Angebot untersagt hat. Vor der Veröffentlichung nach Satz 1 darf die Angebotsunterlage nicht bekannt gegeben werden. Die Bundesanstalt kann vor einer Untersagung

tend the period in accordance with sentence 1 by up to five working days, if the offer document is not complete or in conformity with the provisions of this law or of a legal regulation issued under this law.

(3) The offer document is to be published by:
1. being placed on the Internet and
2. being copied in a supra-regional official stock exchange gazette or by being made available without charge to be given out at a suitable place in Germany; in the latter case, it shall be announced in a supra-regional official stock exchange gazette at which location the offer document is available.

The offeror shall, without delay, send proof of publication under sentence 1 no. 2, to the Supervisory Office.

(4) The offeror shall communicate the offer document to the management board of the target company without delay after the publication in accordance with para. 3 sentence 1. The management board of the target company shall communicate the offer document without delay to the relevant works council or insofar as there is no works council, directly to the employees.

§ 15. Prohibition of a Bid

(1) The Supervisory Office prohibits the bid if
1. the offer document does not contain the data required by § 11 para. 2 or by a legal regulation issued on the basis of § 11 para. 4.

2. the data contained in the offer document obviously violates the provisions of this law or of legal regulations issued on the basis of this law,

3. the offeror has communicated no offer document to the Supervisory Office, in violation of § 14 para. 1 sentence 1,

4. the offeror has not published the offer document, in violation of § 14 para. 2 sentence 1.

(2) The Supervisory Office may prohibit the bid if the offeror has not made the publication in the form prescribed in § 14 para. 3 sentence 1.

(3) If the bid has been prohibited under para. 1 or para. 2, publication of the offer document is prohibited. A legal transaction based on a bid prohibited under para. 1 or 2 is void.

§ 16. Periods for Acceptance, Calling of General Meeting

(1) The period for accepting the bid (acceptance period) may not be less than four weeks and, notwithstanding the provisions of § 21 para. 5 and § 22 para. 2, not more than ten weeks. The acceptance period begins with the publication of the offer document in accordance with § 14 para. 3 sentence 1.

(2) In the case of a takeover offer, the shareholders of the company who have not accepted the bid, may accept the bid within two weeks after the publication in accordance with § 23 para. 1 sentence 1 No. 2 (further accept-

des Angebots die Frist nach Satz 1 um bis zu fünf Werktage verlängern, wenn die Angebotsunterlage nicht vollständig ist oder sonst den Vorschriften dieses Gesetzes oder einer auf Grund dieses Gesetzes erlassenen Rechtsverordnung nicht entspricht.

(3) Die Angebotsunterlage ist zu veröffentlichen durch
1. Bekanntgabe im Internet und
2. Abdruck in einem überregionalen Börsenpflichtblatt oder durch Bereithalten zur kostenlosen Ausgabe bei einer geeigneten Stelle im Inland; im letzteren Fall ist in einem überregionalen Börsenpflichtblatt bekannt zu machen, bei welcher Stelle die Angebotsunterlage bereit gehalten wird.

Der Bieter hat der Bundesanstalt unverzüglich einen Beleg über die Veröffentlichung nach Satz 1 Nr. 2 zu übersenden.

(4) Der Bieter hat die Angebotsunterlage dem Vorstand der Zielgesellschaft unverzüglich nach der Veröffentlichung nach Absatz 3 Satz 1 zu übermitteln. Der Vorstand der Zielgesellschaft hat die Angebotsunterlage unverzüglich dem zuständigen Betriebsrat oder, sofern ein solcher nicht besteht, unmittelbar den Arbeitnehmern zu übermitteln.

§ 15. Untersagung des Angebots

(1) Die Bundesanstalt untersagt das Angebot, wenn
1. die Angebotsunterlage nicht die Angaben enthält, die nach § 11 Abs. 2 oder einer auf Grund des § 11 Abs. 4 erlassenen Rechtsverordnung erforderlich sind,
2. die in der Angebotsunterlage enthaltenen Angaben offensichtlich gegen Vorschriften dieses Gesetzes oder einer auf Grund dieses Gesetzes erlassenen Rechtsverordnung verstoßen,
3. der Bieter entgegen § 14 Abs. 1 Satz 1 der Bundesanstalt keine Angebotsunterlage übermittelt oder
4. der Bieter entgegen § 14 Abs. 2 Satz 1 die Angebotsunterlage nicht veröffentlicht hat.

(2) Die Bundesanstalt kann das Angebot untersagen, wenn der Bieter die Veröffentlichung nicht in der in § 14 Abs. 3 Satz 1 vorgeschriebenen Form vornimmt.

(3) Ist das Angebot nach Absatz 1 oder 2 untersagt worden, so ist die Veröffentlichung der Angebotsunterlage verboten. Ein Rechtsgeschäft auf Grund eines nach Absatz 1 oder 2 untersagten Angebots ist nichtig.

§ 16. Annahmefristen; Einberufung der Hauptversammlung

(1) Die Frist für die Annahme des Angebots (Annahmefrist) darf nicht weniger als vier Wochen und unbeschadet der Vorschriften des § 21 Abs. 5 und § 22 Abs. 2 nicht mehr als zehn Wochen betragen. Die Annahmefrist beginnt mit der Veröffentlichung der Angebotsunterlage gemäß § 14 Abs. 3 Satz 1.

(2) Bei einem Übernahmeangebot können die Aktionäre der Zielgesellschaft, die das Angebot nicht angenommen haben, das Angebot innerhalb von zwei Wochen nach der in § 23 Abs. 1 Satz 1 Nr. 2 genannten

ance period). Sentence 1 shall not apply if the offeror has made the bid dependent on the acquisition of a minimum number of shares and this minimum number of shares has not been achieved on expiry of the acceptance period.

(3) If a shareholders' meeting of the target company is called in connection with the bid after the publication of the offer document, the acceptance period, notwithstanding the provisions of § 21 para. 5 and § 22 para. 2, shall be ten weeks from the publication of the offer document. The management board of the target company shall notify the calling of the general meeting of the target company without delay to the offeror and to the Supervisory Office. The offeror shall without delay publish the communication under sentence 2, stating the expiry of the acceptance period, in a supra-regional official stock exchange gazette. The offeror shall send to the Supervisory Office without delay proof of the publication.

(4) The shareholders' meeting in accordance with para. 3 may be called up to two weeks prior to the day of the meeting. In deviation from § 121 para. 5 of the Stock Corporation Act and any provisions of the articles of association, the company may freely choose the location of the shareholders' meeting. If the period of one month in accordance with § 123 para. 1 of the Stock Corporation Act is abridged, the periods for notice and deposit and the period under § 125 para. 1 sentence 1 of the Stock Corporation Act shall be four days. The company shall facilitate the shareholders in the matter of granting power of attorney to exercise voting rights insofar as this is permissible under the law and the articles of association. Communications to the shareholders, a report under § 186 para. 4 sentence 2 of the Stock Corporation Act and shareholders' motions filed in good time are to be made available to all shareholders and notified to them in summary form. The sending of communications and counter proposals may be remitted if the management board is convinced, with the agreement of the supervisory board, that receipt in time by the shareholders is unlikely. In this case, § 128 para. 2 sentence 2 of the Stock Corporation Act shall apply also to bearer shares in respect of suggestions regarding voting on resolutions.

§ 17. Inadmissibility of Public Demand to Make Bids

A public invitation by the offeror directed at the acquisition of securities of the target company to the owners of the securities to make offers is inadmissible.

§ 18. Conditions; Inadmissibility of the Reservation of the Right to Withdraw and Revoke

(1) Subject to § 25, a bid shall not be made dependent on conditions, the fulfilment of which can be brought about exclusively by the offeror, persons acting in common with the offeror or their subsidiaries, advisors acting for such persons or companies in connection with the bid.

Veröffentlichung (weitere Annahmefrist) annehmen. Satz 1 gilt nicht, wenn der Bieter das Angebot von dem Erwerb eines Mindestanteils der Aktien abhängig gemacht hat und dieser Mindestanteil nach Ablauf der Annahmefrist nicht erreicht wurde.

(3) Wird im Zusammenhang mit dem Angebot nach der Veröffentlichung der Angebotsunterlage eine Hauptversammlung der Zielgesellschaft einberufen, beträgt die Annahmefrist unbeschadet der Vorschriften des § 21 Abs. 5 und § 22 Abs. 2 zehn Wochen ab der Veröffentlichung der Angebotsunterlage. Der Vorstand der Zielgesellschaft hat die Einberufung der Hauptversammlung der Zielgesellschaft unverzüglich dem Bieter und der Bundesanstalt mitzuteilen. Der Bieter hat die Mitteilung nach Satz 2 unter Angabe des Ablaufs der Annahmefrist unverzüglich in einem überregionalen Börsenpflichtblatt zu veröffentlichen. Er hat der Bundesanstalt unverzüglich einen Beleg über die Veröffentlichung zu übersenden.

(4) Die Hauptversammlung nach Absatz 3 kann bis spätestens zwei Wochen vor dem Tag der Versammlung einberufen werden. Abweichend von § 121 Abs. 5 des Aktiengesetzes und etwaigen Bestimmungen der Satzung ist die Gesellschaft bei der Wahl des Versammlungsortes frei. Wird die Monatsfrist des § 123 Abs. 1 des Aktiengesetzes unterschritten, so betragen die Anmelde- und Hinterlegungsfristen und die Frist nach § 125 Abs. 1 Satz 1 des Aktiengesetzes vier Tage. Die Gesellschaft hat den Aktionären die Erteilung von Stimmrechtsvollmachten soweit nach Gesetz und Satzung möglich zu erleichtern. Mitteilungen an die Aktionäre, ein Bericht nach § 186 Abs. 4 Satz 2 des Aktiengesetzes und fristgerecht eingereichte Anträge von Aktionären sind allen Aktionären zugänglich und in Kurzfassung bekannt zu machen. Die Zusendung von Mitteilungen und Gegenanträgen kann unterbleiben, wenn zur Überzeugung des Vorstands mit Zustimmung des Aufsichtsrats der rechtzeitige Eingang bei den Aktionären nicht wahrscheinlich ist. Für Abstimmungsvorschläge gilt § 128 Abs. 2 Satz 2 des Aktiengesetzes in diesem Fall auch bei Inhaberaktien.

§ 17. Unzulässigkeit der öffentlichen Aufforderung zur Abgabe von Angeboten

Eine öffentliche auf den Erwerb von Wertpapieren der Zielgesellschaft gerichtete Aufforderung des Bieters zur Abgabe von Angeboten durch die Inhaber der Wertpapiere ist unzulässig.

§ 18. Bedingungen; Unzulässigkeit des Vorbehalts des Rücktritts und des Widerrufs

(1) Ein Angebot darf vorbehaltlich § 25 nicht von Bedingungen abhängig gemacht werden, deren Eintritt der Bieter, mit ihm gemeinsam handelnde Personen oder deren Tochterunternehmen oder im Zusammenhang mit dem Angebot für diese Personen oder Unternehmen tätige Berater ausschließlich selbst herbeiführen können.

(2) A bid made subject to the reservation that it may be revoked or withdrawn, is inadmissible.

§ 19. Acceptance in the case of a Partial Bid

If, in the case of a bid directed only to the acquisition of a certain portion or a certain number of securities, the portion or number of securities which the offeror can acquire is higher than the portion or the number of securities which the offeror has undertaken to acquire, the declarations of acceptance shall, in principle, be taken into account proportionately.

§ 20. Trading Portfolio

(1) The Supervisory Office shall, on written application by the offeror, permit that securities of the target company not be taken into account as far as the additional data under § 11 para. 4 no. 2, the publication obligations under § 23, the calculation of the voting rights portion under § 29 para. 2 and the determination of consideration under § 31 para. 1, 3 and 4 and the consideration in money under § 31 para. 5 are concerned.

(2) An application for exemption under para. 1 may be made if the offeror, the persons acting in common with it or their subsidiaries

1. hold or intend to hold the securities affected, in order to use the existing or expected difference between the purchase price and the sale price in the short term and are enterprises admitted to trading on an organised market and provide investment services,
2. submit that by the purchase of the securities insofar as shares with voting rights are concerned, it is not intended to exert influence on the management of the company.

(3) Voting rights of shares which due to an exemption under para. 1 are not taken into account, may not be exercised if, when they are taken into account, a bid as a takeover bid would have to be made or an obligation under § 35 para. 1 sentence 1 and para. 2 sentence 1 would arise.

(4) If an offeror no longer intends to hold securities in respect of which an exemption under para. 1 has been issued, for the purposes stated in para. 1 no. 1 or intends to exercise influence on the management of the company, this is to be communicated to the Supervisory Office without delay. The Supervisory Office can revoke the exemption under para. 1 except under the provisions of the Administrative Procedure Act, if the obligation under sentence 1 has not been fulfilled.

§ 21. Change to the Bid

(1) The offeror may up to one working day prior to the expiry of the acceptance period
1. increase the consideration,
2. offer the choice of an alternative consideration,

(2) Ein Angebot, das unter dem Vorbehalt des Widerrufs oder des Rücktritts abgegeben wird, ist unzulässig.

§ 19. Zuteilung bei einem Teilangebot

Ist bei einem Angebot, das auf den Erwerb nur eines bestimmten Anteils oder einer bestimmten Anzahl der Wertpapiere gerichtet ist, der Anteil oder die Anzahl der Wertpapiere, die der Bieter erwerben kann, höher als der Anteil oder die Anzahl der Wertpapiere, die der Bieter zu erwerben sich verpflichtet hat, so sind die Annahmeerklärungen grundsätzlich verhältnismäßig zu berücksichtigen.

§ 20. Handelsbestand

(1) Die Bundesanstalt lässt auf schriftlichen Antrag des Bieters zu, dass Wertpapiere der Zielgesellschaft bei den ergänzenden Angaben nach § 11 Abs. 4 Nr. 2, den Veröffentlichungspflichten nach § 23, der Berechnung des Stimmrechtsanteils nach § 29 Abs. 2 und der Bestimmung der Gegenleistung nach § 31 Abs. 1, 3 und 4 und der Geldleistung nach § 31 Abs. 5 unberücksichtigt bleiben.

(2) Ein Befreiungsantrag nach Absatz 1 kann gestellt werden, wenn der Bieter, die mit ihm gemeinsam handelnden Personen oder deren Tochterunternehmen
1. die betreffenden Wertpapiere halten oder zu halten beabsichtigen, um bestehende oder erwartete Unterschiede zwischen dem Erwerbspreis und dem Veräußerungspreis kurzfristig zu nutzen und

2. darlegen, dass mit dem Erwerb der Wertpapiere, soweit es sich um stimmberechtigte Aktien handelt, nicht beabsichtigt ist, auf die Geschäftsführung der Gesellschaft Einfluss zu nehmen.

(3) Stimmrechte aus Aktien, die auf Grund einer Befreiung nach Absatz 1 unberücksichtigt bleiben, können nicht ausgeübt werden, wenn im Falle ihrer Berücksichtigung ein Angebot als Übernahmeangebot abzugeben wäre oder eine Verpflichtung nach § 35 Abs. 1 Satz 1 und Abs. 2 Satz 1 bestünde.

(4) Beabsichtigt der Bieter Wertpapiere, für die eine Befreiung nach Absatz 1 erteilt worden ist, nicht mehr zu den in Absatz 1 Nr. 1 genannten Zwecken zu halten oder auf die Geschäftsführung der Gesellschaft Einfluss zu nehmen, ist dies der Bundesanstalt unverzüglich mitzuteilen. Die Bundesanstalt kann die Befreiung nach Absatz 1 außer nach den Vorschriften des Verwaltungsverfahrensgesetzes widerrufen, wenn die Verpflichtung nach Satz 1 nicht erfüllt worden ist.

§ 21. Änderung des Angebots

(1) Der Bieter kann bis zu einem Werktag vor Ablauf der Annahmefrist

1. die Gegenleistung erhöhen,
2. wahlweise eine andere Gegenleistung anbieten,

3. reduce the minimum portion or the minimum number of securities or the minimum portion of voting rights, the acquisition of which the offeror had made a condition for the effectiveness of its bid,
4. waive conditions.

Compliance with the period in accordance with sentence 1 shall depend on the publication of the change under para. 2.

(2) The offeror shall publish the change to the bid referring to the right of withdrawal under para. 4 without delay in accordance with § 14 para. 3 sentence 1. § 14 para. 3 sentence 2 and para. 4 shall apply mutatis mutandis.

(3) § 11 para. 1 sentences 2 to 5, para. 3, §§ 12, 13 and § 15 para. 1 no. 2 shall apply mutatis mutandis.

(4) In the event of a change to the bid, the holders of securities in the target company who have accepted the bid prior to the publication of the change in accordance with para. 2, may withdraw from the contract up to the time of expiry of the acceptance period.

(5) In the event of a change to the bid, the acceptance period shall be extended by two weeks insofar as the publication of the change has taken place within the last two weeks prior to the expiry of the bid period. This applies also if the amended bid is in violation of legal regulations.

(6) A further change to the bid within the period of two weeks stated in para. 5 is not admissible.

§ 22. Competing Bids

(1) Competing bids are bids made by a third party during the acceptance period of a bid.

(2) If, in the case of competing bids, the acceptance period for the bid expires prior to the expiry of the acceptance period for the competing bid, the expiry of the acceptance period for the bid shall be determined by the expiry of the acceptance period for the competing bid. This applies also if the competing bid is changed or prohibited or is in breach of legal regulations.

(3) Holders of securities of the target company who have accepted the bid, may withdraw from the contract up to the time of expiry of the acceptance period if the conclusion of the contract has taken place prior to the publication of the offer document of the competing bid.

§ 23. Publication Obligations of the Offeror after Making a Bid

(1) The offeror is obliged to publish and to notify to the Supervisory Office, in accordance with § 14 para. 3 sentence 1, the number of all securities of the target company to which it, persons acting in common with it and their subsidiaries, are entitled including the amount of each shareholding and of the voting rights portions to which it is entitled and those attributed to it according to § 30, and the number of securities which are the object of the bid concerned in acceptance declarations received by it, including the amount of securities and voting rights,

3. den Mindestanteil oder die Mindestzahl der Wertpapiere oder den Mindestanteil der Stimmrechte, von dessen Erwerb der Bieter die Wirksamkeit seines Angebots abhängig gemacht hat, verringern oder
4. auf Bedingungen verzichten.

Für die Wahrung der Frist nach Satz 1 ist auf die Veröffentlichung der Änderung nach Absatz 2 abzustellen.

(2) Der Bieter hat die Änderung des Angebots unter Hinweis auf das Rücktrittsrecht nach Absatz 4 unverzüglich gemäß § 14 Abs. 3 Satz 1 zu veröffentlichen. § 14 Abs. 3 Satz 2 und Abs. 4 gilt entsprechend.

(3) § 11 Abs. 1 Satz 2 bis 5, Abs. 3, §§ 12, 13 und 15 Abs. 1 Nr. 2 gelten entsprechend.

(4) Im Falle einer Änderung des Angebots können die Inhaber von Wertpapieren der Zielgesellschaft, die das Angebot vor Veröffentlichung der Änderung nach Absatz 2 angenommen haben, von dem Vertrag bis zum Ablauf der Annahmefrist zurücktreten.

(5) Im Falle einer Änderung des Angebots verlängert sich die Annahmefrist um zwei Wochen, sofern die Veröffentlichung der Änderung innerhalb der letzten zwei Wochen vor Ablauf der Angebotsfrist erfolgt. Dies gilt auch, falls das geänderte Angebot gegen Rechtsvorschriften verstößt.

(6) Eine erneute Änderung des Angebots innerhalb der in Absatz 5 genannten Frist von zwei Wochen ist unzulässig.

§ 22. Konkurrierende Angebote

(1) Konkurrierende Angebote sind Angebote, die während der Annahmefrist eines Angebots von einem Dritten abgegeben werden.

(2) Läuft im Falle konkurrierender Angebote die Annahmefrist für das Angebot vor Ablauf der Annahmefrist für das konkurrierende Angebot ab, bestimmt sich der Ablauf der Annahmefrist für das Angebot nach dem Ablauf der Annahmefrist für das konkurrierende Angebot. Dies gilt auch, falls das konkurrierende Angebot geändert oder untersagt wird oder gegen Rechtsvorschriften verstößt.

(3) Inhaber von Wertpapieren der Zielgesellschaft, die das Angebot angenommen haben, können bis zum Ablauf der Annahmefrist vom Vertrag zurücktreten, sofern der Vertragsschluss vor Veröffentlichung der Angebotsunterlage des konkurrierenden Angebots erfolgte.

§ 23. Veröffentlichungspflichten des Bieters nach Abgabe des Angebots

(1) Der Bieter ist verpflichtet, die Anzahl sämtlicher ihm, den mit ihm gemeinsam handelnden Personen und deren Tochterunternehmen zustehenden Wertpapiere der Zielgesellschaft einschließlich der Höhe der jeweiligen Anteile und der ihm zustehenden und nach § 30 zuzurechnenden Stimmrechtsanteile sowie die sich aus den ihm zugegangenen Annahmeerklärungen ergebende Anzahl der Wertpapiere, die Gegenstand des Angebots sind, einschließlich der Höhe der Wertpapier- und Stimmrechtsanteile

1. weekly, after publication of the offer document and, in the last week prior to the expiry of the acceptance period, daily,
2. without delay after the expiry of the acceptance period, and
3. without delay after the expiry of a further acceptance period.

§ 14 para. 3 sentence 2 and § 31 para. 6 apply mutatis mutandis.

(2) If, in the course of a takeover bid in which the offeror has acquired control over the target company, or in the course of a mandatory offer, the offeror, persons acting in common with it or their subsidiary companies, acquire shares of the target company outside the bid procedure, and in the context of mandatory offers of the offeror, after the publication of the offer document and before expiry of one year after publication in accordance with para. 1 no. 2, the offeror shall publish the amount of shares and the proportion of voting rights acquired stating the nature and amount of the consideration paid for each share without delay in accordance with § 14 para. 3 sentence 1, and shall notify same to the Supervisory Office. § 31 para. 6 shall apply mutatis mutandis.

§ 24. Cross-Border Bids

If the offeror in the case of cross-border bids also has to observe the regulations of another state outside the European Economic Area, and if it is unreasonable therefore that the offeror should make a bid to all holders of securities, the Supervisory Office can, on application by the offeror, permit certain holders of securities having residence, registered office or usual abode in that state to be excluded from the bid.

§ 25. Resolution of the Shareholders' Meeting of the Offeror

If the bid made by the offeror is subject to a resolution of its shareholders' meeting, it shall procure the passing of the said resolution without delay at the latest by the fifth working day prior to expiry of the acceptance period.

§ 26. Waiting Period

(1) If a bid has been prohibited under § 15 para. 1 or 2, a new bid by the offeror prior to the expiry of one year is not admissible. The same applies if the offeror has made a bid subject to the acquisition of a minimum number of securities and this minimum number has not been achieved on the expiration of the acceptance period. Sentences 1 and 2 shall not apply if the offeror is obliged to make publication under § 35 para. 1 sentence 1 and obliged to make a bid under § 35 para. 2 sentence 1.

(2) The Supervisory Office may, on written application, exempt the offeror from the prohibition contained in para. 1 sentences 1 and 2, if the target company agrees to the exemption.

1. nach Veröffentlichung der Angebotsunterlage wöchentlich sowie in der letzten Woche vor Ablauf der Annahmefrist täglich,
2. unverzüglich nach Ablauf der Annahmefrist und
3. unverzüglich nach Ablauf der weiteren Annahmefrist

gemäß § 14 Abs. 3 Satz 1 zu veröffentlichen und der Bundesanstalt mitzuteilen. § 14 Abs. 3 Satz 2 und § 31 Abs. 6 gelten entsprechend.

(2) Erwerben bei Übernahmeangeboten, bei denen der Bieter die Kontrolle über die Zielgesellschaft erlangt hat, und bei Pflichtangeboten der Bieter, mit ihm gemeinsam handelnde Personen oder deren Tochterunternehmen nach der Veröffentlichung der Angebotsunterlage und vor Ablauf eines Jahres nach der Veröffentlichung gemäß Absatz 1 Nr. 2 außerhalb des Angebotsverfahrens Aktien der Zielgesellschaft, so hat der Bieter die Höhe der erworbenen Aktien- und Stimmrechtsanteile unter Angabe der Art und Höhe der für jeden Anteil gewährten Gegenleistung unverzüglich gemäß § 14 Abs. 3 Satz 1 zu veröffentlichen und der Bundesanstalt mitzuteilen. § 31 Abs. 6 gilt entsprechend.

§ 24. Grenzüberschreitende Angebote

Hat der Bieter bei grenzüberschreitenden Angeboten zugleich die Vorschriften eines anderen Staates außerhalb des Europäischen Wirtschaftsraums einzuhalten und ist dem Bieter deshalb ein Angebot an alle Inhaber von Wertpapieren unzumutbar, kann die Bundesanstalt dem Bieter auf Antrag gestatten, bestimmte Inhaber von Wertpapieren mit Wohnsitz, Sitz oder gewöhnlichem Aufenthalt in dem Staat von dem Angebot auszunehmen.

§ 25. Beschluss der Gesellschafterversammlung des Bieters

Hat der Bieter das Angebot unter der Bedingung eines Beschlusses seiner Gesellschafterversammlung abgegeben, hat er den Beschluss unverzüglich, spätestens bis zum fünften Werktag vor Ablauf der Annahmefrist, herbeizuführen.

§ 26. Sperrfrist

(1) Ist ein Angebot nach § 15 Abs. 1 oder 2 untersagt worden, ist ein erneutes Angebot des Bieters vor Ablauf eines Jahres unzulässig. Gleiches gilt, wenn der Bieter ein Angebot von dem Erwerb eines Mindestanteils der Wertpapiere abhängig gemacht hat und dieser Mindestanteil nach Ablauf der Annahmefrist nicht erreicht wurde. Die Sätze 1 und 2 gelten nicht, wenn der Bieter zur Veröffentlichung nach § 35 Abs. 1 Satz 1 und zur Abgabe eines Angebots nach § 35 Abs. 2 Satz 1 verpflichtet ist.

(2) Die Bundesanstalt kann den Bieter auf schriftlichen Antrag von dem Verbot des Absatzes 1 Satz 1 und 2 befreien, wenn die Zielgesellschaft der Befreiung zustimmt.

§ 27. The Opinion of the Board of Management and of the Supervisory Board of the Company

(1) The management board and the supervisory board of the target company shall issue a reasoned opinion on the bid and also on each amendment to it. This opinion must in particular refer to
1. the nature and amount of the consideration offered,
2. the foreseeable consequences of a successful bid for the target company, the employees and their representation, the conditions of employment and the locations of facilities of the company,
3. the objectives pursued by the offeror with the bid,
4. the intention of members of the management board and of the supervisory board, insofar as they are holders of securities of the target company, to accept the bid.

(2) If the relevant works council, or insofar as such does not exist, the employees of the target company directly, present an opinion on the bid to the management board, the management board shall, without their obligation under para. 3 sentence 1 being affected thereby, attach the latter opinion to its opinion.

(3) The management board and the supervisory board of the target company shall publish the opinion without delay after the communication of the offer document and any changes to it by the offeror according to § 14 para. 3 sentence 1. They shall simultaneously communicate the opinion to the relevant works council or if such does not exist directly to the employees. The management board and the supervisory board of the target company shall without delay submit evidence of publication in accordance with § 14 para. 3 sentence 1 no. 2 to the Supervisory Office.

§ 28. Advertising

(1) For the purpose of preventing abuse in advertising in connection with bids for the purchase of securities, the Supervisory Office may forbid certain types of advertising.

(2) Prior to general measures under para. 1, the commission is to be heard.

Part 4.
Takeover Bids

§ 29. Definitions

(1) Takeover bids are bids directed towards the acquisition of control.

(2) Control is the holding of at least 30 percent of the voting rights of the target company.

§ 27. Stellungnahme des Vorstands und Aufsichtsrats der Zielgesellschaft

(1) Der Vorstand und der Aufsichtsrat der Zielgesellschaft haben eine begründete Stellungnahme zu dem Angebot sowie zu jeder seiner Änderungen abzugeben. Die Stellungnahme muss insbesondere eingehen auf
1. die Art und Höhe der angebotenen Gegenleistung,
2. die voraussichtlichen Folgen eines erfolgreichen Angebots für die Zielgesellschaft, die Arbeitnehmer und ihre Vertretungen, die Beschäftigungsbedingungen und die Standorte der Zielgesellschaft,
3. die vom Bieter mit dem Angebot verfolgten Ziele,
4. die Absicht der Mitglieder des Vorstands und des Aufsichtsrats, soweit sie Inhaber von Wertpapieren der Zielgesellschaft sind, das Angebot anzunehmen.

(2) Übermitteln der zuständige Betriebsrat oder, sofern ein solcher nicht besteht, unmittelbar die Arbeitnehmer der Zielgesellschaft dem Vorstand eine Stellungnahme zu dem Angebot, hat der Vorstand unbeschadet seiner Verpflichtung nach Absatz 3 Satz 1 diese seiner Stellungnahme beizufügen.

(3) Der Vorstand und der Aufsichtsrat der Zielgesellschaft haben die Stellungnahme unverzüglich nach Übermittlung der Angebotsunterlage und deren Änderungen durch den Bieter gemäß § 14 Abs. 3 Satz 1 zu veröffentlichen. Sie haben die Stellungnahme gleichzeitig dem zuständigen Betriebsrat oder, sofern ein solcher nicht besteht, unmittelbar den Arbeitnehmern zu übermitteln. Der Vorstand und der Aufsichtsrat der Zielgesellschaft haben der Bundesanstalt unverzüglich einen Beleg über die Veröffentlichung gemäß § 14 Abs. 3 Satz 1 Nr. 2 zu übersenden.

§ 28. Werbung

(1) Um Missständen bei der Werbung im Zusammenhang mit Angeboten zum Erwerb von Wertpapieren zu begegnen, kann die Bundesanstalt bestimmte Arten der Werbung untersagen.

(2) Vor allgemeinen Maßnahmen nach Absatz 1 ist der Beirat zu hören.

Abschnitt 4.
Übernahmeangebote

§ 29. Begriffsbestimmungen

(1) Übernahmeangebote sind Angebote, die auf den Erwerb der Kontrolle gerichtet sind.

(2) Kontrolle ist das Halten von mindestens 30 Prozent der Stimmrechte an der Zielgesellschaft.

§ 30. Attribution of Voting Rights

(1) Voting rights of the offeror are equal to voting rights from shares in the target company, which are
1. held by a subsidiary of the offeror,
2. held by a third party and held for the account of the offeror,
3. transferred by the offeror to a third party as security, unless the third party is entitled to exercise the voting rights from these shares and announces the intention of exercising the voting rights independently of the instructions of the offeror,
4. over which a right of enjoyment in favour of the offeror exists,
5. which the offeror can acquire by declaration of intent,
6. which are entrusted to the offeror insofar as the offeror may exercise the voting rights of these shares according to its discretion, if no special instructions of the shareholder are given.

As far as the attribution in sentence 1 nos. 2 to 6 is concerned, a subsidiary company of the offeror is equated with the offeror. Voting rights of a subsidiary company will be attributed to the offeror in their full amount.

(2) Voting rights of a third party from shares of the target company with whom the offeror or its subsidiary co-ordinates its conduct in relation to the company on the basis of an agreement or in any other manner will be attributed in their full amount to the offeror with the exception of agreements on the exercise of voting rights in particular cases. For the calculation of the third party's portion of the voting rights share, para. 1 applies mutatis mutandis.

§ 31. Consideration

(1) The offeror shall offer the shareholders of the target company an adequate consideration. In determining an adequate consideration, in principle, the average stock exchange price of the shares of the target company, and acquisitions of shares of the target company by the offeror, by persons acting in common with it or their subsidiaries shall be taken into account.

(2) The consideration shall be in cash in Euro or in liquid shares which are admitted for trading on an organised market. If holders of shares carrying voting rights are offered consideration by means of shares, these shares must also carry a voting right.

(3) The offeror shall offer the shareholders of the target company consideration in cash in Euro if it, persons acting in common with it or their subsidiaries have purchased in return for consideration in cash
1. in the three months prior to the publication in accordance with § 10 para. 3 sentence 1, a total of at least five percent of the shares or voting rights in the target company, or
2. after the publication in accordance with § 10 para. 3 sentence 1 and prior to the expiry of the acceptance period, a total of at least one percent of the shares or voting rights in the target company.

§ 30. Zurechnung von Stimmrechten

(1) Stimmrechten des Bieters stehen Stimmrechte aus Aktien der Zielgesellschaft gleich,
1. die einem Tochterunternehmen des Bieters gehören,
2. die einem Dritten gehören und von ihm für Rechnung des Bieters gehalten werden,
3. die der Bieter einem Dritten als Sicherheit übertragen hat, es sei denn, der Dritte ist zur Ausübung der Stimmrechte aus diesen Aktien befugt und bekundet die Absicht, die Stimmrechte unabhängig von den Weisungen des Bieters auszuüben,
4. an denen zugunsten des Bieters ein Nießbrauch bestellt ist,
5. die der Bieter durch eine Willenserklärung erwerben kann,
6. die dem Bieter anvertraut sind, sofern er die Stimmrechte aus diesen Aktien nach eigenem Ermessen ausüben kann, wenn keine besonderen Weisungen des Aktionärs vorliegen.

Für die Zurechnung nach Satz 1 Nr. 2 bis 6 stehen dem Bieter Tochterunternehmen des Bieters gleich. Stimmrechte des Tochterunternehmens werden dem Bieter in voller Höhe zugerechnet.

(2) Dem Bieter werden auch Stimmrechte eines Dritten aus Aktien der Zielgesellschaft in voller Höhe zugerechnet, mit dem der Bieter oder sein Tochterunternehmen sein Verhalten in Bezug auf die Zielgesellschaft auf Grund einer Vereinbarung oder in sonstiger Weise abstimmt; ausgenommen sind Vereinbarungen über die Ausübung von Stimmrechten in Einzelfällen. Für die Berechnung des Stimmrechtsanteils des Dritten gilt Absatz 1 entsprechend.

§ 31. Gegenleistung

(1) Der Bieter hat den Aktionären der Zielgesellschaft eine angemessene Gegenleistung anzubieten. Bei der Bestimmung der angemessenen Gegenleistung sind grundsätzlich der durchschnittliche Börsenkurs der Aktien der Zielgesellschaft und Erwerbe von Aktien der Zielgesellschaft durch den Bieter, mit ihm gemeinsam handelnder Personen oder deren Tochterunternehmen zu berücksichtigen.

(2) Die Gegenleistung hat in einer Geldleistung in Euro oder in liquiden Aktien zu bestehen, die zum Handel an einem organisierten Markt zugelassen sind. Werden Inhabern stimmberechtigter Aktien als Gegenleistung Aktien angeboten, müssen diese Aktien ebenfalls ein Stimmrecht gewähren.

(3) Der Bieter hat den Aktionären der Zielgesellschaft eine Geldleistung in Euro anzubieten, wenn er, mit ihm gemeinsam handelnde Personen oder deren Tochterunternehmen
1. in den drei Monaten vor der Veröffentlichung gemäß § 10 Abs. 3 Satz 1 insgesamt mindestens 5 Prozent der Aktien oder Stimmrechte an der Zielgesellschaft oder
2. nach der Veröffentlichung gemäß § 10 Abs. 3 Satz 1 und vor Ablauf der Annahmefrist insgesamt mindestens 1 Prozent der Aktien oder Stimmrechte an der Zielgesellschaft

gegen Zahlung einer Geldleistung erworben haben.

(4) If the offeror, persons acting in common with it or their subsidiaries, purchase shares of the target company after publication of the offer document and prior to the publication in accordance with § 23 para. 1 sentence 1 no. 2, and if a higher value consideration is paid or agreed for such shares then the consideration owed to the recipients of the bid of each share class, shall be increased in value by the amount of the difference.

(5) If the offeror, persons acting in common with it or their subsidiaries, purchase shares of the target company, otherwise than on the stock exchange, within one year after the publication in accordance with § 23 para. 1 sentence 1 no. 2 and if consideration for such shares of higher value than that stated in the bid is paid or agreed, the offeror is obliged to pay the holders of the shares who accepted the bid, a consideration in cash in Euro in the amount of the difference. Sentence 1 shall not apply to the purchase of shares in the context of a legal obligation to pay compensation to shareholders of the company and shall not apply to the purchase of assets or part of the assets of the target company through merger, division or transfer of assets.

(6) Agreements on the basis of which the transfer of the ownership of shares can be demanded shall also constitute purchase within the meaning of paras. 3 to 5. The exercise of rights flowing from a rights issue on the basis of a capital increase in the target company shall not be deemed to be a purchase.

(7) The Federal Ministry of Finance can, by legal regulation which does not require the approval of the Bundesrat, issue more detailed regulations as to the adequacy of consideration under para. 1, in particular the taking into account of the average stock exchange price of the shares of the target company and the purchases of shares of the target company by the offeror, persons acting in common with it or their subsidiary companies and the period of time decisive therefor, and as to exceptions from the principle stated in para. 1 sentence 2 and the determination of the difference under para. 4 and 5. The Federal Ministry of Finance may delegate the authority by regulation having the force of law to the Supervisory Office.

§ 32. Inadmissibility of Partial Bids

A takeover offer which extends only to part of the shares of the target company is inadmissible notwithstanding the provisions of § 24.

§ 33. Acts of the Board of Management of the target Company

(1) After publication of the decision to make a bid until the publication of the result in accordance with § 23 para. 1 sentence 1 no. 2, the management board of the target company may not take any action which could prevent the bid being successful. This does not apply to actions which would also have been taken in the course of due and diligent management of a company which is not affected by a takeover bid, seeking a competitive bid or to actions to which the supervisory board of the target company has agreed.

(4) Erwerben der Bieter, mit ihm gemeinsam handelnde Personen oder deren Tochterunternehmen nach Veröffentlichung der Angebotsunterlage und vor der Veröffentlichung gemäß § 23 Abs. 1 Satz 1 Nr. 2 Aktien der Zielgesellschaft und wird hierfür wertmäßig eine höhere als die im Angebot genannte Gegenleistung gewährt oder vereinbart, erhöht sich die den Angebotsempfängern der jeweiligen Aktiengattung geschuldete Gegenleistung wertmäßig um den Unterschiedsbetrag.

(5) Erwerben der Bieter, mit ihm gemeinsam handelnde Personen oder deren Tochterunternehmen innerhalb eines Jahres nach der Veröffentlichung gemäß § 23 Abs. 1 Satz 1 Nr. 2 außerhalb der Börse Aktien der Zielgesellschaft und wird hierfür wertmäßig eine höhere als die im Angebot genannte Gegenleistung gewährt oder vereinbart, ist der Bieter gegenüber den Inhabern der Aktien, die das Angebot angenommen haben, zur Zahlung einer Geldleistung in Euro in Höhe des Unterschiedsbetrages verpflichtet. Satz 1 gilt nicht für den Erwerb von Aktien im Zusammenhang mit einer gesetzlichen Verpflichtung zur Gewährung einer Abfindung an Aktionäre der Zielgesellschaft und für den Erwerb des Vermögens oder von Teilen des Vermögens der Zielgesellschaft durch Verschmelzung, Spaltung oder Vermögensübertragung.

(6) Dem Erwerb im Sinne der Absätze 3 bis 5 gleichgestellt sind Vereinbarungen, auf Grund derer die Übereignung von Aktien verlangt werden kann. Als Erwerb gilt nicht die Ausübung eines gesetzlichen Bezugsrechts auf Grund einer Erhöhung des Grundkapitals der Zielgesellschaft.

(7) Das Bundesministerium der Finanzen kann durch Rechtsverordnung, die nicht der Zustimmung des Bundesrates bedarf, nähere Bestimmungen über die Angemessenheit der Gegenleistung nach Absatz 1, insbesondere die Berücksichtigung des durchschnittlichen Börsenkurses der Aktien der Zielgesellschaft und der Erwerbe von Aktien der Zielgesellschaft durch den Bieter, mit ihm gemeinsam handelnder Personen oder deren Tochterunternehmen und die hierbei maßgeblichen Zeiträume sowie über Ausnahmen von dem in Absatz 1 Satz 2 genannten Grundsatz und die Ermittlung des Unterschiedsbetrages nach den Absätzen 4 und 5 erlassen. Das Bundesministerium der Finanzen kann die Ermächtigung durch Rechtsverordnung auf die Bundesanstalt übertragen.

§ 32. Unzulässigkeit von Teilangeboten

Ein Übernahmeangebot, das sich nur auf einen Teil der Aktien der Zielgesellschaft erstreckt, ist unbeschadet der Vorschrift des § 24 unzulässig.

§ 33. Handlungen des Vorstands der Zielgesellschaft

(1) Nach Veröffentlichung der Entscheidung zur Abgabe eines Angebots bis zur Veröffentlichung des Ergebnisses nach § 23 Abs. 1 Satz 1 Nr. 2 darf der Vorstand der Zielgesellschaft keine Handlungen vornehmen, durch die der Erfolg des Angebots verhindert werden könnte. Dies gilt nicht für Handlungen, die auch ein ordentlicher und gewissenhafter Geschäftsleiter einer Gesellschaft, die nicht von einem Übernahmeangebot betroffen ist, vorgenommen hätte, für die Suche nach einem konkurrierenden Angebot

(2) If the general meeting authorises the management board prior to the time stated in para. 1 sentence 1 to take actions which are within the competence of the general meeting, with the object of preventing takeover bids, the nature of such actions is to be determined in the authorisation. The authorisation may be granted for a maximum of eighteen months. The resolution of the general meeting shall require a majority consisting of at least three quarters of the capital represented at the taking of the resolution; the articles of association may specify a greater majority of capital and further requirements. Acts of the management board based on an authorisation in accordance with sentence 1 shall require the approval of the supervisory board.

(3) The offeror and persons acting in common with it are forbidden to make, or hold out the prospect of, unjustified payments in money or other unjustified benefits in money's worth to members of the management board or of the supervisory board of the target company in connection with the bid.

§ 34. Application of the Provisions of Part 3

The provisions of Part 3 shall apply to takeover bids unless it is otherwise provided in the above provisions.

Part 5.
Mandatory Offers

§ 35. Obligation to Publish and Make an Offer

(1) Whoever obtains control of a target company directly or indirectly shall publish this fact without delay, at the latest within seven calendar days in accordance with § 10 para. 3 sentences 1 and 2, stating the amount of its share of the voting rights. The said period commences at the point in time at which the offeror acquires knowledge, or in the circumstances must have acquired knowledge, that it has acquired control of the target company. The attributed voting rights for each basis of attribution in accordance with § 30 shall be stated separately in the publication. § 10 para. 2, 3 sentence 3 and para. 4 to 6 shall apply mutatis mutandis.

(2) The offeror shall within four weeks after the publication of the fact that control of a target company has been acquired, communicate an offer document to the Supervisory Office and publish an offer in accordance with § 14 para. 2 sentence 1. § 14 para. 2 sentence 2, para. 3 and para. 4 shall apply mutatis mutandis. The target company's own shares, shares in the target company which belong to a dependent enterprise or to an enterprise in which the target company holds the majority, and shares of the target company which belong to a third party but are, however, held for the account of the target company or for a dependent enterprise or one in which the target company holds the majority, shall be excluded from the obligation under sentence 1.

sowie für Handlungen, denen der Aufsichtsrat der Zielgesellschaft zugestimmt hat.

(2) Ermächtigt die Hauptversammlung den Vorstand vor dem in Absatz 1 Satz 1 genannten Zeitraum zur Vornahme von Handlungen, die in die Zuständigkeit der Hauptversammlung fallen, um den Erfolg von Übernahmeangeboten zu verhindern, sind diese Handlungen in der Ermächtigung der Art nach zu bestimmen. Die Ermächtigung kann für höchstens 18 Monate erteilt werden. Der Beschluss der Hauptversammlung bedarf einer Mehrheit, die mindestens drei Viertel des bei der Beschlussfassung vertretenen Grundkapitals umfasst; die Satzung kann eine größere Kapitalmehrheit und weitere Erfordernisse bestimmen. Handlungen des Vorstands auf Grund einer Ermächtigung nach Satz 1 bedürfen der Zustimmung des Aufsichtsrats.

(3) Dem Bieter und mit ihm gemeinsam handelnden Personen ist es verboten, Vorstands- oder Aufsichtsratsmitgliedern der Zielgesellschaft im Zusammenhang mit dem Angebot ungerechtfertigte Geldleistungen oder andere ungerechtfertigte geldwerte Vorteile zu gewähren oder in Aussicht zu stellen.

§ 34. Anwendung der Vorschriften des Abschnitts 3

Für Übernahmeangebote gelten die Vorschriften des Abschnitts 3, soweit sich aus den vorstehenden Vorschriften nichts anderes ergibt.

Abschnitt 5.
Pflichtangebote

§ 35. Verpflichtung zur Veröffentlichung und zur Abgabe eines Angebots

(1) Wer unmittelbar oder mittelbar die Kontrolle über eine Zielgesellschaft erlangt, hat dies unter Angabe der Höhe seines Stimmrechtsanteils unverzüglich, spätestens innerhalb von sieben Kalendertagen, gemäß § 10 Abs. 3 Satz 1 und 2 zu veröffentlichen. Die Frist beginnt mit dem Zeitpunkt, zu dem der Bieter Kenntnis davon hat oder nach den Umständen haben musste, dass er die Kontrolle über die Zielgesellschaft erlangt hat. In der Veröffentlichung sind die nach § 30 zuzurechnenden Stimmrechte für jeden Zurechnungstatbestand getrennt anzugeben. § 10 Abs. 2, 3 Satz 3 und Abs. 4 bis 6 gilt entsprechend.

(2) Der Bieter hat innerhalb von vier Wochen nach der Veröffentlichung der Erlangung der Kontrolle über eine Zielgesellschaft der Bundesanstalt eine Angebotsunterlage zu übermitteln und nach § 14 Abs. 2 Satz 1 ein Angebot zu veröffentlichen. § 14 Abs. 2 Satz 2, Abs. 3 und 4 gilt entsprechend. Ausgenommen von der Verpflichtung nach Satz 1 sind eigene Aktien der Zielgesellschaft, Aktien der Zielgesellschaft, die einem abhängigen oder im Mehrheitsbesitz stehenden Unternehmen der Zielgesellschaft gehören, und Aktien der Zielgesellschaft, die einem Dritten gehören, jedoch für Rechnung der Zielgesellschaft, eines abhängigen oder eines im Mehrheitsbesitz stehenden Unternehmens der Zielgesellschaft gehalten werden.

(3) If control of the target company is acquired on the basis of a takeover offer, no obligation under para. 1 sentence 1 and para. 2 sentence 1 arises.

§ 36. Voting Rights not taken into Account

The Supervisory Office shall admit, on written application, that voting rights from shares of the target company not be taken into account in the calculation of the share of voting rights, if the shares are acquired by means of
1. devolution, distribution of an estate or voluntary gift between spouses, life-partners or relatives in the direct line and up to the third degree or by means of a distribution of assets due to the dissolution of a marriage or life-partnership,
2. transformation of legal form, or
3. restructuring within a group of companies.

§ 37. Exemption from the Publication Obligation and from the Making of an Offer

(1) The Supervisory Office may, on written application, exempt the offeror from the obligations under § 35 para. 1 sentence 1 and para. 2 sentence 1, insofar as such an exemption appears to be justified having regard to the nature of the acquisition, the objective intended by the acquisition of control, the non-maintenance of the control threshold after the acquisition of control, the relative participation in the target company or the actual possibility of exercising control having regard to the interests of the applicant and of the holders of shares of the target company.

(2) The Federal Ministry of Finance may, by legal regulation which does not require the approval of the Bundesrat, issue more detailed provisions concerning the exemption from the obligations under § 35 para. 1 sentence 1, para. 2 sentence 1. The Federal Ministry of Finance may delegate this authority by legal regulation to the Supervisory Office.

§ 38. Right to Interest

The offeror is obliged to pay the shareholders of the target company interest at five percentage points per annum above the then current base interest rate according to § 247 Civil Code on the consideration for the period of the breach, if
1. the offeror in breach of § 35 para. 1 sentence 1 does not make the publication in accordance with § 10 para. 3 sentence 1,
2. the offeror does not make an offer under § 14 para. 3 sentence 1, in breach of § 35 para. 2 sentence 1, or
3. the offeror is forbidden from making an offer within the meaning of § 35 para. 2 sentence 1 according to § 15 para. 1 nos. 1, 2 or 3.

§ 39. Application of the Provisions of Parts 3 and 4

With the exception of § 10 para. 1 sentence 1, § 14 para. 1 sentence 1, § 16 para. 2, § 18 para. 1, Secs. 19, 25, 26 and 34, the provisions of parts 3 and 4 shall apply mutatis mutandis to bids in accordance with § 35 para. 2 sentence 1.

(3) Wird die Kontrolle über die Zielgesellschaft auf Grund eines Übernahmeangebots erworben, besteht keine Verpflichtung nach Absatz 1 Satz 1 und Absatz 2 Satz 1.

§ 36. Nichtberücksichtigung von Stimmrechten

Die Bundesanstalt lässt auf schriftlichen Antrag zu, dass Stimmrechte aus Aktien der Zielgesellschaft bei der Berechnung des Stimmrechtsanteils unberücksichtigt bleiben, wenn die Aktien erlangt wurden durch
1. Erbgang, Erbauseinandersetzung oder unentgeltliche Zuwendung unter Ehegatten, Lebenspartnern oder Verwandten in gerader Linie und bis zum dritten Grade oder durch Vermögensauseinandersetzung aus Anlass der Auflösung einer Ehe oder Lebenspartnerschaft,
2. Rechtsformwechsel oder
3. Umstrukturierungen innerhalb eines Konzerns.

§ 37. Befreiung von der Verpflichtung zur Veröffentlichung und zur Abgabe eines Angebots

(1) Die Bundesanstalt kann auf schriftlichen Antrag den Bieter von den Verpflichtungen nach § 35 Abs. 1 Satz 1 und Abs. 2 Satz 1 befreien, sofern dies im Hinblick auf die Art der Erlangung, die mit der Erlangung der Kontrolle beabsichtigte Zielsetzung, ein nach der Erlangung der Kontrolle erfolgendes Unterschreiten der Kontrollschwelle, die Beteiligungsverhältnisse an der Zielgesellschaft oder die tatsächliche Möglichkeit zur Ausübung der Kontrolle unter Berücksichtigung der Interessen des Antragstellers und der Inhaber der Aktien der Zielgesellschaft gerechtfertigt erscheint.

(2) Das Bundesministerium der Finanzen kann durch Rechtsverordnung, die nicht der Zustimmung des Bundesrates bedarf, nähere Bestimmungen über die Befreiung von den Verpflichtungen nach § 35 Abs. 1 Satz 1, Abs. 2 Satz 1 erlassen. Das Bundesministerium der Finanzen kann die Ermächtigung durch Rechtsverordnung auf die Bundesanstalt übertragen.

§ 38. Anspruch auf Zinsen

Der Bieter ist den Aktionären der Zielgesellschaft für die Dauer des Verstoßes zur Zahlung von Zinsen auf die Gegenleistung in Höhe von fünf Prozentpunkten auf das Jahr über dem jeweiligen Basiszinssatz nach § 247 des Bürgerlichen Gesetzbuches verpflichtet, wenn
1. er entgegen § 35 Abs. 1 Satz 1 keine Veröffentlichung gemäß § 10 Abs. 3 Satz 1 vornimmt,
2. er entgegen § 35 Abs. 2 Satz 1 kein Angebot gemäß § 14 Abs. 3 Satz 1 abgibt oder
3. ihm ein Angebot im Sinne des § 35 Abs. 2 Satz 1 nach § 15 Abs. 1 Nr. 1, 2 oder 3 untersagt worden ist.

§ 39. Anwendung der Vorschriften des Abschnitts 3 und 4

Für Angebote nach § 35 Abs. 2 Satz 1 gelten mit Ausnahme von § 10 Abs. 1 Satz 1, § 14 Abs. 1 Satz 1, § 16 Abs. 2, § 18 Abs. 1, §§ 19, 25, 26 und 34 die Vorschriften der Abschnitte 3 und 4 sinngemäß.

Part 6.
Procedure

§ 40. The Authority of the Federal Supervisory Office to Investigate

(1) The offeror, persons acting in common with it and their subsidiaries, shall at the request of the Supervisory Office, provide information and documents required by the Supervisory Office for the supervision of compliance with the obligations
1. under § 10 para. 1 to 5 sentence 1, § 14 para. 1 to 4 sentence 1, § 21 para. 2, §§ 23, 27 para. 2 and 3 and § 31 para. 1 to 6 or on the basis of a legal regulation issued under § 31 para. 7, § 35 para. 1 and 2 sentences 1 and 2, and
2. under § 11 para. 1 or to examine whether the offer document contains the data required under § 11 para. 2 or according to a legal regulation issued under § 11 para. 4 and 5.

(2) The target company shall, on the request of the Supervisory Office, provide information and documents required by the Supervisory Office for the supervision of compliance with the obligations under § 10 para. 5 sentence 2, § 14 para. 4 sentence 2, §§ 27 and 33.

(3) The target company, its shareholders and former shareholders and enterprises providing investment services shall, at the request of the Supervisory Office, provide information and documents required by the Supervisory Office for the supervision of compliance with the obligations under § 31 para. 1, also in connection with a legal regulation under para. 7, and § 35 para. 1 and 2. This shall also apply mutatis mutandis to persons and enterprises whose voting rights are attributed to the offeror under § 30.

(4) The German stock exchanges shall, at the request of the Supervisory Office, provide information and documents required by the Supervisory Office for the supervision of compliance with the obligations under § 31 para. 1, 4 and 5, in each case also in connection with a legal regulation issued under para. 7.

(5) A person obliged to provide information, may refuse information in answer to such questions, the answers to which would expose him or a relative specified in § 383 para. 1 nos. 1 to 3 of the Code of Civil Procedure to the danger of criminal investigation or proceedings under the Act on Breaches of Administrative Rules.[6] The person so obliged shall be informed of his right to refuse to give the information.

§ 41. Objections Procedure

(1) Prior to the filing of an appeal to a court,[7] the legality and appropriateness of rulings of the Supervisory Office shall be reviewed in an objections procedure. Such a review shall not be required if the relieving reply or the decision on the objection contains, for the first time, conditions more

---

[6] Ordnungswiedrigkeitengesetz.
[7] Beschwerde.

Abschnitt 6
Verfahren

§ 40. Ermittlungsbefugnisse der Bundesanstalt

(1) Der Bieter, die mit ihm gemeinsam handelnden Personen sowie deren Tochterunternehmen haben auf Verlangen der Bundesanstalt Auskünfte zu erteilen und Unterlagen vorzulegen, die die Bundesanstalt benötigt zur Überwachung der Einhaltung der Pflichten
1. nach § 10 Abs. 1 bis 5 Satz 1, § 14 Abs. 1 bis 4 Satz 1, § 21 Abs. 2, §§ 23, 27 Abs. 2 und 3 und § 31 Abs. 1 bis 6 oder auf Grund einer nach § 31 Abs. 7 erlassenen Rechtsverordnung, § 35 Abs. 1 und 2 Satz 1 und 2 und
2. nach § 11 Abs. 1 oder zur Prüfung, ob die Angebotsunterlage die Angaben enthält, die nach § 11 Abs. 2 oder einer auf Grund des § 11 Abs. 4 und 5 erlassenen Rechtsverordnung erforderlich sind.

(2) Die Zielgesellschaft hat auf Verlangen der Bundesanstalt Auskünfte zu erteilen und Unterlagen vorzulegen, die die Bundesanstalt zur Überwachung der Einhaltung der Pflichten nach § 10 Abs. 5 Satz 2, § 14 Abs. 4 Satz 2, §§ 27 und 33 benötigt.

(3) Die Zielgesellschaft, deren Aktionäre und ehemaligen Aktionäre sowie Wertpapierdienstleistungsunternehmen haben auf Verlangen der Bundesanstalt Auskünfte zu erteilen und Unterlagen vorzulegen, die die Bundesanstalt zur Überwachung der Einhaltung der Pflichten nach § 31 Abs. 1, auch in Verbindung mit einer Rechtverordnung nach Abs. 7, und § 35 Abs. 1 und 2 benötigt. Dies gilt entsprechend für Personen und Unternehmen, deren Stimmrechte dem Bieter nach § 30 zuzurechnen sind.

(4) Die inländischen Börsen haben auf Verlangen der Bundesanstalt Auskünfte zu erteilen und Unterlagen vorzulegen, die die Bundesanstalt zur Überwachung der Einhaltung der Pflichten nach § 31 Abs. 1, 4 und 5, jeweils auch in Verbindung mit einer Rechtsverordnung nach Abs. 7, benötigt.

(5) Der zur Erteilung einer Auskunft Verpflichtete kann die Auskunft auf solche Fragen verweigern, deren Beantwortung ihn selbst oder einen der in § 383 Abs. 1 Nr. 1 bis 3 der Zivilprozessordnung bezeichneten Angehörigen der Gefahr strafgerichtlicher Verfolgung oder eines Verfahrens nach dem Gesetz über Ordnungswidrigkeiten aussetzen würde. Der Verpflichtete ist über sein Recht zur Verweigerung der Auskunft zu belehren.

§ 41. Widerspruchsverfahren

(1) Vor Einlegung der Beschwerde sind Rechtmäßigkeit und Zweckmäßigkeit der Verfügungen der Bundesanstalt in einem Widerspruchsverfahren nachzuprüfen. Einer solchen Nachprüfung bedarf es nicht, wenn der Abhilfebescheid oder der Widerspruchsbescheid erstmalig eine Beschwer enthält. Für das Widerspruchsverfahren gelten die §§ 68 bis 73 der Verwaltungsgerichtsordnung, soweit in diesem Gesetz nichts Abweichendes geregelt ist.

onerous for the objector. §§ 68 to 73 of the Rules of Procedure of the Administrative Courts[8] shall apply to the objections procedure unless otherwise provided in this law.

(2) The Supervisory Office shall make its decision within a period of two weeks from the receipt of the objection. In cases of special factual or legal difficulties or in the case of many objection procedures, the Supervisory Office may extend this period of time by unappealable decision.

(3) The participants shall co-operate in clarifying the factual position, as required by a process conducive to a rapid conclusion of the procedure. Time limits may be set for the parties, after the expiry of which further submissions will not be taken into account.

(4) The objections committee may transfer the procedure without oral hearing by unappealable decision to the chairman for his sole decision. This transfer is only admissible if the matter does not reveal significant difficulties in regard to the facts or the legal aspects, and the decision will not be of fundamental significance.

§ 42. Immediate Enforceability

An objection against measures of the Supervisory Office under § 4 para. 1 sentence 3, § 15 para. 1 or 2, § 28 para. 1 or § 40 para. 1 to 4 shall not have suspensory effect.

§ 43. Notification and Service

(1) Rulings which are made vis-á-vis a person with residence or a company with registered office outside the territory of application of this law, shall be notified by the Federal Supervisory Office to the person who has been nominated as authorised representative. If no person is so named, the notification shall be made by publication in the Federal Gazette (Bundesanzeiger).

(2) If a ruling is to be served, service in the case of persons with residence or companies with registered office outside the territory of application of this law shall be made on the person named as authorised representative. If no person is so named, service shall be effected by publication of the notice in the Federal Gazette (Bundesanzeiger).

§ 44. The Federal Supervisory Office's Right of Publication

The Federal Supervisory Office may publish its rulings under § 4 para. 1 sentence 3, § 10 para. 2 sentence 3, § 15 para. 1 and 2, § 20 para. 1, § 28 para. 1, § 36 or § 37 para. 1, also in conjunction with a legal regulation under para. 2, at the expense of the addressee of the ruling, in the Federal Gazette (Bundesanzeiger).

---

[8] Verwaltungsgerichtsordnung.

(2) Die Bundesanstalt trifft ihre Entscheidung innerhalb einer Frist von zwei Wochen ab Eingang des Widerspruchs. Bei besonderen tatsächlichen oder rechtlichen Schwierigkeiten oder bei einer Vielzahl von Widerspruchsverfahren kann die Bundesanstalt die Frist durch unanfechtbaren Beschluss verlängern.

(3) Die Beteiligten haben an der Aufklärung des Sachverhaltes mitzuwirken, wie es einem auf Förderung und raschen Abschluss des Verfahrens bedachten Vorgehen entspricht. Den Beteiligten können Fristen gesetzt werden, nach deren Ablauf weiterer Vortrag unbeachtet bleibt.

(4) Der Widerspruchsausschuss kann das Verfahren ohne mündliche Verhandlung dem Vorsitzenden durch unanfechtbaren Beschluss zur alleinigen Entscheidung übertragen. Diese Übertragung ist nur zulässig, sofern die Sache keine wesentlichen Schwierigkeiten in tatsächlicher und rechtlicher Hinsicht aufweist und die Entscheidung nicht von grundsätzlicher Bedeutung sein wird.

§ 42. Sofortige Vollziehbarkeit

Der Widerspruch gegen Maßnahmen der Bundesanstalt nach § 4 Abs. 1 Satz 3, § 15 Abs. 1 oder 2, § 28 Abs. 1 oder § 40 Abs. 1 bis 4 hat keine aufschiebende Wirkung.

§ 43. Bekanntgabe und Zustellung

(1) Verfügungen, die gegenüber einer Person mit Wohnsitz oder einem Unternehmen mit Sitz außerhalb des Geltungsbereichs dieses Gesetzes ergehen, gibt die Bundesanstalt der Person bekannt, die als Bevollmächtigte benannt wurde. Ist kein Bevollmächtigter benannt, so erfolgt die Bekanntgabe durch öffentliche Bekanntmachung im Bundesanzeiger.

(2) Ist die Verfügung zuzustellen, so erfolgt die Zustellung bei Personen mit Wohnsitz oder Unternehmen mit Sitz außerhalb des Geltungsbereichs dieses Gesetzes an die Person, die als Bevollmächtigte benannt wurde. Ist kein Bevollmächtigter benannt, so erfolgt die Zustellung durch öffentliche Bekanntmachung im Bundesanzeiger.

§ 44. Veröffentlichungsrecht der Bundesanstalt

Die Bundesanstalt kann ihre Verfügungen nach § 4 Abs. 1 Satz 3, § 10 Abs. 2 Satz 3, § 15 Abs. 1 und 2, § 20 Abs. 1, § 28 Abs. 1, § 36 oder § 37 Abs. 1, auch in Verbindung mit einer Rechtsverordnung nach Abs. 2, auf Kosten des Adressaten der Verfügung im Bundesanzeiger veröffentlichen.

§ 45. Communications to the Federal Supervisory Office

Applications and communications to the Federal Supervisory Office shall be made in writing. Communication by electronic data transmission is admissible provided the sender can be identified without any doubt.

§ 46. Penalties

The Federal Supervisory Office can enforce its rulings made under this law by sanctions in accordance with the provisions of the Administrative Enforcement Act.[9] It can also apply sanctions against legal persons of public law. Objections and appeals against the threat and determination of penalties under §§ 13 and 14 of the Administrative Enforcement Act do not have suspensory effect. The amount of penalties shall be up to 500,000 Euro, in deviation from § 11 of the Administrative Enforcement Act.

§ 47. Costs

The Federal Supervisory Office imposes charges (fees and outlay) for official acts arising under § 10 para. 2 sentence 3, §§ 14 and 15 para. 1 or 2, §§ 20, 24, 28 para. 1, §§ 36, 37 para. 1 also in connection with a legal regulation under para. 2, or § 41 in conjunction with § 6. The Federal Ministry of Finance shall determine, by legal regulation which does not require the approval of the Bundesrat, the items charged for individually and the amount of costs. The Federal Ministry of Finance may delegate this authority by legal regulation to the Federal Supervisory Office.

Part 7. Legal Remedies

§ 48. Admissibility, Jurisdiction

(1) An appeal shall lie against rulings of the Federal Supervisory Office. It may rely on new facts and evidence.

(2) The appeal may be taken by the participants in the procedure before the Federal Supervisory Office.

(3) An appeal may also be taken against the failure of the Federal Supervisory Office to issue a ruling to which the applicant believes it has a right. It shall also be deemed a failure to issue if the Federal Supervisory Office has not decided on the application for the issue of a ruling within a reasonable period without adequate grounds. The failure to decide on the application shall then be deemed to be equivalent to a refusal.

(4) An appeal shall be decided exclusively by the Oberlandesgericht[10] in Frankfurt am Main which has jurisdiction over the location of the registered office of the Federal Supervisory Office.

---

[9] Verwaltungs-Vollstreckungsgesetz.
[10] Regional Court of Appeal.

§ 45. Mitteilungen an die Bundesanstalt

Anträge und Mitteilungen an die Bundesanstalt haben in schriftlicher Form zu erfolgen. Eine Übermittlung im Wege der elektronischen Datenfernübertragung ist zulässig, sofern der Absender zweifelsfrei zu erkennen ist.

§ 46. Zwangsmittel

Die Bundesanstalt kann Verfügungen, die nach diesem Gesetz ergehen, mit Zwangsmitteln nach den Bestimmungen des Verwaltungs-Vollstreckungsgesetzes durchsetzen. Sie kann auch Zwangsmittel gegen juristische Personen des öffentlichen Rechts anwenden. Widerspruch und Beschwerde gegen die Androhung und Festsetzung der Zwangsmittel nach den §§ 13 und 14 des Verwaltungs-Vollstreckungsgesetzes haben keine aufschiebende Wirkung. Die Höhe des Zwangsgeldes beträgt abweichend von § 11 des Verwaltungs-Vollstreckungsgesetzes bis zu 500 000 Euro.

§ 47. Kosten

Die Bundesanstalt erhebt für Amtshandlungen auf Grund von § 10 Abs. 2 Satz 3, §§ 14 und 15 Abs. 1 oder 2, §§ 20, 24, 28 Abs. 1, §§ 36, 37 Abs. 1, auch in Verbindung mit einer Rechtsverordnung nach Abs. 2, oder § 41 in Verbindung mit § 6 Kosten (Gebühren und Auslagen). Das Bundesministerium der Finanzen bestimmt die Kostentatbestände im Einzelnen und die Höhe der Kosten durch Rechtsverordnung, die nicht der Zustimmung des Bundesrates bedarf. Das Bundesministerium der Finanzen kann die Ermächtigung durch Rechtsverordnung auf die Bundesanstalt übertragen.

Abschnitt 7. Rechtsmittel

§ 48. Statthaftigkeit, Zuständigkeit

(1) Gegen Verfügungen der Bundesanstalt ist die Beschwerde statthaft. Sie kann auch auf neue Tatsachen und Beweismittel gestützt werden.

(2) Die Beschwerde steht den am Verfahren vor der Bundesanstalt Beteiligten zu.

(3) Die Beschwerde ist auch gegen die Unterlassung einer beantragten Verfügung der Bundesanstalt statthaft, auf deren Vornahme der Antragsteller ein Recht zu haben behauptet. Als Unterlassung gilt es auch, wenn die Bundesanstalt den Antrag auf Vornahme der Verfügung ohne zureichenden Grund in angemessener Frist nicht beschieden hat. Die Unterlassung ist dann einer Ablehnung gleich zu erachten.

(4) Über die Beschwerde entscheidet ausschließlich das für den Sitz der Bundesanstalt in Frankfurt am Main zuständige Oberlandesgericht.

§ 49. Suspensory Effect

An appeal has suspensory effect if, by the ruling under appeal, an exemption under § 10 para. 1 sentence 3 or § 37 para. 1, also in conjunction with a legal regulation under para. 2, or a non-recognition of a share of voting rights under § 36, is revoked.

§ 50. Order of Immediate Enforcement

(1) The Federal Supervisory Office may, in the cases under § 49, order the immediate enforcement of the ruling if this is required in the public interest or in the preponderate interest of a participant.

(2) A ruling under para. 1 can be made prior to the filing of an appeal.

(3) On application, the appeal court may order or re-instate the suspensory effect of an objection or appeal in whole or in part, if

1. the preconditions for the ruling under para. 1 did not exist or no longer exist,
2. serious doubt exists as to the legality of the ruling under appeal, or
3. enforcement would result in an inequitable hardship for the party affected which is not required by predominant public interests.

(4) An application under para. 3 is admissible prior to the filing of the appeal. The facts which will be relied upon in the application, have to be credibly established[11] by the applicant. If the ruling has been enforced at the time of the decision, the court can order that the enforcement be revoked. The order of suspensory effect may be made dependent on provision of a security or on other conditions. It can also be subject to a time-limit.

(5) Decisions on applications under para. 3 may be changed or set aside at any time. Insofar as the applications are granted by such decisions, they are not subject to appeal.

§ 51. Time-Limits and Form

(1) The appeal shall be filed in writing with the appeal court within a statutory period of one month. The said period begins with the promulgation or service of the reply to the objection by the Federal Supervisory Office.

(2) If no ruling is issued on an application, the appeal is not subject to any time-limit.

(3) Grounds shall be given for the appeal. The time-limit for submitting grounds for the appeal shall be one month. It shall begin with the filing of the appeal and can be extended by the presiding judge of the appeal court on application.

---

[11] Glaubhaftmachung.

§ 49. Aufschiebende Wirkung

Die Beschwerde hat aufschiebende Wirkung, soweit durch die angefochtene Verfügung eine Befreiung nach § 10 Abs. 1 Satz 3 oder § 37 Abs. 1, auch in Verbindung mit einer Rechtsverordnung nach Abs. 2, oder eine Nichtberücksichtigung von Stimmrechtsanteilen nach § 36 widerrufen wird.

§ 50. Anordnung der sofortigen Vollziehung

(1) Die Bundesanstalt kann in den Fällen des § 49 die sofortige Vollziehung der Verfügung anordnen, wenn dies im öffentlichen Interesse oder im überwiegenden Interesse eines Beteiligten geboten ist.

(2) Die Anordnung nach Absatz 1 kann bereits vor der Einreichung der Beschwerde getroffen werden.

(3) Auf Antrag kann das Beschwerdegericht die aufschiebende Wirkung von Widerspruch oder Beschwerde ganz oder teilweise anordnen oder wiederherstellen, wenn
1. die Voraussetzungen für die Anordnung nach Absatz 1 nicht vorgelegen haben oder nicht mehr vorliegen,
2. ernstliche Zweifel an der Rechtmäßigkeit der angefochtenen Verfügung bestehen oder
3. die Vollziehung für den Betroffenen eine unbillige, nicht durch überwiegende öffentliche Interessen gebotene Härte zur Folge hätte.

(4) Der Antrag nach Absatz 3 ist schon vor Einreichung der Beschwerde zulässig. Die Tatsachen, auf die der Antrag gestützt wird, sind vom Antragsteller glaubhaft zu machen. Ist die Verfügung im Zeitpunkt der Entscheidung schon vollzogen, kann das Gericht auch die Aufhebung der Vollziehung anordnen. Die Anordnung der aufschiebenden Wirkung kann von der Leistung einer Sicherheit oder von anderen Auflagen abhängig gemacht werden. Sie kann auch befristet werden.

(5) Beschlüsse über Anträge nach Absatz 3 können jederzeit geändert oder aufgehoben werden. Soweit durch sie den Anträgen entsprochen ist, sind sie unanfechtbar.

§ 51. Frist und Form

(1) Die Beschwerde ist binnen einer Notfrist von einem Monat bei dem Beschwerdegericht schriftlich einzureichen. Die Frist beginnt mit der Bekanntgabe oder der Zustellung des Widerspruchsbescheides der Bundesanstalt.

(2) Ergeht auf einen Antrag keine Verfügung, so ist die Beschwerde an keine Frist gebunden.

(3) Die Beschwerde ist zu begründen. Die Frist für die Beschwerdebegründung beträgt einen Monat; sie beginnt mit der Einlegung der Beschwerde und kann auf Antrag von dem Vorsitzenden des Beschwerdegerichts verlängert werden.

(4) The grounds of appeal must contain
1. the declaration to what extent the ruling is appealed and amendment to it or its setting aside is applied for, and
2. specification of the facts and evidence upon which the appeal is based.

§ 52. Participants in the Appeal

The appellant and the Federal Supervisory Office shall be the parties participating in the appeal.

§ 53. Compulsory Legal Representation

The parties must be represented before the appeal court by a lawyer admitted to practice before a German court, or a teacher of law at a German university within the meaning of the University Framework Act, qualified for judicial office. The Federal Supervisory Office may be represented by a permanent official qualified for judicial office.

§ 54. Oral Hearing

(1) The appeal court decides on the appeal in oral hearing; with the agreement of the parties the decision can also be made without oral hearing.

(2) If the participants at the hearing do not appear in spite of having been informed in time, or are not duly represented, the matter can nevertheless be dealt with and decided upon.

§ 55. Principle of Investigation

(1) The appeal court investigates the facts ex officio.

(2) The court shall endeavour to ensure that formal errors are removed, that unclear applications are clarified, that relevant applications are made, that inadequate factual statements are supplemented, and that all explanations significant for the determination and adjudication of the matter are given.

(3) The appeal court may order the parties to make submissions on issues which require clarification, to specify evidence and to present documents and other evidence in their possession, within a period to be determined. If the said period is not complied with, the matter may be decided on the basis of the position reached without taking into account the evidence which has not been produced.

§ 56. Appeal Decision; Obligation to Present Documents

(1) The appeal court decides by ruling in accordance with its free conclusion arrived at as a result of the entire procedure. The ruling may rely only on facts and evidence upon which the participants could make submissions. The appeal court can deviate therefrom if interested parties summoned do

(4) Die Beschwerdebegründung muss enthalten
1. die Erklärung, inwieweit die Verfügung angefochten und ihre Abänderung oder Aufhebung beantragt wird, und
2. die Angabe der Tatsachen und Beweismittel, auf die sich die Beschwerde stützt.

§ 52. Beteiligte am Beschwerdeverfahren

An dem Verfahren vor dem Beschwerdegericht sind der Beschwerdeführer und die Bundesanstalt beteiligt.

§ 53. Anwaltszwang

Vor dem Beschwerdegericht müssen die Beteiligten sich durch einen bei einem deutschen Gericht zugelassenen Rechtsanwalt oder Rechtslehrer an einer deutschen Hochschule im Sinne des Hochschulrahmengesetzes mit Befähigung zum Richteramt als Bevollmächtigten vertreten lassen. Die Bundesanstalt kann sich durch einen Beamten auf Lebenszeit mit Befähigung zum Richteramt vertreten lassen.

§ 54. Mündliche Verhandlung

(1) Das Beschwerdegericht entscheidet über die Beschwerde auf Grund mündlicher Verhandlung; mit Einverständnis der Beteiligten kann ohne mündliche Verhandlung entschieden werden.

(2) Sind die Beteiligten in dem Verhandlungstermin trotz rechtzeitiger Benachrichtigung nicht erschienen oder gehörig vertreten, so kann gleichwohl in der Sache verhandelt und entschieden werden.

§ 55. Untersuchungsgrundsatz

(1) Das Beschwerdegericht erforscht den Sachverhalt von Amts wegen.

(2) Das Gericht hat darauf hinzuwirken, dass Formfehler beseitigt, unklare Anträge erläutert, sachdienliche Anträge gestellt, ungenügende tatsächliche Angaben ergänzt, ferner alle für die Feststellung und Beurteilung des Sachverhalts wesentlichen Erklärungen abgegeben werden.

(3) Das Beschwerdegericht kann den Beteiligten aufgeben, sich innerhalb einer zu bestimmenden Frist über aufklärungsbedürftige Punkte zu äußern, Beweismittel zu bezeichnen und in ihren Händen befindliche Urkunden sowie andere Beweismittel vorzulegen. Bei Versäumung der Frist kann nach Lage der Sache ohne Berücksichtigung der nicht beigebrachten Beweismittel entschieden werden.

§ 56. Beschwerdeentscheidung; Vorlagepflicht

(1) Das Beschwerdegericht entscheidet durch Beschluss nach seiner freien, aus dem Gesamtergebnis des Verfahrens gewonnenen Überzeugung. Der Beschluss darf nur auf Tatsachen und Beweismittel gestützt werden, zu denen die Beteiligten sich äußern konnten. Das Beschwerdegericht kann

not permit inspection of files because of justifiable interests of the participants or of third parties, and, therefore, the content of such files were not submitted to the court. This shall not apply to interested parties who participate in the legal relationship in dispute in such a manner that the decision has to be rendered in a uniform manner vis-á-vis them, as well.

(2) If the appeal court finds that the ruling of the Federal Supervisory Office is inadmissible or unjustified, it shall set it aside. If the ruling has already been dealt with by withdrawal or in any other manner, the appeal court shall on application, state that the ruling of the Federal Supervisory Office was inadmissible or unjustified, if the appellant has a legitimate interest in such a statement being made.

(3) If the appeal court finds that the refusal or failure to issue a ruling is inadmissible or unjustified, it shall pronounce the obligation of the Federal Supervisory Office to issue the ruling applied for.

(4) The ruling shall also be inadmissible and unjustified if the Federal Supervisory Office has abused its discretion, in particular, if it has exceeded the legal limits of its discretion or has breached the meaning and purpose of this law in exercising its discretion.

(5) The court shall issue a reasoning of its ruling and shall serve the ruling on the participants.

(6) If the appeal court intends to deviate from a decision of the Oberlandesgericht[12] or of the Bundesgerichtshof,[13] it shall submit the matter to the Bundesgerichtshof.[14] The Bundesgerichtshof[15] instead of the Oberlandesgericht[16] shall decide the matter.

§ 57. Inspection of Files

(1) The participants referred to in § 52 may inspect the files of the appeal court and obtain duplicates, extracts and copies from the office at their expense. § 299 para. 3 of the Code of Civil Procedure shall apply mutatis mutandis.

(2) Inspection of preliminary files, ancillary files, expert reports and documents concerning information may be made only with the consent of the offices to whom the files belong or which obtained the information. The Federal Supervisory Office shall refuse consent to the inspection of documents belonging to it if this is necessary for good reason, in particular for the protection of the justified interests of participants or of third parties. If inspection is refused or if it is inadmissible, such documents may be relied on in the decision only insofar as their content has been submitted. The ap-

---

[12] Regional Court of Appeal.
[13] Federal Supreme Court.
[14] Federal Supreme Court.
[15] Federal Supreme Court.
[16] Regional Court of Appeal.

hiervon abweichen, soweit Beigeladenen aus berechtigten Interessen der Beteiligten oder dritter Personen Akteneinsicht nicht gewährt und der Akteninhalt aus diesen Gründen auch nicht vorgetragen worden ist. Dies gilt nicht für solche Beigeladene, die an dem streitigen Rechtsverhältnis derart beteiligt sind, dass die Entscheidung auch ihnen gegenüber nur einheitlich ergehen kann.

(2) Hält das Beschwerdegericht die Verfügung der Bundesanstalt für unzulässig oder unbegründet, so hebt es die Verfügung auf. Hat sich die Verfügung vorher durch Zurücknahme oder auf andere Weise erledigt, so spricht das Beschwerdegericht auf Antrag aus, dass die Verfügung der Bundesanstalt unzulässig oder unbegründet gewesen ist, wenn der Beschwerdeführer ein berechtigtes Interesse an dieser Feststellung hat.

(3) Hält das Beschwerdegericht die Ablehnung oder Unterlassung der Verfügung für unzulässig oder unbegründet, so spricht es die Verpflichtung der Bundesanstalt aus, die beantragte Verfügung vorzunehmen.

(4) Die Verfügung ist auch dann unzulässig oder unbegründet, wenn die Bundesanstalt von ihrem Ermessen fehlerhaft Gebrauch gemacht hat, insbesondere wenn sie die gesetzlichen Grenzen des Ermessens überschritten oder durch die Ermessensentscheidung Sinn und Zweck dieses Gesetzes verletzt hat.

(5) Der Beschluss ist zu begründen und den Beteiligten zuzustellen.

(6) Will das Beschwerdegericht von einer Entscheidung eines Oberlandesgerichts oder des Bundesgerichtshofs abweichen, so legt es die Sache dem Bundesgerichtshof vor. Der Bundesgerichtshof entscheidet anstelle des Oberlandesgerichts.

§ 57. Akteneinsicht

(1) Die in § 52 bezeichneten Beteiligten können die Akten des Beschwerdegerichts einsehen und sich durch die Geschäftsstelle auf ihre Kosten Ausfertigungen, Auszüge und Abschriften erteilen lassen. § 299 Abs. 3 der Zivilprozessordnung gilt entsprechend.

(2) Einsicht in Vorakten, Beiakten, Gutachten und Unterlagen über Auskünfte ist nur mit Zustimmung der Stellen zulässig, denen die Akten gehören oder die die Äußerung eingeholt haben. Die Bundesanstalt hat die Zustimmung zur Einsicht in die ihr gehörigen Unterlagen zu versagen, soweit dies aus wichtigen Gründen, insbesondere zur Wahrung von berechtigten Interessen Beteiligter oder dritter Personen, geboten ist. Wird die Einsicht abgelehnt oder ist sie unzulässig, dürfen diese Unterlagen der Entscheidung nur insoweit zugrunde gelegt werden, als ihr Inhalt vor-

peal court may, by ruling, order the presentation of facts or evidence, the maintenance of confidentiality in respect of which has been demanded for good reasons, in particular in order to protect legitimate interests of the participants or of third parties, after hearing those affected by their presentation, provided the decision is dependent on such facts or evidence, no other possibility of clarification of the facts exists and provided that, after considering all the circumstances of the particular case, the significance of the matter for ensuring the propriety of the proceeding outweighs the interests of the affected party in the maintenance of confidentiality. The ruling shall be reasoned. In the proceeding in accordance with sentence 4, the affected party need not be represented by a lawyer.

§ 58. Application of the Provisions of the Court Constitution Act[17] and the Code of Civil Procedure

Except as otherwise provided, the following shall apply in the proceedings before the appeal court
1. the provisions of §§ 169 to 197 of the Court Constitution Act on hearings in public, the presence of police at the hearings, the language of the courts, discussion and agreement, and
2. the provisions of the Code of Civil Procedure on the exclusion and refusal of a judge, on legal representation and assistance, on service ex officio, on summonses, dates and periods of notice, on the ordering of the personal attendance of the parties, on the fusion of several cases, on dealing with the evidence of witnesses and experts and on the other methods of taking evidence, on the reinstatement in the former position notwithstanding the expiry of a time limit.

Part 8. Penalties

§ 59. Forfeiture of Rights

Rights from shares, which belong to the offeror, to parties acting in common with it or their subsidiary companies, or from which voting rights are attributed in accordance with § 30 para. 1 sentence 1 no. 2 to it, to persons acting in common with it or their subsidiary companies, shall not apply for the time in which the obligations under § 35 para. 1 or 2 are not complied with. This does not apply to claims under § 58 para. 4 of the Stock Corporation Act and § 271 of the Stock Corporation Act, if the publication or the bid under § 35 para. 1 sentence 1 or para. 2 sentence 1 has not been intentionally omitted and has been made good.

§ 60. Fines

(1) An administrative offence shall be committed by any person who intentionally or carelessly,

---

[17] Gerichtsverfassungsgesetz.

getragen worden ist. Das Beschwerdegericht kann die Offenlegung von Tatsachen oder Beweismitteln, deren Geheimhaltung aus wichtigen Gründen, insbesondere zur Wahrung von berechtigten Interessen Beteiligter oder Dritter verlangt wird, nach Anhörung des von der Offenlegung Betroffenen durch Beschluss anordnen, soweit es für die Entscheidung auf diese Tatsachen oder Beweismittel ankommt, andere Möglichkeiten der Sachaufklärung nicht bestehen und nach Abwägung aller Umstände des Einzelfalles die Bedeutung der Sache für die Sicherung eines ordnungsgemäßen Verfahrens das Interesse des Betroffenen an der Geheimhaltung überwiegt. Der Beschluss ist zu begründen. In dem Verfahren nach Satz 4 muss sich der Betroffene nicht anwaltlich vertreten lassen.

§ 58. Geltung von Vorschriften des Gerichtsverfassungsgesetzes und der Zivilprozessordnung

Im Verfahren vor dem Beschwerdegericht gelten, soweit nichts anderes bestimmt ist, entsprechend
1. die Vorschriften der §§ 169 bis 197 des Gerichtsverfassungsgesetzes über Öffentlichkeit, Sitzungspolizei, Gerichtssprache, Beratung und Abstimmung und
2. die Vorschriften der Zivilprozessordnung über Ausschließung und Ablehnung eines Richters, über Prozessbevollmächtigte und Beistände, über die Zustellung von Amts wegen, über Ladungen, Termine und Fristen, über die Anordnung des persönlichen Erscheinens der Parteien, über die Verbindung mehrerer Prozesse, über die Erledigung des Zeugen- und Sachverständigenbeweises sowie über die sonstigen Arten des Beweisverfahrens, über die Wiedereinsetzung in den vorigen Stand gegen die Versäumung einer Frist.

Abschnitt 8. Sanktionen

§ 59. Rechtsverlust

Rechte aus Aktien, die dem Bieter, mit ihm gemeinsam handelnden Personen oder deren Tochterunternehmen gehören oder aus denen ihm, mit ihm gemeinsam handelnden Personen oder deren Tochterunternehmen Stimmrechte gemäß § 30 Abs. 1 Satz 1 Nr. 2 zugerechnet werden, bestehen nicht für die Zeit, für welche die Pflichten nach § 35 Abs. 1 oder 2 nicht erfüllt werden. Dies gilt nicht für Ansprüche nach § 58 Abs. 4 des Aktiengesetzes und § 271 des Aktiengesetzes, wenn die Veröffentlichung oder das Angebot nach § 35 Abs. 1 Satz 1 oder Abs. 2 Satz 1 nicht vorsätzlich unterlassen wurde und nachgeholt worden ist.

§ 60. Bußgeldvorschriften

(1) Ordnungswidrig handelt, wer vorsätzlich oder leichtfertig

1. in breach of
   a) § 10 para. 1 sentence 1, § 14 para. 2 sentence 1 or § 35 para. 1 sentence 1 or para. 2 sentence 1, or
   b) § 21 para. 2 sentence 1, § 23 para. 1 sentence 1 or para. 2 sentence 1 or § 27 para. 3 sentence 1,

   does not, or not accurately, or not completely or not in the prescribed form or not within the correct period, publish a notice, and
2. in breach of
   a) § 10 para. 2 sentence 1, also in conjunction with § 35 para. 1 sentence 4, § 14 para. 1 sentence 1 or § 35 para. 2 sentence 1,
   b) § 10 para. 5, also in conjunction with § 35 para. 1 sentence 4 or § 14 para. 4 also in conjunction with § 21 para. 2 sentence 2 or § 35 para. 2 sentence 2, or
   c) § 27 para. 3 sentence 2,

   does not issue a communication, an instruction or a transmission, does not do so accurately, completely, in the prescribed manner or within the prescribed period,
3. in breach of § 10 para. 3 sentence 3, also in conjunction with § 35 para. 1 sentence 4, or § 14 para. 2 sentence 2, also in conjunction with § 35 para. 2 sentence 2, makes a publication or issues an offer document,
4. in breach of § 10 para. 4 sentence 1, also in conjunction with § 35 para. 1 sentence 4, does not send a published notice, does not do so correctly, completely or within the prescribed period,
5. in breach of § 14 para. 3 sentence 2 also in conjunction with § 21 para. 2 sentence 2, § 23 para. 1 sentence 2 or § 35 para. 2 sentence 2, or in breach of § 27 para. 3 sentence 3 does not send evidence, does not send it completely or within the prescribed period,
6. makes a publication in breach of § 15 para. 3,
7. issues a bid in breach of § 26 para. 1 sentences 1 or 2, or
8. in breach of § 33 para. 1 sentence 1 takes an action referred to there without the authority of the general meeting.

(2) Any person will be guilty of an administrative offence who intentionally or negligently
1. acts in breach of an enforceable ruling under § 28 para. 1, or
2. in breach of § 40 para. 1, 2 or 3 sentence 1, also in connection with sentence 2, does not give information, does not give it accurately, completely or within the prescribed period, or who does not present a document, does not do so accurately, completely or within the prescribed period.

(3) The administrative offence may in the cases of para. 1 no. 1a, nos. 3, 6 to 8 be penalised by a fine of up to one million Euro, in the cases of para. 1 no. 1b, no. 2a and no. 4 with a fine of up to five hundred thousand Euro, in the remaining cases with a fine of up to two hundred thousand Euro.

§ 61. The Competent Administrative Authority

The Federal Supervisory Office is the competent administrative authority within the meaning of § 36 para. 1 no. 1 of the Act on Administrative Offences.

1. entgegen
   a) § 10 Abs. 1 Satz 1, § 14 Abs. 2 Satz 1 oder § 35 Abs. 1 Satz 1 oder Abs. 2 Satz 1 oder
   b) § 21 Abs. 2 Satz 1, § 23 Abs. 1 Satz 1 oder Abs. 2 Satz 1 oder § 27 Abs. 3 Satz 1
   eine Veröffentlichung nicht, nicht richtig, nicht vollständig, nicht in der vorgeschriebenen Weise oder nicht rechtzeitig vornimmt,
2. entgegen
   a) § 10 Abs. 2 Satz 1, auch in Verbindung mit § 35 Abs. 1 Satz 4, § 14 Abs. 1 Satz 1 oder § 35 Abs. 2 Satz 1,
   b) § 10 Abs. 5, auch in Verbindung mit § 35 Abs. 1 Satz 4, oder § 14 Abs. 4, auch in Verbindung mit § 21 Abs. 2 Satz 2 oder § 35 Abs. 2 Satz 2, oder
   c) § 27 Abs. 3 Satz 2
   eine Mitteilung, Unterrichtung oder Übermittlung nicht, nicht richtig, nicht vollständig, nicht in der vorgeschriebenen Weise oder nicht rechtzeitig vornimmt,
3. entgegen § 10 Abs. 3 Satz 3, auch in Verbindung mit § 35 Abs. 1 Satz 4, oder § 14 Abs. 2 Satz 2, auch in Verbindung mit § 35 Abs. 2 Satz 2, eine Veröffentlichung vornimmt oder eine Angebotsunterlage bekannt gibt,
4. entgegen § 10 Abs. 4 Satz 1, auch in Verbindung mit § 35 Abs. 1 Satz 4, eine Veröffentlichung nicht, nicht richtig, nicht vollständig oder nicht rechtzeitig übersendet,
5. entgegen § 14 Abs. 3 Satz 2, auch in Verbindung mit § 21 Abs. 2 Satz 2, § 23 Abs. 1 Satz 2 oder § 35 Abs. 2 Satz 2, oder entgegen § 27 Abs. 3 Satz 3 einen Beleg nicht, nicht richtig oder nicht rechtzeitig übersendet,
6. entgegen § 15 Abs. 3 eine Veröffentlichung vornimmt,
7. entgegen § 26 Abs. 1 Satz 1 oder 2 ein Angebot abgibt oder
8. entgegen § 33 Abs. 1 Satz 1 eine dort genannte Handlung vornimmt.

(2) Ordnungswidrig handelt, wer vorsätzlich oder fahrlässig

1. einer vollziehbaren Anordnung nach § 28 Abs. 1 zuwiderhandelt oder
2. entgegen § 40 Abs. 1, 2 oder 3 Satz 1, auch in Verbindung mit Satz 2, eine Auskunft nicht, nicht richtig, nicht vollständig oder nicht rechtzeitig erteilt oder eine Unterlage nicht, nicht richtig, nicht vollständig oder nicht rechtzeitig vorlegt.

(3) Die Ordnungswidrigkeit kann in den Fällen des Absatzes 1 Nr. 1 Buchstabe a, Nr. 3, 6 bis 8 mit einer Geldbuße bis zu einer Million Euro, in den Fällen des Absatzes 1 Nr. 1 Buchstabe b, Nr. 2 Buchstabe a und Nr. 4 mit einer Geldbuße bis zu fünfhunderttausend Euro, in den übrigen Fällen mit einer Geldbuße bis zu zweihunderttausend Euro geahndet werden.

§ 61. Zuständige Verwaltungsbehörde

Verwaltungsbehörde im Sinne des § 36 Abs. 1 Nr. 1 des Gesetzes über Ordnungswidrigkeiten ist die Bundesanstalt.

§ 62. Jurisdiction of the Oberlandesgericht[18] in Court Proceedings

(1) In court proceedings in relation to an administrative offence under § 60, the Oberlandesgericht[19] Frankfurt am Main with jurisdiction over the location of the registered office of the Federal Supervisory Office shall decide; this court shall also decide on an application for a court decision (§ 62 of the Act on Administrative Offences), in the cases of § 52 para. 2 sentence 3 and of § 69 para. 1 sentence 2 of the Act on Administrative Offences. § 140 para. 1 no. 1 of the Code of Criminal Procedure in connection with § 46 para. 1 of the Act on Administrative Offences shall not apply.

(2) The Oberlandesgericht,[20] consisting of three members including the presiding member, shall decide.

§ 63. Appeal on a Point of Law to the Bundesgerichtshof

An appeal on a point of law (§ 79 of the Act on Administrative Offences) shall be decided by the Bundesgerichtshof.[21] If the court sets aside the decision appealed against, without deciding on the matter itself, it shall return the matter to the Oberlandesgericht[22] the decision of which has been set aside.

§ 64. Reinstatement with Fine

In a procedure for reinstatement against the ruling on a fine imposed by the Federal Supervisory Office (§ 85 para. 4 of the Act on Administrative Offences), the court with jurisdiction under § 62 para. 1 shall decide.

§ 65. Court Decision on Enforcement

Court decisions necessary for enforcement (§ 104 of the Act on Administrative Offences) shall be issued by the court having jurisdiction under § 63 para. 1.

Part 9.
Court Jurisdiction; Transitional Arrangements

§ 66. The Court in Matters of the Purchase of Securities and of Takeovers

(1) In the case of civil legal disputes which arise out of this law, the Landgerichte[23] shall have exclusive jurisdiction irrespective of the value of the matter in dispute. Sentence 1 shall also apply to claims referred to in § 12 para. 6 and to a case in which the decision in a legal dispute is wholly or partially dependent upon a decision which is to be made under this law.

---

[18] Regional Court of Appeal.
[19] Regional Court of Appeal.
[20] Regional Court of Appeal.
[21] Federal Supreme Court.
[22] Regional Court of Appeal.
[23] District Court.

§ 62. Zuständigkeit des Oberlandesgerichts im gerichtlichen Verfahren

(1) Im gerichtlichen Verfahren wegen einer Ordnungswidrigkeit nach § 60 entscheidet das für den Sitz der Bundesanstalt in Frankfurt am Main zuständige Oberlandesgericht; es entscheidet auch über einen Antrag auf gerichtliche Entscheidung (§ 62 des Gesetzes über Ordnungswidrigkeiten) in den Fällen des § 52 Abs. 2 Satz 3 und des § 69 Abs. 1 Satz 2 des Gesetzes über Ordnungswidrigkeiten. § 140 Abs. 1 Nr. 1 der Strafprozessordnung in Verbindung mit § 46 Abs. 1 des Gesetzes über Ordnungswidrigkeiten findet keine Anwendung.

(2) Das Oberlandesgericht entscheidet in der Besetzung von drei Mitgliedern mit Einschluss des vorsitzenden Mitglieds.

§ 63. Rechtsbeschwerde zum Bundesgerichtshof

Über die Rechtsbeschwerde (§ 79 des Gesetzes über Ordnungswidrigkeiten) entscheidet der Bundesgerichtshof. Hebt er die angefochtene Entscheidung auf, ohne in der Sache selbst zu entscheiden, so verweist er die Sache an das Oberlandesgericht, dessen Entscheidung aufgehoben wird, zurück.

§ 64. Wiederaufnahme gegen Bußgeldbescheid

Im Wiederaufnahmeverfahren gegen den Bußgeldbescheid der Bundesanstalt (§ 85 Abs. 4 des Gesetzes über Ordnungswidrigkeiten) entscheidet das nach § 62 Abs. 1 zuständige Gericht.

§ 65. Gerichtliche Entscheidung bei der Vollstreckung

Die bei der Vollstreckung notwendig werdenden gerichtlichen Entscheidungen (§ 104 des Gesetzes über Ordnungswidrigkeiten) werden von dem nach § 62 Abs. 1 zuständigen Gericht erlassen.

Abschnitt 9.
Gerichtliche Zuständigkeit; Übergangsregelungen

§ 66. Gerichte für Wertpapiererwerbs- und Übernahmesachen

(1) Für bürgerliche Rechtsstreitigkeiten, die sich aus diesem Gesetz ergeben, sind ohne Rücksicht auf den Wert des Streitgegenstandes die Landgerichte ausschließlich zuständig. Satz 1 gilt auch für die in § 12 Abs. 6 genannten Ansprüche und für den Fall, dass die Entscheidung eines Rechtsstreits ganz oder teilweise von einer Entscheidung abhängt, die nach diesem Gesetz zu treffen ist. Für Klagen, die auf Grund dieses Gesetzes oder wegen der in § 12 Abs. 6 genannten Ansprüche erhoben werden, ist auch das Landgericht zuständig, in dessen Bezirk die Zielgesellschaft ihren Sitz hat.

The Landgericht[24] in whose area the company has its registered office also has jurisdiction in court proceedings which are taken on the basis of this law or because of the claims referred to in § 12 para. 6.

(2) Court disputes are commercial matters within the meaning of §§ 93 to 114 of the Court Constitution Act.

(3) The governments of the Länder[25] are authorised to allot jurisdiction by legal regulation, in civil legal disputes for which the Landgerichte[26] have exclusive jurisdiction, pursuant to para. 1, to one Landgericht[27] for the areas of several Landgerichte,[28] if such a concentration serves the legal process in matters of the acquisition of securities and of take-overs. They are further authorised to allot to one or several of the Oberlandesgerichte,[29] if there is more than one Oberlandesgericht[30] in that Land, decisions on appeals and reviews of decisions of the Landgerichte[31] having jurisdiction under para. 1 in civil legal proceedings. The governments of the Länder may delegate this authority to the justice administrations of the Länder. By agreements between the Länder, jurisdiction of a Landgericht[32] for particular areas or the entire area of several Länder may be established.

§ 67. The Oberlandesgericht[33] Panel for Matters Concerning the Acquisition of Securities and Takeovers

In legal matters in which it has jurisdiction under § 48 para. 4, § 62 para. 1, §§ 64 and 65, the Oberlandesgericht[34] shall decide by means of a panel for matters concerning the purchase of securities and takeovers.

§ 68. Transitional Provisions

(1) The objections committee shall, until the appointment of honorary advisory members on the basis of proposals of the commission under § 5 para. 3 sentence 3, at the latest by 30 June 2002, consist exclusively of the persons named in § 6 para. 2 sentence 1 nos. 1 and 2.

(2) This law shall not, subject to para. 3, apply to bids which have been published before January 1, 2002.

(3) A person who acquires control after January 1, 2002 on the basis of a bid which was published prior to January 1, 2002, shall observe the obligations under § 35 para. 1 sentence 1 and para. 2 sentence 1. The Federal Super-

---

[24] District Court.
[25] the federal German states.
[26] District Court.
[27] District Court.
[28] District Court.
[29] Court of Appeal.
[30] Court of Appeal.
[31] District Court.
[32] District Court.
[33] Court of Appeal.
[34] Court of Appeal.

(2) Die Rechtsstreitigkeiten sind Handelssachen im Sinne der §§ 93 bis 114 des Gerichtsverfassungsgesetzes.

(3) Die Landesregierungen werden ermächtigt, durch Rechtsverordnung bürgerliche Rechtsstreitigkeiten, für die nach Absatz 1 ausschließlich die Landgerichte zuständig sind, einem Landgericht für die Bezirke mehrerer Landgerichte zuzuweisen, wenn eine solche Zusammenfassung der Rechtspflege in Wertpapiererwerbs- und Übernahmesachen dienlich ist. Sie werden ferner ermächtigt, die Entscheidungen über Berufungen und Beschwerden gegen Entscheidungen der nach Absatz 1 zuständigen Landgerichte in bürgerlichen Rechtsstreitigkeiten einem oder einigen der Oberlandesgerichte zuzuweisen, wenn in einem Land mehrere Oberlandesgerichte errichtet sind. Die Landesregierungen können die Ermächtigungen auf die Landesjustizverwaltungen übertragen. Durch Staatsverträge zwischen den Ländern kann die Zuständigkeit eines Landgerichts für einzelne Bezirke oder das gesamte Gebiet mehrerer Länder begründet werden.

§ 67. Senat für Wertpapiererwerbs- und Übernahmesachen beim Oberlandesgericht

In den ihm nach § 48 Abs. 4, § 62 Abs. 1, §§ 64 und 65 zugewiesenen Rechtssachen entscheidet das Oberlandesgericht durch einen Wertpapiererwerbs- und Übernahmesenat.

§ 68. Übergangsregelungen

(1) Der Widerspruchsausschuss besteht bis zur Bestellung von ehrenamtlichen Beisitzern auf Grund von Vorschlägen des Beirats nach § 5 Abs. 3 Satz 3, spätestens bis zum 30. Juni 2002, ausschließlich aus den in § 6 Abs. 2 Satz 1 Nr. 1 und 2 genannten Personen.

(2) Dieses Gesetz findet vorbehaltlich Absatz 3 keine Anwendung auf Angebote, die vor dem 1. Januar 2002 veröffentlicht wurden.

(3) Wer nach dem 1. Januar 2002 die Kontrolle auf Grund eines Angebots erlangt, das vor dem 1. Januar 2002 veröffentlicht wurde, hat die Verpflichtungen nach § 35 Abs. 1 Satz 1 und Abs. 2 Satz 1 einzuhalten. Die

visory Office releases the offeror on written application, from the obligations under sentence 1, if the bid corresponds to the requirements of §§ 31 and 32. The objections committee shall decide on objections against rulings of the Federal Supervisory Office under sentence 2.

Bundesanstalt befreit den Bieter auf schriftlichen Antrag von den Verpflichtungen nach Satz 1, wenn das Angebot den Vorgaben nach §§ 31 und 32 entspricht. Über Widersprüche gegen Verfügungen der Bundesanstalt nach Satz 2 entscheidet der Widerspruchsausschuss.

Appendix 2
Public Offer Regulation

Regulation as to the content of the offer document, the consideration in the case of takeover offers and mandatory offers and the release from the obligation to publish and to make a bid

(Unoffinal Translation of the German „WpÜG-Angebotsverordnung" (2002) by NÖRR STIEFENHÖFER LUTZ)

Table of Contents

Part 1. Scope of Application

§ 1 Scope of Application 204

Part 2. Content of the Offer Document

§ 2 Additional Information in the Offer Document 206

Part 3. Consideration in the case of Takeover Offers and Mandatory Offers

§ 3 Principles 208
§ 4 Taking account of prior purchases 208
§ 5 Domestic stock exchange prices taken into consideration 210
§ 6 Foreign stock exchange prices taken into consideration 210
§ 7 Determination of the value of the consideration 212

Part 4. Exemption from the Obligation to Publish and Make an Offer

§ 8 Application 212
§ 9 Ground for exemption 212
§ 10 Content of the application 214
§ 11 Documents to be submitted with the application 214
§ 12 Examination of the completeness of the application 214

Part 5. Final Provision

§ 13 Legal Effect 214

Part 1. Scope of Application

§ 1. Scope of Application

This regulation applies to bids in accordance with § 2 para. 1 Takeover Act.

Anhang 2
WpÜG-Angebotsverordnung

Verordnung über den Inhalt der Angebotsunterlage, die Gegenleistung bei Übernahmeangeboten und Pflichtangeboten und die Befreiung von der Verpflichtung zur Veröffentlichung und zur Abgabe eines Angebots (WpÜG-Angebotsverordnung)

vom 27. Dezember 2001 (BGBl. I S. 4263), geändert durch Verordnung vom 29. April 2002 (BGBl. I S. 1495)

Inhaltsübersicht

Erster Abschnitt. Anwendungsbereich
§ 1 Anwendungsbereich 205

Zweiter Abschnitt. Inhalt der Angebotsunterlage
§ 2 Ergänzende Angaben der Angebotsunterlage 207

Dritter Abschnitt. Gegenleistung bei Übernahmeangeboten und Pflichtangeboten
§ 3 Grundsatz 209
§ 4 Berücksichtigung von Vorerwerben 209
§ 5 Berücksichtigung inländischer Börsenkurse 211
§ 6 Berücksichtigung ausländischer Börsenkurse 211
§ 7 Bestimmung des Wertes der Gegenleistung 213

Vierter Abschnitt. Befreiung von der Verpflichtung zur Veröffentlichung und zur Abgabe eines Angebots
§ 8 Antragstellung 213
§ 9 Befreiungstatbestände 213
§ 10 Antragsinhalt 215
§ 11 Antragsunterlagen 215
§ 12 Prüfung der Vollständigkeit des Antrags 215

Fünfter Abschnitt. Schlussvorschrift
§ 13 Inkrafttreten 215

Erster Abschnitt. Anwendungsbereich

§ 1. Anwendungsbereich

Diese Verordnung ist auf Angebote gemäß § 2 Abs. 1 des Wertpapiererwerbs- und Übernahmegesetzes anzuwenden.

Part Two. Content of the Offer Document

§ 2. Additional Information in the Offer Document

The offeror shall provide the following additional information in its offer document:

1. The names and address of registered offices of persons acting in common with the offeror and of persons whose voting rights from shares of the target company under § 30 Takeover Act are considered to be equal to the voting rights of the offeror or are to be attributed to him, and if the third persons are corporations, their legal form,

2. Data in accordance with § 7 of the Prospectus Act together with the Prospectus Regulation, insofar as shares are offered as consideration. If within the twelve months prior to the publication of the offer document a sales prospectus, a prospectus on the basis of which the shares were admitted to trading to a stock exchange with an official quotation, or a company report was published in German in Germany, in respect of these shares, it shall suffice to give the data which was published in the prospectus or in the company report and to state where this is obtainable, and the data on changes which have occurred since the publication of the prospectus or the company report.

3. The method used for determining the consideration and the grounds as to why this method is appropriate, as well as a statement of the exchange ratio or of the consideration which is derived by application of various methods, insofar as various methods were applied. The weighting given to the various methods in the determination of the exchange ratio or of the consideration is to be given and the value on which they are based, the reasons for the significance of the weighting and which special difficulties arose in determining the consideration.

4. The measures which those in receipt of the bid must take in order to accept it and in order to receive the consideration for the securities, which are subject matter of the bid as well as a statement of the costs connected with these measures for the recipients of the bid and the time at which those who have accepted the bid will receive the consideration.

5. The number of securities held by the bidder and those acting in common with it and their subsidiaries, and amount of voting rights held by said parties stating the share of voting rights attributable to each separately according to the basis of attribution, in accordance with § 30 Takeover Act,

6. In the case of partial offers, the share or number of securities of the target company which are the subject matter of the bid as well as the allotments in accordance with § 19 Takeover Act,

Zweiter Abschnitt. Inhalt der Angebotsunterlage

§ 2. Ergänzende Angaben der Angebotsunterlage

Der Bieter hat in seine Angebotsunterlage folgende ergänzende Angaben aufzunehmen:
1. Name oder Firma und Anschrift oder Sitz der mit dem Bieter gemeinsam handelnden Personen und der Personen, deren Stimmrechte aus Aktien der Zielgesellschaft nach § 30 des Wertpapiererwerbsund Übernahmegesetzes Stimmrechten des Bieters gleichstehen oder ihm zuzurechnen sind, sowie, wenn es sich bei diesen Personen um Gesellschaften handelt, die Rechtsform;
2. Angaben nach § 7 des Verkaufsprospektgesetzes in Verbindung mit der Verkaufsprospekt-Verordnung, sofern Wertpapiere als Gegenleistung angeboten werden; wurde für diese Wertpapiere innerhalb von zwölf Monaten vor Veröffentlichung der Angebotsunterlage ein Verkaufsprospekt, ein Prospekt, auf Grund dessen die Wertpapiere zum Börsenhandel mit amtlicher Notierung zugelassen worden sind, oder ein Unternehmensbericht im Inland in deutscher Sprache veröffentlicht, genügt die Angabe, dass ein Prospekt oder ein Unternehmensbericht veröffentlicht wurde und wo dieser erhältlich ist, sowie die Angabe der seit der Veröffentlichung des Prospekts oder des Unternehmensberichts eingetretenen Änderungen;
3. die zur Festsetzung der Gegenleistung angewandten Bewertungsmethoden und die Gründe, warum die Anwendung dieser Methoden angemessen ist, sowie die Angabe, welches Umtauschverhältnis oder welcher Gegenwert sich bei der Anwendung verschiedener Methoden, sofern mehrere angewandt worden sind, jeweils ergibt; zugleich ist darzulegen, welches Gewicht den verschiedenen Methoden bei der Bestimmung des Umtauschverhältnisses oder des Gegenwerts und der ihnen zugrunde liegenden Werte beigemessen worden ist, welche Gründe für die Gewichtung bedeutsam waren, und welche besonderen Schwierigkeiten bei der Bewertung der Gegenleistung aufgetreten sind;
4. die Maßnahmen, die die Adressaten des Angebots ergreifen müssen, um dieses anzunehmen und um die Gegenleistung für die Wertpapiere zu erhalten, die Gegenstand des Angebots sind, sowie Angaben über die mit diesen Maßnahmen für die Adressaten verbundenen Kosten und den Zeitpunkt, zu dem diejenigen, die das Angebot angenommen haben, die Gegenleistung erhalten;
5. die Anzahl der vom Bieter und von mit ihm gemeinsam handelnden Personen und deren Tochterunternehmen bereits gehaltenen Wertpapiere sowie die Höhe der von diesen gehaltenen Stimmrechtsanteile unter Angabe der ihnen jeweils nach § 30 des Wertpapiererwerbs- und Übernahmegesetzes zuzurechnenden Stimmrechtsanteile getrennt für jeden Zurechnungstatbestand;
6. bei Teilangeboten der Anteil oder die Anzahl der Wertpapiere der Zielgesellschaft, die Gegenstand des Angebots sind, sowie Angaben über die Zuteilung nach § 19 des Wertpapiererwerbs- und Übernahmegesetzes;

7. The nature and extent of the consideration granted or agreed by the parties and companies named at no. 5. in each case for the purchase of securities of the target company, insofar as the purchase has taken place within three months prior to the publication in accordance with § 10 para. 3 clause 1 of the Takeover Act or prior to the publication of the offer document under § 14 para. 3 clause 1 Takeover Act. Agreements on the basis of which the transfer of ownership of securities can be demanded, is equated with acquisition.

8. Details of the necessity and status of official consents and proceedings, in particular those under competition law, in connection with the acquisition of the securities of the target company.

9. Reference to the acceptance period in the case of a change to the bid under § 21 para. 5 Takeover Act and the acceptance period in the case of competing bids under § 22 para. 2 Takeover Act as well as, in the case of takeover offers, reference to the further acceptance period under § 16 para. 2 Takeover Act.

10. Reference to where the offer document under § 14 para. 3 clause 1 Takeover Act will be published.

11. Reference to the right of withdrawal under § 21 para. 4 and § 22 para. 3 Takeover Act

12. The law to which contracts between the offeror and the owners of securities in the target company arising out of the acceptance of bids are subject.

Part 3. Consideration in the case of Takeover Offers and Mandatory Offers

§ 3. Principles

In the case of takeover offers and mandatory offers, the offeror shall offer the shareholders of the target company an adequate consideration. The amount of the consideration may not be less than the minimum value determined in accordance with §§ 4 to 6. It is to be determined separately for shares which do not belong to the same class.

§ 4. Taking account of prior purchases

The consideration for the shares of the target company must correspond at least to the value of the highest consideration granted or agreed by the offeror, a person acting in common with it or their subsidiaries for the purchase of shares in the target company within the three months prior to the publication under § 14 para. 2 clause 1 or § 35 para. 2 clause 1 of the Takeover Act. § 31 para. 6 of the Takeover Act applies accordingly.

7. Art und Umfang der von den in Nummer 5 genannten Personen und Unternehmen jeweils für den Erwerb von Wertpapieren der Zielgesellschaft gewährten oder vereinbarten Gegenleistung, sofern der Erwerb innerhalb von drei Monaten vor der Veröffentlichung gemäß § 10 Abs. 3 Satz 1 des Wertpapiererwerbsund Übernahmegesetzes oder vor der Veröffentlichung der Angebotsunterlage gemäß § 14 Abs. 3 Satz 1 des Wertpapiererwerbs- und Übernahmegesetzes erfolgte; dem Erwerb gleichgestellt sind Vereinbarungen, auf Grund derer die Übereignung der Wertpapiere verlangt werden kann;
8. Angaben zum Erfordernis und Stand behördlicher, insbesondere wettbewerbsrechtlicher Genehmigungen und Verfahren im Zusammenhang mit dem Erwerb der Wertpapiere der Zielgesellschaft;
9. der Hinweis auf die Annahmefrist im Falle einer Änderung des Angebots nach § 21 Abs. 5 des Wertpapiererwerbs- und Übernahmegesetzes und die Annahmefrist im Falle konkurrierender Angebote nach § 22 Abs. 2 des Wertpapiererwerbs- und Übernahmegesetzes sowie im Falle von Übernahmeangeboten der Hinweis auf die weitere Annahmefrist nach § 16 Abs. 2 des Wertpapiererwerbs- und Übernahmegesetzes;
10. der Hinweis, wo die Angebotsunterlage gemäß § 14 Abs. 3 Satz 1 des Wertpapiererwerbs- und Übernahmegesetzes veröffentlicht wird;
11. der Hinweis auf das Rücktrittsrecht nach § 21 Abs. 4 und § 22 Abs. 3 des Wertpapiererwerbs- und Übernahmegesetzes und
12. Angaben darüber, welchem Recht die sich aus der Annahme des Angebots ergebenden Verträge zwischen dem Bieter und den Inhabern der Wertpapiere der Zielgesellschaft unterliegen.

Dritter Abschnitt. Gegenleistung bei Übernahmeangeboten und Pflichtangeboten

§ 3. Grundsatz

Bei Übernahmeangeboten und Pflichtangeboten hat der Bieter den Aktionären der Zielgesellschaft eine angemessene Gegenleistung anzubieten. Die Höhe der Gegenleistung darf den nach den §§ 4 bis 6 festgelegten Mindestwert nicht unterschreiten. Sie ist für Aktien, die nicht derselben Gattung angehören, getrennt zu ermitteln.

§ 4. Berücksichtigung von Vorerwerben

Die Gegenleistung für die Aktien der Zielgesellschaft muss mindestens dem Wert der höchsten vom Bieter, einer mit ihm gemeinsam handelnden Person oder deren Tochterunternehmen gewährten oder vereinbarten Gegenleistung für den Erwerb von Aktien der Zielgesellschaft innerhalb der letzten drei Monate vor der Veröffentlichung nach § 14 Abs. 2 Satz 1 oder § 35 Abs. 2 Satz 1 des Wertpapiererwerbs- und Übernahmegesetzes entsprechen. § 31 Abs. 6 des Wertpapiererwerbs- und Übernahmegesetzes gilt entsprechend.

§ 5. Domestic stock exchange prices taken into consideration

1. If the shares in the target company are admitted to trading on a domestic stock exchange, the consideration must correspond at least to the weighted average domestic stock exchange price of these shares within the three months prior to the publication under § 10 para. 1 clause 1 or § 35 para. 1 clause 1 Takeover Act.
2. If the shares in the target company at the time of the publication under § 10 para. 1 clause 1 or § 35 para. 1 clause 1 Takeover Act have not yet been admitted for three months to trading on a domestic stock exchange, the value of the consideration must correspond at least to the weighted average domestic stock exchange price since the introduction of the shares to trading.
3. The weighted average domestic stock exchange price is the average price weighted in accordance with turnover reported as stock exchange transactions to the Federal Supervisory Office under § 9 of the Securities Trading Act.
4. If for the shares of the target company during the last three months prior to the publication under § 10 para. 1 clause 1 or § 35 para. 1 clause 1 Takeover Act a stock exchange price has been fixed on less than one third of the trading days, and if several stock exchange prices fixed in succession to each other differ from each other by more than five percent, the amount of the consideration shall correspond to the value ascertained by a valuation of the target company.

§ 6. Foreign stock exchange prices taken into consideration

1. If the shares of the target company are exclusively admitted to trading on an organized market in the sense of § 2 para. 1 Takeover Act in another state of the European Economic Area in the sense of § 2 para. 8 Takeover Act, the consideration must correspond at least to the average stock exchange price during the last three months prior to the publication under § 10 para. 1 clause 1 or § 35 para. 1 clause 1 Takeover Act of the organized market with the highest turnover in the shares of the target company.
2. If the shares of the target company at the time of the publication under § 10 para. 1 clause 1 or § 35 para. 1 clause 1 Takeover Act have not yet been admitted for three months to trading on a market in the meaning of para. 1 hereof, the value of the consideration must correspond at least to the average stock exchange price since the introduction of the shares to trading in that market.
3. The average stock exchange price is the average price of the daily final auction of the shares of the target company on the organized market. If on the organized market under para. 1 above no final auction takes place, the average price shall be determined based on other prices appropriate for the determination of an average price, fixed daily on a stock exchange.

§ 5. Berücksichtigung inländischer Börsenkurse

(1) Sind die Aktien der Zielgesellschaft zum Handel an einer inländischen Börse zugelassen, muss die Gegenleistung mindestens dem gewichteten durchschnittlichen inländischen Börsenkurs dieser Aktien während der letzten drei Monate vor der Veröffentlichung nach § 10 Abs. 1 Satz 1 oder § 35 Abs. 1 Satz 1 des Wertpapiererwerbsund Übernahmegesetzes entsprechen.

(2) Sind die Aktien der Zielgesellschaft zum Zeitpunkt der Veröffentlichung nach § 10 Abs. 1 Satz 1 oder § 35 Abs. 1 Satz 1 des Wertpapiererwerbs- und Übernahmegesetzes noch keine drei Monate zum Handel an einer inländischen Börse zugelassen, so muss der Wert der Gegenleistung mindestens dem gewichteten durchschnittlichen inländischen Börsenkurs seit der Einführung der Aktien in den Handel entsprechen.

(3) Der gewichtete durchschnittliche inländische Börsenkurs ist der nach Umsätzen gewichtete Durchschnittskurs der der Bundesanstalt für Finanzdienstleistungsaufsicht (Bundesanstalt) nach § 9 des Wertpapierhandelsgesetzes als börslich gemeldeten Geschäfte.

(4) Sind für die Aktien der Zielgesellschaft während der letzten drei Monate vor der Veröffentlichung nach § 10 Abs. 1 Satz 1 oder § 35 Abs. 1 Satz 1 des Wertpapiererwerbs- und Übernahmegesetzes an weniger als einem Drittel der Börsentage Börsenkurse festgestellt worden und weichen mehrere nacheinander festgestellte Börsenkurse um mehr als 5 Prozent voneinander ab, so hat die Höhe der Gegenleistung dem anhand einer Bewertung der Zielgesellschaft ermittelten Wert des Unternehmens zu entsprechen.

§ 6. Berücksichtigung ausländischer Börsenkurse

(1) Sind die Aktien der Zielgesellschaft ausschließlich zum Handel an einem organisierten Markt im Sinne des § 2 Abs. 7 des Wertpapiererwerbs- und Übernahmegesetzes in einem anderen Staat des Europäischen Wirtschaftsraums im Sinne des § 2 Abs. 8 des Wertpapiererwerbsund Übernahmegesetzes zugelassen, muss die Gegenleistung mindestens dem durchschnittlichen Börsenkurs während der letzten drei Monate vor der Veröffentlichung nach § 10 Abs. 1 Satz 1 oder § 35 Abs. 1 Satz 1 des Wertpapiererwerbs- und Übernahmegesetzes des organisierten Marktes mit den höchsten Umsätzen in den Aktien der Zielgesellschaft entsprechen.

(2) Sind die Aktien der Zielgesellschaft zum Zeitpunkt der Veröffentlichung nach § 10 Abs. 1 Satz 1 oder § 35 Abs. 1 Satz 1 des Wertpapiererwerbs- und Übernahmegesetzes noch keine drei Monate zum Handel an einem Markt im Sinne des Absatzes 1 zugelassen, so muss der Wert der Gegenleistung mindestens dem durchschnittlichen Börsenkurs seit Einführung der Aktien in den Handel an diesem Markt entsprechen.

(3) Der durchschnittliche Börsenkurs ist der Durchschnittskurs der börsentäglichen Schlussauktion der Aktien der Zielgesellschaft an dem organisierten Markt. Wird an dem organisierten Markt nach Absatz 1 keine Schlussauktion durchgeführt, ist der Durchschnittskurs auf der Grundlage anderer, zur Bildung eines Durchschnittskurses geeigneter Kurse, die börsentäglich festgestellt werden, zu bestimmen.

4. If the prices on the organized market according to para. 1 above are given in a currency other than Euro, the average price used for the calculation of the minimum price on the basis of the relevant daily prices shall be converted into Euro.

5. The basis on which the average stock exchange price is calculated is to be documented in detail.

6. § 5 para. 4 is applicable.

§ 7. Determination of the value of the consideration

If the consideration offered by the offeror is in shares, §§ 5 and 6 shall be applied for the determination of the value of such shares.

Part 4. Exemption from the Obligation to Publish and Make an Offer

§ 8. Application

The application for exemption from the obligation to publish an offer under § 35 para. 1 clause 1 Takeover Act and to make an offer under § 35 para. 2 clause 1 Takeover Act shall be made by the offeror to the Federal Supervisory Office. The application can be made prior to the acquisition of control over the target company and within seven calendar days after the time at which the offeror has become aware or should have become aware that it has acquired control of the target company.

§ 9. Ground for exemption

The Federal Supervisory Office can, in particular, issue an exemption from the obligation stated in § 8 clause 1 in the case of the acquisition of control over a target company

1. through inheritance or in connection with a resolution of an inheritance, insofar as the deceased and the offeror are not related in the meaning of § 26 no. 1 Takeover Act,
2. by gift, insofar as the donor and the offeror are not related within the meaning of § 36 no. 1 Takeover Act,
3. in connection with the reconstruction of the target company,
4. for the purpose of securing debts,
5. because of reduction in the total number of voting rights in the target company,
6. without this being the intention of the offeror, insofar as without delay, the number of securities required will fall below the threshold of § 29 para. 2 Takeover Act.

(4) Werden die Kurse an dem organisierten Markt nach Absatz 1 in einer anderen Währung als in Euro angegeben, sind die zur Bildung des Mindestpreises herangezogenen Durchschnittskurse auf der Grundlage des jeweiligen Tageskurses in Euro umzurechnen.

(5) Die Grundlagen der Berechnung des durchschnittlichen Börsenkurses sind im Einzelnen zu dokumentieren.

(6) § 5 Abs. 4 ist anzuwenden.

§ 7. Bestimmung des Wertes der Gegenleistung

Besteht die vom Bieter angebotene Gegenleistung in Aktien, sind für die Bestimmung des Wertes dieser Aktien die §§ 5 und 6 entsprechend anzuwenden.

Vierter Abschnitt. Befreiung von der Verpflichtung zur Veröffentlichungund zur Abgabe eines Angebots

§ 8. Antragstellung

Der Antrag auf Befreiung von der Pflicht zur Veröffentlichung nach § 35 Abs. 1 Satz 1 des Wertpapiererwerbsund Übernahmegesetzes und zur Abgabe eines Angebots nach § 35 Abs. 2 Satz 1 des Wertpapiererwerbs- und Übernahmegesetzes ist vom Bieter bei der Bundesanstalt zu stellen. Der Antrag kann vor Erlangung der Kontrolle über die Zielgesellschaft und innerhalb von sieben Kalendertagen nach dem Zeitpunkt gestellt werden, zu dem der Bieter Kenntnis davon hat oder nach den Umständen haben musste, dass er die Kontrolle über die Zielgesellschaft erlangt hat.

§ 9. Befreiungstatbestände

Die Bundesanstalt kann insbesondere eine Befreiung von den in § 8 Satz 1 genannten Pflichten erteilen bei Erlangung der Kontrolle über die Zielgesellschaft
1. durch Erbschaft oder im Zusammenhang mit einer Erbauseinandersetzung, sofern Erblasser und Bieter nicht verwandt im Sinne des § 36 Nr. 1 des Wertpapiererwerbs- und Übernahmegesetzes sind,
2. durch Schenkung, sofern Schenker und Bieter nicht verwandt im Sinne des § 36 Nr. 1 des Wertpapiererwerbs- und Übernahmegesetzes sind,
3. im Zusammenhang mit der Sanierung der Zielgesellschaft,
4. zum Zwecke der Forderungssicherung,
5. auf Grund einer Verringerung der Gesamtzahl der Stimmrechte an der Zielgesellschaft,
6. ohne dass dies vom Bieter beabsichtigt war, soweit die Schwelle des § 29 Abs. 2 des Wertpapiererwerbs- und Übernahmegesetzes nach der Antragstellung unverzüglich wieder unterschritten wird.

An exemption can also be granted if
1. a third party has the right to dispose over a higher share of voting rights, which are neither equated with those of the offeror nor with those acting in common with it in accordance with § 30 Takeover Act or attributable to it
2. on the basis of the capital entitled to voting rights which was represented at the immediately past three ordinary general meetings, it is not to be expected that the offeror can dispose in the general meeting of the target company over more than 50% of the represented voting rights,
3. the control over a target company within the meaning of § 2 para. 3 Takeover Act has been acquired indirectly by the acquisition of control over a company and the book value of the participation of the company in the target company is less than 20% of the book value of the assets of the company.

§ 10. Content of the application

The application must contain the following data:
1. name and residence or registered office of the applicant
2. name, registered office and legal form of the target company
3. the number of shares and voting rights held by the offeror and persons acting in common with it and those voting rights attributable to them in accordance with § 30 Takeover Act
4. the day on which the threshold in accordance with § 39 para. 2 Takeover Act was exceeded and
5. the facts grounding the application.

§ 11. Documents to be submitted with the application

The documents necessary for the assessment and processing of the application shall be filed without delay with the Federal Supervisory Office.

§ 12. Examination of the completeness of the application

The Federal Supervisory Office shall, after receipt of the application and the documents, examine whether they comply with the requirements of §§ 10 and 11. If the application or the documents are not complete, the Federal Supervisory Office shall request the applicant to immediately supplement the application or the documents within a reasonable period. If this request is not complied with within the period set by the Federal Supervisory Office, the application shall be deemed to have been withdrawn.

Part 5. Final Provision

§ 13. Legal Effect

This regulation comes into effect on 1st January 2002.

Eine Befreiung kann ferner erteilt werden, wenn
1. ein Dritter über einen höheren Anteil an Stimmrechten verfügt, die weder dem Bieter noch mit diesem gemeinsam handelnden Personen gemäß § 30 des Wertpapiererwerbs- und Übernahmegesetzes gleichstehen oder zuzurechnen sind,
2. auf Grund des in den zurückliegenden drei ordentlichen Hauptversammlungen vertretenen stimmberechtigten Kapitals nicht zu erwarten ist, dass der Bieter in der Hauptversammlung der Zielgesellschaft über mehr als 50 Prozent der vertretenen Stimmrechte verfügen wird,
3. auf Grund der Erlangung der Kontrolle über eine Gesellschaft mittelbar die Kontrolle an einer Zielgesellschaft im Sinne des § 2 Abs. 3 des Wertpapiererwerbs- und Übernahmegesetzes erlangt wurde und der Buchwert der Beteiligung der Gesellschaft an der Zielgesellschaft weniger als 20 Prozent des buchmäßigen Aktivvermögens der Gesellschaft beträgt.

§ 10. Antragsinhalt

Der Antrag muss folgende Angaben enthalten:
1. Name oder Firma und Wohnsitz oder Sitz des Antragstellers,
2. Firma, Sitz und Rechtsform der Zielgesellschaft,
3. Anzahl der vom Bieter und den gemeinsam handelnden Personen bereits gehaltenen Aktien und Stimmrechte und die ihnen nach § 30 des Wertpapiererwerbs- und Übernahmegesetzes zuzurechnenden Stimmrechte,
4. Tag, an dem die Schwelle des § 29 Abs. 2 des Wertpapiererwerbs- und Übernahmegesetzes überschritten wurde, und
5. die den Antrag begründenden Tatsachen.

§ 11. Antragsunterlagen

Die zur Beurteilung und Bearbeitung des Antrags erforderlichen Unterlagen sind unverzüglich bei der Bundesanstalt einzureichen.

§ 12. Prüfung der Vollständigkeit des Antrags

Die Bundesanstalt hat nach Eingang des Antrags und der Unterlagen zu prüfen, ob sie den Anforderungen der §§ 10 und 11 entsprechen. Sind der Antrag oder die Unterlagen nicht vollständig, so hat die Bundesanstalt den Antragsteller unverzüglich aufzufordern, den Antrag oder die Unterlagen innerhalb einer angemessenen Frist zu ergänzen. Wird der Aufforderung innerhalb der von der Bundesanstalt gesetzten Frist nicht entsprochen, gilt der Antrag als zurückgenommen.

Fünfter Abschnitt. Schlussvorschrift

§ 13. Inkrafttreten

Diese Verordnung tritt am 1. Januar 2002 in Kraft.

Glossary

Action to Set Aside
(„Anfechtungsklage")

A resolution of the shareholders' meeting is generally not invalid *per se* if it violates the law or the articles of association. It is, however, voidable by means of an action to set it aside *(Anfechtungsklage)*. A successful action to set aside will void the shareholders' resolution. Such a judgment is effective for and against all shareholders and members of the management and supervisory boards.

An action to set aside may generally be filed by any shareholder who participated in the shareholders' meeting, or by the management board.

Appointment of Management Board Members

The appointment and removal of management board members falls within the responsibility of the supervisory board.

Appointment of Supervisory Board Members

The members of the supervisory board (except for representatives elected by the employees) are elected by the shareholders' meeting, unless certain shareholders are entitled to appoint a specific number of members under the articles of association (quite common in private companies).

The members of the supervisory board (except for representatives elected by the employees) may be removed from office prior to the end of their term by means of a resolution of the shareholders' meeting requiring a ¾ voting majority.

Moreover, members may be removed by the competent court *(„Amtsgericht")* for good cause.

Authorized (unissued) Capital
(„Genehmigtes Kapital")

The management board of the corporation may be authorized by the shareholders' meeting to increase the share capital up to an amount fixed in the shareholders' resolution (no more than 50% of the registered share capital).

Thereby, the shareholders may give the management board freedom to issue new shares, *inter alia*, necessary to preserve the company's liquidity or as acquisition currency.

Civil Code
(„*Bürgerliches Gesetzbuch*")

Code governing general civil law, effective as of 1900, in important parts completely revised in 2001/2002.

Coal and Steel Codetermination Act
(„*Montanmitbestimmungsgesetz*")

The Coal and Steel Codetermination Act, applicable to enterprises in the coal or steel industries, provides for equal representation of the employees and shareholders on the supervisory board. To prevent a deadlock, an additional member may be appointed who must have the confidence of both capital and labor.

Codetermination Act 1976
(„*Mitbestimmungsgesetz 1976*")

The Codetermination Act 1976 applies to corporations with more than 2000 employees. The supervisory board shall have an equal number of employee representatives and shareholder representatives. In the case of a stalemate, the chairman (generally appointed by the shareholder representatives) has two votes.

Commercial Register
(„*Handelsregister*")

Public register evidencing the commercial and legal status of companies and certain partnerships (most important entries: nominal share capital, authorized unissued capital, members of the management board).

Company Agreements
(„*Unternehmensverträge*")

This legal term comprises in particular control and profit transfer agreements (see this index).

Compensation Assessment Proceeding
(„*Spruchverfahren*" oder „*Spruchstellenverfahren*")

In a court proceeding which is specifically provided for in the Reorganization Act, the shareholders may claim certain compensation. This refers, in particular, to determining the conversion ratio and certain compensation claims of dissenting shareholders in the case of mergers. This procedure implies an interest in excluding disruptive law suits against the validity of the merger by shareholders who are not adequately compensated or who have not been compensated. The Compensation Assessment Proceeding cannot prevent or delay a merger. The shareholder can achieve only an improvement in the conversion ratio or in the level of cash compensation.

Control Agreement
(„*Beherrschungsvertrag*")

An agreement in which one company submits to the management of another company is a "control agreement." Under this type of agreement the controlling enterprise has the right to give instructions to the management of the controlled company in all aspects of the business. Compliance may be refused only in certain exceptional circumstances.

In many instances, control agreements include profit transfer agreements (see this index).

Corporate Disclosure Requirements

The Securities Trading Act (see this index) requires that listed companies, without undue delay, publish facts that are relevant for their business and financial situation, and may have an impact on the share price (§ 15). The Takeover Act contains several disclosure requirements in the context of public offers.

Federal Constitutional Court
(*„Bundesverfassungsgericht"*)

The Federal Constitutional Court sees that government authorities and lower courts act in conformity with the Federal Constitution (*„Grundgesetz"*-*"Basic Law"*). It even has the power to declare an Act of Parliament null and void. The decisions of the Court are non-appealable and binding on all other courts and institutions of the federal and state governments.

Federal Supervisory Office
(*„Bundesanstalt für Finanzdienstleistungsaufsicht";*
BAFin)

Federal Supervisory Office for Financial Services. This office is a central supervisory authority for banking, insurance and securities trading services.

Federal Supreme Court
(*„Bundesgerichtshof"*)

The Federal Supreme Court is the highest instance for civil and criminal cases. It is only responsible for appeals on points of law and not for questions of fact.

General Partnership
(*„Offene Handelsgesellschaft"*)

The general partnership is a partnership formed for the purpose of jointly operating a commercial enterprise and (in contrast to a limited partnership) with unlimited liability of all partners.

The organization is based on the personal bonds between the partners.

Integration
(*„Eingliederung"*)

Integration takes place when one stock corporation becomes organizationally integrated into its parent company (so-called "principal corporation"), while retaining its status as a legal entity. The principal company may give instructions to the management board of the integrated company not only with respect to the strategic management but also with respect to daily business operations. It simultaneously assumes responsibility for instructions given. Moreover, the principal company is jointly and severally liable for all liabilities of the integrated company, whether incurred before or after the integration (note: this financial responsibility exceeds the liability of parent companies under control or profit transfer agreements where the parent is liable only for losses incurred during the term of the agreement).

Joint Works Council
(„Gesamtbetriebsrat")

The Codetermination Act (see this index) provides that all work councils existing within a particular enterprise or groups of enterprises shall form a joint works council. The joint works council is responsible for those matters that relate to the enterprise or group of enterprises as a whole, and which cannot be handled by the local works council in their works.

Limited Liability Company
(„Gesellschaft mit beschränkter Haftung")

A Limited Liability Company is a corporation with its own legal identity and a corporate organization. The minimum amount of the nominal share capital is € 25,000. The nominal share capital of the company must be fully covered by the share capital contributions paid by the shareholders. Creditors of the corporation have recourse only to corporate assets. The shareholders are not personally responsible for the company's liabilities.

GmbH shareholdings have to be transferred by means of a notarial deed (§ 15 para. 3, 4 Act on Limited Liability Companies). For this reason it is not possible to trade shares of a Limited Liability Company on a stock exchange.

(Note: The limited liability company under German law is a real corporation that must not be confused with limited liability companies which are, in some jurisdictions, merely flow-through entities for tax purposes and are not legal persons.)

Maintenance of Capital Rules
(„Kapitalerhaltungsgrundsätze")

The Stock Corporation Act (as well as the Limited Liability Company Act) adheres to the fundamental principle that the registered (nominal) share capital must be fully paid in and maintained. These rules are designed to ensure that the net assets of the corporation will cover at least the nominal share capital. Therefore, stock corporations may only distribute the annual profit or profit carried forward as regular dividends to their shareholders.

Management Board
("Vorstand")

The responsibilities of the management board in Germany differ slightly from the competences of the management board in U.S. companies. Though the management board has exclusive authority and control of the strategic and daily business management, it does not have authority for certain structural measures that may be available to the board of a U.S. corporation:

- The board may not change or amend the articles of association and by-laws (U.S.: see § 10.02 and § 10.03 Model Business Corporation Act 1984 (MCBA 1984)).
- The board may not issue shares or exclude shareholders' pre-emptive rights unless authorized by the shareholders' meeting (U.S.: see § 6.21 MBCA 1984).
- The board may not declare dividends; this falls within the responsibility of the annual shareholders' meeting (U.S.: see § 6.40 MBCA 1984).

If required by the articles or resolved by the supervisory board, certain legal acts or management transactions require the prior consent of the supervisory board.

The management board must report on its activities to the supervisory board.

Mandatory Offer/
Mandatory Bid
("Pflichtangebot")

If a shareholder has acquired the control of a publicly quoted company (30% of the votes), it is obliged to make a public bid (mandatory offer) to acquire the remaining shares. The procedure for the mandatory offer is regulated in detail in the Takeover Act. If the offeror acquired the control by means of a public offer, it does not have to make a mandatory offer.

Ordinary Shares
(Common Shares)
("Stammaktien")

Ordinary shares *("Stammaktien")* confer all regular shareholder rights (in particular voting and profit sharing right). Preference shares *("Vorzugsaktien")* do not grant voting rights, but rather preferred profit sharing rights.

Own Shares/ Treasury Shares (*„Eigene Aktien"*)

The Stock Corporation Act allows the acquisition by a company of its own shares (sometimes called "Treasury Shares") only in certain specific circumstances (up to a maximum of 10% of the share capital and only with approval of the shareholders' meeting). The rights attached to shares (voting rights, profit sharing rights) are suspended when the corporation holds its own shares.

Partnership Limited by Shares (*„Kommanditgesellschaft auf Aktien", KGaA*)

A hybrid company form that is a combination between a partnership and a corporation. It has one or several general partners who are personally responsible for all liabilities of the partnership and manage the company; in this respect it resembles a partnership. On the other hand, it has shareholders, who are not personally liable for the company's liabilities and do not have management responsibilities; in this respect it resembles a stock corporation.

Despite the personal responsibility of the general partners, the partnership limited by shares is a legal entity with its own legal personality.

It is a rather rare form of a business association, and its foundation is in most cases based on tax reasons, as it combines corporate taxation in respect of the shareholders and partnership taxation regarding the general partners.

Pre-emptive Rights (*„Bezugsrechte"*)

In general, all shareholders are entitled, pro rata, to purchase or subscribe for shares issued in connection with a capital increase. This right, which is transferable, ensures that the shareholders may retain their proportionate interest in the corporation. The elimination of pre-emptive rights, which is an encroachment on the ownership position of the stockholder, requires special justification. It can be justified by significant and reasonable business interests, if the resulting benefit for the corporation and its stockholders outweigh the dilution of the shareholders position. This is usually the case for business acquisitions with shares as acquisition currency, or when new investors are obtained.

Preference Shares (*„Vorzugsaktien"*)

Preference shares entitle the holder to a preferred share of profit and dividends. However, preference shares do not confer voting rights.

Profit Transfer Agreement („*Gewinnabführungsvertrag*")	An agreement between two companies under which one company agrees to transfer its entire profit to another company is a "Profit Transfer Agreement." Such an agreement must provide for adequate compensation for the outside shareholders by periodic payments. Usually, profit transfer agreements are combined with "control agreements" (see this index).
Public Offer Regulation („*Angebotsverordnung*")	The Public Offer Regulation was issued by the Federal Finance Ministry on December 27, 2001 and came into force on January 1, 2002 concurrently with the Takeover Act. It regulates certain aspects of the takeover procedure, in particular regarding the amount of consideration, and the conditions on which exemption from the obligation to make a mandatory bid may be granted by the Federal Supervisory Office. The statutory basis for its issue is § 31 para. 7 Takeover Act.
Receiving Entity („*Aufnehmender Rechtsträger*")	See upstream merger (this index)
Reorganization Act („*Umwandlungsgesetz*")	The Reorganization Act governs procedures for legal reorganizations of companies. Most important are corporate mergers and the change of the legal form of a company.
Securities Trading Act („*Wertpapierhandelsgesetz*," *WpHG*)	The Securities Trading Act mainly regulates preventative combating of insider trading, and corporate disclosure requirements for the protection of shareholders and investors along with the authority of the Federal Supervisory Office (see this index).
Share Capital („*Stammkapital*" / „*Grundkapital*")	The share capital and par value of the shares must be denominated in Euro. The minimum nominal amount of the registered capital is € 50,000 for stock corporations, and € 25,000 for limited liability companies.
Shareholders' Meeting („*Hauptversammlung*")	The shareholders' meeting is the forum for the shareholders to exercise their voting and information rights. They cannot influence the day-to-day business, but decisions concerning the legal and financial structure of the corporation, such as capital increases, mergers, liquidation, changes of the articles, and similar

matters, require shareholder approval. Additionally, shareholders are able to express their view on the quality of the management by resolutions approving or disapproving of the discharge by the board members of their responsibilities (Entlastung). The shareholders' meeting elects the members of the supervisory board.

Shop Constitution Act (*„Betriebsverfassungsgesetz 1952"*)

Under the Shop Constitution Act 1952 one third of the members of the supervisory board must be employees' representatives, except for corporations with less than 500 employees; for corporations that were incorporated before August 10, 1994, this is applicable only if these corporations are family controlled (§ 76 para. 6 Shop Constitution Act).

Sound Business Judgment (*„Sorgfalt eines ordentlichen Kaufmanns"*)

Standard of care exercised by a diligent and prudent business executive (§ 93 Stock Corporation Act); when exercising this duty the management has a relatively broad business discretion (Business Judgment Rule).

Stock Corporation (*„Aktiengesellschaft"*)

The stock corporation possesses legal personality. The corporation is strictly separate from its shareholders and, accordingly, creditors of the corporation have recourse only to corporate assets. The stock corporation has three bodies: the shareholders' meeting, the management board, and the supervisory board. The management board alone bears responsibility for managing corporate activities.

Stock Exchange Act (*„Börsengesetz"*)

The Stock Exchange Act includes provisions for the supervision of the stock exchange and for the admission of securities to stock exchange trading.

Supervisory Board (*„Aufsichtsrat"*)

The Supervisory Board appoints the members of the management board, and is responsible for the supervision of the conduct of the business by the management board. This supervisory function extends to all business activity.

The management board's duty to report enables the supervisory board to properly fulfil its supervisory function.

The supervisory board may require that the management board carry out certain transactions only with the consent of the supervisory board. Transactions may be made subject to such consent requirements in the articles or by resolution of the supervisory board.

Takeover Act (The Act on the Purchase of Securities and on Takeovers) („*Wertpapiererwerbs- und Übernahmegesetz,*" *WpÜG*)	The Takeover Act provides for a standardized procedure for public tender offers including ample protection of the target and its shareholders, such as minimum price rules and disclosure requirements.
Takeover Code („*Übernahmekodex der Börsensachverständigenkommission*")	The Takeover Code 1995 of the Stock Exchange Expert Commission. It had no binding legal power; its application was based on a voluntary self-obligation of publicly traded companies. As of December 31, 2001, 802 of 913 companies listed on German stock exchanges had subscribed to the Takeover Code.
Takeover Offer („*Übernahmeangebot*")	The takeover offer is a public tender offer aimed at acquiring control of the target under the Takeover Act. Control over a corporation is achieved when one shareholder holds at least 30% of the voting rights.
Target („*Zielgesellschaft*")	The company, the securities of which are the subject of a public tender offer, is referred to by the Takeover Act as the target.
Transferring Entity („*Übertragender Rechtsträger*")	See upstream merger (this index)
Upstream Merger („*Verschmelzung durch Aufnahme*")	By means of an upstream merger, the entire assets of one company (transferring entity) are transferred to another existing company (receiving entity). The transferring entity ceases to exist and its shareholders obtain shares in the receiving entity (share exchange), unless the transferring entity is already a 100% subsidiary of the receiving entity. An upstream merger may be used as "cold delisting" of minority shareholders.
Voting Rights („*Stimmrecht*")	With the exception of certain preference shares, each issued share confers a voting right. The number of votes allocated to each share is determined by the par value. Multiple voting rights („*Mehrfachstimmrechte*") exceeding those proportionately attributable to the par value of a share are prohibited.

Works (*„Betrieb"*)	Codetermination under German law (Codetermination Act 1976; Coal and Steel Determination Act; Shop Constitution Act; see this index) is not organized according to legal entities; the relevant organizational units are "works", i.e., particular separate operating units. Each works usually has its own works council.
13th EU-Directive on Public Takeover Offers	On July 4th 2001 the European Parliament rejected the 13th EU-Directive on public takeover offers by a 273:273 vote. Germany voted against the directive as it feared that German stock corporations would be put at a disadvantage, because general German corporate law, by forbidding maximum- or plural votes as well as Poison Pills, does not provide for efficient ways to defend a company against a hostile takeover. In contrast, other European countries allow golden shares that provide a sort of veto. Therefore, the German government took the view that takeover regulations should provide for other effective defense tactics, which the EU-Directive did not include.

Sachverzeichnis

Acceptance period, *see* offer document
Ad-hoc defensive strategies, *see* defensive tactics
Advertising campaigns, *see* defensive tactics
Amendment of the offer, *see* offer document
Average-price rule, *see* consideration

Bootstrap offer, *see* offensive tactics
Business judgment rule, *see* defensive tactics

City Code on Takeovers and Mergers, 131 et seq.
- Generally, 131, 134 et seq.
- Application, 133 et seq.
- Conflict of laws, 133
- Mandatory offers, 135 et seq.
- Principles, 134 et seq.
- Sanctions, 132
- Self regulation, 131 et seq.
Codetermination („Mitbestimmung"), 2 et seq., 56, 105 (fn. 80)
Compensation assessment proceeding („Spruchstellenverfahren"), *see* mergers of equals, *see* squeeze-out
Conflict of law (international offers), *see* Takover Offers under the Takeover Act
Consideration, *see also* mandatory bids
- Generally, 73 et seq.
- Amount, 75 et seq.
- Average-price rule, 75, 76 et seq.
- Cash consideration, 74 et seq.
- Control premium, 79
- Discounted cash flow (DCF) valuation method, 75 et seq.
- Due diligence, 76
- Fixed conversion ratio, 32
- Fixed value, 32
- Form of consideration, 73 et seq.
- Improved bids, 78 et seq.
- Income valuation approach, 75 et seq.
- Liquid shares, 73 et seq.
- Most favored status of a bid, 78 et seq.
- Options, 78 et seq., 80
- Variable consideration, 32, 77 et seq.
- Voting shares, 74
- Preference shares, 74
- Remedies, 81 et seq.
- Thinly traded stocks, 75, 76
- Toe holds, 74 et seq.
Control, *see* takeover offers under the Takeover Act
Control premium, *see* consideration
Controlling interest, *see* mandatory bids
Conversation ratio, *see* consideration
Convertible bonds, *see* squeeze-out
Corporate Governance, 1 et seq.
- Codetermination („Mitbestimmung"), 2 et seq., 56, 105 (fn. 80)
- Management board („Vorstand"), 4
- Shareholders' meeting, 4 et seq.
- Supervisory board („Aufsichtsrat"), 2 et seq.
- Registered authorized officer („Prokurist"), 1
- Two-tier board system, 1 et seq., 56
Corporate Governance Code of Best Practice, 48
Cross-border mergers, *see* mergers of equals
Cross-shareholdings, *see* defensive tactics

Defense document, *see* defensive tactics
Defensive tactics, *see also* neutrality
- Generally, 45, 51 et seq.
- Ad-hoc defensive strategies, 51, 59 et seq.
- Advertising campaigns, *see* public relations activities
- Authorized unissued capital, 59
- Business judgment rule, 45
- Cross-shareholdings, 57 et seq.
- Defense document, 50 et seq., 60 et seq.
- Employee stock option plans (ESOPs), 57
- Federal Supervisory Office, 89
- Fiduciary duties, 69 et seq.
- Issue of new shares, 66, 67

- Level playing flield, 51, 59
- Liability issues, 61 et seq., 63
- Poison pills, 52 et seq.
- Practical issues, 71
- Neutrality, *see* main index
- Public relations activities, 60 et seq., 62, 89
- Purchase of the target's own shares, 66, 67
- Remedies of the target's shareholders, 61 et seq., 69 et seq.
- Remedies of the bidder, 71
- *Revlon* doctrine, 46, 47, 49
- Sale of assets („crown jewels"), 67
- „Saturday Night Special," 60
- Shareholder rights plans, *see* poison pills
- Staggered boards, 56 et seq.
- Statements of the target's boards, *see* defense document
- Structural defense strategies, 51, 52 et seq., 73
- U. S. law, 45 et seq.
- *Unocal* doctrine, 46, 47
- White knight, 65

Delisting, *see* squeeze-out
Discounted cash flow (DCF) valuation method, *see* consideration, *see* mergers of equals, *see* squeeze-out
Due diligence, *see* consideration

Efficient capital markets and takeover rules, 11 et seq.
Employee stock option plans (ESOPs), *see* defensive tactics
Equal treatment of shareholders, *see* takeover offers under the Takeover Act
European Union, Takover Directive, 8 et seq., 49
Exchange ratio, *see* mergers of equals
Extrinsic value, *see* mergers of equals, *see* squeeze-out

Fair bid procedure, *see* takeover offers under the Takeover Act
Federal Supervisory Office, 89 et seq.
Financial assistance, 43, 75 (Fn. 337)
Financing confirmation, *see* offer document

Golden handshakes, *see* offensive tactics
Golden parachutes, *see* offensive tactics

Golden shares, *see* shares and capital
Greenmailing, *see* offensive tactics

Holzmüller doctrine, 63
Hostile takeover bids, examples, 53

Improved bids, *see* consideration
International application of the Takeover Act, *see* takeover offers under the Takeover Act
International offers, *see* takeover offers under the Takeover Act
Intrinsic value, *see* mergers of equals, *see* squeeze-out

Leveraged buyout, *see* offensive tactics

Mandatory bids, 83 et seq.
- Generally, 83 et seq.
- City Code on Takeovers and Mergers, 135 et seq.
- Consideration, 88
- Controlling interest, 83 et seq.
- Exemptions, 86 et seq.
- Federal Supervisory Office, sanctions, 89, 90
- Merger transactions, 84 et seq.
- Private cause of action, 89
- Remedies, 89
- Sanctions, 88 et seq.

Merger control, *see* mergers of equals
Mergers of equals, 93 et seq.
- Generally, 93 et seq., 97
- Action to set aside (Anfechtungsklage), 95, 110
- Affiliated companies, 108
- Antitrust issues, 95 et seq.
- Capitalized earnings valuation method, 99, 101, 107
- Capital increase, 109
- Collective bargaining agreements, 104
- Compensation assessment proceeding (Spruchstellenverfahren), 95, 111
- Cross-border mergers, 111 et seq.
- Discounted cash flow (DCF) valuation method, 99, 101
- Dissenters' rights, 104
- Dominated/non-dominated mergers, 100
- Employees, 104, 105
- Exchange ratio, 97 et seq., 103, 107
- Extrinsic value, 97 et seq., 107
- Forms of mergers, 94 et seq.

- Intrinsic value, 97 et seq., 99 et seq.
- Liquidation value, 102
- Merger agreement, 103 et seq.
- Merger audit, 106
- Merger control, 95 et seq.
- Merger report, 106
- Merger resolution, 108 et seq.
- Registration in the commercial register, 109
- Relationship between Takeover Act and Reorganization Act, 84 et seq., 94
- Relative valuation of merging entities, 100 et seq.
- Shareholders' protection, 109 et seq.
- Synergy effects, 101 et seq., 106
- Upstream merger, 93, 100
- Valuation date, 102
- Works council, 105

Neutrality, 47 et seq.
- Generally, 47 et seq., 55
- Exceptions, 48 et seq.
- – Approval by the supervisory board, 49, 68 et seq., 72
- – Going-concern exception, 49 et seq.
- – Ongoing business operations, 49 et seq.
- – Shareholders' resolutions, 48 et seq., 65 et seq., 72
- Practical issues, 71 et seq.

Offer document, 30 et seq.
- Acceptance period, 37 et seq.
- Amendment of the offer, 38
- Content of the offer document, 33 et seq.
- Conditions, 30 et seq.
- Financing confirmation, 34, 36 et seq.
- Liability issues, 36 et seq.
- „Fence sitting provision" („Zaunkönigregelung"), 39 et seq.
- Extension of the acceptance period, 39
- Further acceptance period, 39

Offensive tactics, 40 et seq.
- Bootstrap offer, 44
- Golden handshakes, 45
- Golden parachutes, 45
- Greenmailing, 42 et seq.
- Leveraged buyout, 43 et seq.
- Proxy fights, 42
- Two-tier offers, 40 et seq., 60, 83

Options, *see* consideration, *see* squeeze-out
Poison pills, *see* defensive tactics
Public offers, 27 et seq.
- Announcement to make an offer, 27
- Federal Supervisory Office, sanctions in the case of illegal offers, 90
- Partial takeover offers, 33
- „Water-level" announcements, 38

Preference shares, *see* consideration, *see* shares and capital
Pre-emptive rights, *see* shares and capital
Procedural overview, *see* takover offers under the Takeover Act
Proxy fights, *see* offensive tactics
Regulation 14E, 64
Reorganization Act („Umwandlungsgesetz"), 93 et seq.
Remedies, *see* defensive tactics, *see* consideration, *see* mandatory bids
Revlon doctrine, *see* defensive tactics
Self-tender offers, *see* takeover offers under the Takeover Act

Shares and capital, 5 et seq.
- Authorized capital (*see also:* defensive steps), 6, 59
- Contingent capital increase (Bedingtes Kapital), 6, 57
- Golden shares, 5
- Issue of new shares, 5, 66
- Pre-emptive rights, 5, 66
- Preferential dividends, 5
- Voting shares/preference shares, 5

Squeeze-out, 116 et seq.
- Generally, 116 et seq.
- Action to set aside („Anfechtungsklage"), 126
- Attribution of shares, 119 et seq., 127
- Audit, 121 et seq.
- Capitalized earnings valuation method, 125
- Compensation, 121 et seq., 124 et seq.
- Compensation assessment proceeding („Spruchstellenverfahren"), 126 et seq.
- Control and profit transfer agreements, 117 et seq.
- Convertible bonds, 124
- Delisting, 117, 128 et seq.
- Discounted cash flow (DCF) valution method, 125
- Extrinsic value, 125

- Integration, 116
- Intrinsic value, 125
- Options, 124
- Other countries, 127 et seq.
- Pooling of shares, 120 et seq., 127
- Procedure, 119 et seq.
- Rationale, 118 et seq.
- Registration in the commercial register, 123
- Shareholders' resolution, 122
- Squeeze-out asset deal, 116 et seq.
- Transfer of the shares, 123

Staggered boards, *see* defensive tactics
Structural defense strategies, *see* defensive tactics

Takeover Act, structure, *see* takeover offers under the Takeover Act
Takeover Code 1995 („Übernahmekodex"), 7 et seq., 12, 60, 83
Takeover offers under the Takeover Act
- Generally, 15 et seq.
- Admission to public trading, 15
- Attribution of shares, 16 et seq.
- Conflict of law (international offers), 19 et seq.
- Control, 15 et seq.
- Equal treatment of shareholders, 21 et seq.
- Fair bid procedure, 13
- General principles, 21 et seq.
- International application of the Takeover Act, 17 et seq.
- International offers, 18 et seq.
- Market manipulation, prohibition against, 21, 24
- Mandatory offers, 17
- Objective, 13
- Partial takeover offers, 33
- Procedural Overview, 24 et seq., 34 et seq.
- Protection for minority shareholders, 13
- Public offer, definition, 13 et seq.
- Scope of application of the Takeover Act, 13 et seq.
- Securities of the target, definition, 14 et seq.
- Self-tender offers, 14 et seq.
- Takeover Act, structure, 20 et seq.
- Transparency, 13, 21, 22
- „Water-Level" announcements, 38

Thinly traded stocks, *see* consideration
Transparency, *see* takeover offers under the Takeover Act
Toe holds, *see* consideration
Two-tier offers, *see* offensive tactics
Unocal doctrine, *see* defensive tactics

Upstream merger, *see* merger of equals

White knight, *see* defensive tactics
Williams Act, 42